At the crossroads of cultures

UNESCO

CULTURES and TIME

L. Gardet A. J. Gurevich A. Kagame
C. Larre G. E. R. Lloyd A. Neher R. Panikkar
G. Pàttaro P. Ricoeur

The Unesco Press
Paris 1976

Published by The Unesco Press
7 Place de Fontenoy, 75700 Paris
Printed by Les Presses de l'Imprimerie Bussière,
Saint-Amand (Cher)

ISBN 92-3-101200-2
French edition : 92-3-201200-6
Spanish edition : 92-3-201200-X

PREFACE

This collection of studies written by specialists is the first of a series of four publications forming part of a Unesco project under the title 'At the Crossroads of Cultures'. The aim of this project is to establish communication in depth between contemporary cultures, centred on a number of fundamental concepts which are of prime importance in everyday life and which, at the same time, are the essential substance of any systematic view of the world.

Time is the key notion of this first publication. The series has thus been launched by a theme which is sufficiently central and topical to enable ideas on it to be pooled or, at least, to give rise to a lively interchange of questions in the hope of arriving at a more informed understanding.

Today, when time is filled with significant action and history is rapidly gathering speed, an understanding of the root causes of the diverse rhythms of life, thought and action seems very much to the point for such diversity is an obstacle to understanding only if the reasons for it are not perceived. Moreover, it is a matter of urgency to achieve such understanding, because the dynamism of history, which is becoming increasingly all-embracing, sweeps along and ineluctably synchronizes different periods of time as they are variously experienced.

Hence the importance of establishing a typology of experiences of time as they are viewed by widely differing cultures, which is the purpose of the present volume. The next publication, which will adopt a more systematic approach, will be concerned with the treatment of temporality in various contemporary philosophies and schools of thought. It will also analyse the effects of sudden encounters between different ways of experiencing time, which cause certain societies to be pathologically conscious of time without always understanding why or, consequently, knowing what remedies to apply.

Lastly there are plans for a third publication dealing with recent changes in the concept of time to be noted in the scientific sphere. Further topics are in mind for later work, such as the nature and rhythm of history and the categories of action.

The opinions expressed are those of the authors and not necessarily those of Unesco.

NOTES ON THE AUTHORS

PAUL RICOEUR. Born in Valence, France, in 1913. *Agrégé* in philosophy, doctorate in literature. Worked at the Centre National de la Recherche Scientifique. Taught history of philosophy at Strasbourg; professor of philosophy at Paris University. Former Dean of the Faculté des Lettres of Nanterre University. Member of the editorial board of *Esprit*.

Publications include: *Philosophie de la Volonté: I. Le Volontaire et l'Involontaire, II. L'Homme Faillible, III. La Symbolique du Mal*; *Histoire et Vérité*; *Platon et Aristote*; *De l'Interprétation, Essai sur Freud*; *Le Conflit des Interprétations.*

CLAUDE LARRE. Sinologist. Graduated in literature, law, theology. Doctorate in Chinese philosophy. Qualifications in Chinese, Japanese, Vietnamese. Professor of Chinese philosophy at the Centre d'Études et de Recherches Philosophiques, Paris. Represents the Institut Ricci (Centre d'Études Chinoises) in Paris.

Publications include: *Mao Tsé-toung et la Vieille Chine*, a study on the *Houai Nan tseu* and a new translation of *Lao Tzu.*

RAIMUNDO PANIKKAR. Born in Barcelona in 1918 of an Indian father and a Spanish mother. Academic studies in science and philosophy in Spain, Germany, Italy and India. Doctorates in science, philosophy, theology. Former research fellow at the universities of Mysore and Varanasi (Benares). Former professor at the universities of Madrid, Rome, Cambridge and Harvard. Former lecturer on Indian philosophy in Latin America. Professor of philosophy and religious studies at the University of California (Santa Barbara). Former member of the Spanish High Council of Scientific Research; co-founder of its journal *Arbor;* co-founder and member of the Spanish Philosophical Society. Member: Academic Council of the Ecumenical Institute for Advanced Theological Study, Jerusalem; American Society for the Study of Religion; Vice-Chairman of the Indian Theological Association; Vice-President of the Teilhard de Chardin Centre for the Future of Man (London); International Institute of Philosophy.

Publications include: three doctoral theses, *El Concepto de Naturaleza, Ontonomía de la Ciencia, The Unknown Christ of Hinduism*; as well as *Kultmysterium in Hinduismus und Christentum*; *Māyā e Apocalisse. L'Incontro dell'Induismo e del Cristianesimo*;

Kerygma und Indien. Zur Heilsgeschichtlichen Problematik der Christlichen Begegnung mit Indien; *Técnica y Tiempo. La Tecnocronía*; *El Silencio del Dios. Un Mensaje del Buddha al Mundo Actual. Contribución al Estudio del Ateismo Religioso*; *The Trinity and World Religions. Icon—Person—Mystery*; *Worship and Secular Man.*

Contributions to various periodicals: 'Letter to a Christian Artist', in: *The Madras Cultural Academy*; 'The Existential Phenomenology of Truth', in: *Philosophy Today*; 'The Integration of Indian Philosophical and Religious Thought', in: *Religion and Society.*

BETTINA BÄUMER. Born in 1940 in Salszburg, Austria. Academic studies in theology, philosophy, history of religions and indology, in Salzburg, Vienna, Rome and Munich. Doctorate in philosophy. Since 1967, research in Sanskrit, Indian philosophy, Hinduism. Former lecturer at Benares Hindu University. Now Assistant Professor, University of Vienna.

Articles and publications include: *Schöpfung als Spiel. Der Begriff līlā im Hinduismus, Seine Philosophische und Theologische Bedeutung*; 'Le Nom Secret dans l'Hindouisme', in: E. Castelli (ed.), *L'Analyse du Langage Théologique. Le Nom de Dieu* ; 'Meditationspraxis im Heutigen Indien', in: *Stimmen der Zeit* (Munich).

ALEXIS KAGAME Ph.D. Professor at the National University of Rwanda and a correspondent at the Institut pour la Recherche Scientifique en Afrique Centrale. Member of: the Académie Royale des Sciences d'Outre-Mer (Brussels); Institut International des Civilisations Différentes; the African International Institute (London); the American Academy of Political and Social Science.

Publications in French include: *Introduction aux Grands Genres Lyriques de l'Ancien Rwanda*; *Un Abrégé de l'Ethno-histoire du Rwanda*; *La Poésie Dynastique au Rwanda*; *Les Institutions Politiques du Rwanda Précolonial*; *Les Organisations Socio-familiales de l'Ancien Rwanda*; *La Philosophie Bantu-Rwandaise de l'Être*; *La Naissance de l'Univers*; *Le Colonialisme face à la Doctrine Missionnaire à l'Heure du Vatican II*; *Le Rwanda 1900–1950*; and *La Mentalité Religieuse Préchrétienne des Bantu*, as well as numerous publications in Kinyarwanda.

G. E. R. LLOYD. University lecturer in classics at King's College, Cambridge University. Born in London, 1933, and educated at Charterhouse. Has graduated at King's College, Cambridge, where he later took his M.A. and Ph.D., and in 1957 became a Fellow.

Publications include: *Polarity and Analogy: Two Types of Argumentation in Early Greek Thought*; *Aristotle: the Growth and Structure of his Thought*; *Early Greek Science: Thales to Aristotle*; *Greek Science After Aristotle*; as well as contributions to such periodicals as *Phronesis, Journal of Hellenic Studies, Classical Review, Gnomon, Cambridge Review, The Times Literary Supplement, British Journal for the Philosophy of Science, History of Science*, and *Proceedings of the Cambridge Philological Society*; and to the *Encyclopedia of Philosophy*, the *Dictionary of the History of Ideas*, and *Literature and Western Civilisation.*

ANDRÉ NEHER. Born in Obernai, France, in 1914. Director of the Institute of Hebraic Studies at the Université des Sciences Humaines of Strasbourg. Member of the academic councils of universities: Brussels, Jerusalem, Tel-Aviv and Haifa.

Publications include: *L'Essence du Prophétisme*; *L'Existence Juive Histoire; Biblique du Peuple d'Israël*; *Le Puits de l'Exil, la Théologie Dialectique du Maharal de Prague*; *L'Exil de la Parole, du Silence Biblique au Silence d'Auschwitz.*

Contributions to the *Encyclopédie Française*, *Encyclopédie de la Pléiade*, *Encyclopaedia Judaica*, *Encyclopédie Hébraïque*, and the Unesco *Journal of World History.*

GERMANO PÀTTARO. Professor at the Patriarchal Seminary in Venice.

Articles and publications include: '*Kérigme* et *Didakè:* Continuité et Discontinuité du Témoignage', in: *Le Témoignage—Actes du Colloque Organisé par le Centre International d'Études Humanistes et par l'Institut d'Études Philosophiques de Rome* (*1972*), edited by E. Castelli.

LOUIS GARDET Christian philosopher. Specializes in comparative religion and cultures (particularly Moslem). Numerous visits to Islamic countries (including the Near and Middle East, the Maghreb, India and Pakistan). Visiting professor at the universities of Rabat, Algiers, Cairo, Beirut. Editor (with Etienne Gilson) of *Études Musulmanes*, Paris. Current contributor to the *Encyclopédie de l'Islam.*

Publications include: *La Pensée Religieuse d'Avicenne*; *La Cité Musulmane, Vie Sociale et Politique*; *Expériences Mystiques en Terres non Chrétiennes*; *Connaître l'Islam*; *Les Grands Problèmes de la Théologie musulmane: Dieu et la Destinée de l'Homme*; *L'Islam, Religion et Communauté*; *La Mystique*; *Études de Philosophie et de Mystique Comparées*; *Introduction à la Théologie Musulmane—Essai de Théologie Comparée*; *Mystique Musulmane—Aspects et Tendances, Expériences et Techniques.*

ABDELMAJID MEZIANE. Associate professor at the Faculté des Lettres of Algiers University.

Articles and publications in French include: 'Histoire et Personnalité'; 'L'Engrenage des Traditionalismes'; 'Le Faux Confort des Orthodoxies'; 'Miettes Culturelles et Culture Révolutionnaire', all four in *Révolution Africaine* (Algiers). In Arabic: (Cultural Crises in Algeria), in *Al Moujahid* (Algiers); (Ideological Rape), in *Achaab* (Algiers) — (French translation by R. P. Gaspar in *Revue Ibla* (Tunis)); (The Rising Tide of Alienation) and (Resistance and Culture in Algeria), in *Al Assāla* (Algiers).

A. J. GUREVICH. Researcher at the Institute of World History of the U.S.S.R. Academy of Sciences. Professor of history at Moscow University. Specializes in the history of Western Europe (particularly Scandinavia) and the social psychology of the early mediaeval period in Western Europe.

Publications (in Russian): (*The Raids of the Vikings*); (*Free Peasantry of Feudal Norway*); (*Problems of the Genesis of Feudalism in Western Europe*); (*History and Saga*); (*Categories of Mediaeval Culture*). Articles (in French) in : *Annales E.S.C.*, *Diogène*; in English in *Mediaeval Scandinavia*, *Arkiv for Nordisk Filologi*, etc.

CONTENTS

INTRODUCTION

Paul Ricoeur

The reader of the essays collected here under the title *Cultures and Time* finds himself confronted by a series of perplexing questions. It is as such a reader that I shall attempt to formulate these questions.[1]

Before asking ourselves what conclusions are to be drawn from the discovery of this cultural diversity, it is important to understand what it means, to grasp its multifarious roots. It is not, in fact, as easy as it may appear to acknowledge whole-heartedly that behind our modernity, in the underlying strata on which our culture rests, there is a basic cleavage, a fundamental disagreement which colours all our awareness of what history has made of us. History has created us many and various: the realization of this must be heightened to the point at which it becomes a radical quandary, a dilemma seemingly lacking all solution.

'Grammatical' diversity

The distinctive nature of the cultures considered in the present volume is treated at several different levels by the different authors of these essays. By the same token, there are several levels of diversity. I shall endeavour to survey them in a certain order, taking as my starting-point the diversity inherent in the vocabulary and the syntax of time. For brevity's sake, I shall call this the level of grammatical diversity. This diversity is, to be sure, by no means the only linguistic factor involved. Other linguistic constraints, which are not properly speaking 'grammatical', will be discussed below. We must, nevertheless, start from this point. The irreducible pluralism innate in the diversity of tongues is evinced by the manner itself in which the authors of these essays have, by tacit or overt agreement, treated their subject. All lay stress on the close relationship between the conception of time and history and the configurations of language. The author of the study 'The Empirical Apperception of Time and the Conception of History in Chinese Thought' states at the very outset: 'The way in which a people experiences the conditions and limitations affecting its life is reflected in its language and its behaviour' (p. 35). The distinction between language and behaviour is itself identified by the author in terms of the imprint it has left upon the Chinese tongue.

There can, therefore, be no question of separating out some personal experience of time and history, experience which would doubtless be that of the Chinese, but which one could universalize, by seeking in oneself its unexpressed equivalent. No, the meaning is so bound up in the arrangement of the words, in the form of a poem or the conventional style of a painting, that no short-cut exists which might dispense us from going the long way round, by way of the Chinese 'characters'. And there is no universal characteristic by means of which these can be made intelligible to all.

The extent to which meaning is bound up in words, in verbal artefacts, in plastic representations and patterns of behaviour is also described by the author of the essay 'Time and History in the Tradition of India'. The interplay of the two higher powers, *kāla* (time) and karma (action), is not something for which we can immediately create a conceptual equivalent in our own system of thought. 'Indian philosophy', the author observes, 'took an interest in time, starting primarily from a consideration of grammar and language, but also (this is striking in Yoga) on the basis of a spiritual desire to transcend time' (p. 70). Let us, for the time being, leave aside this second aspect, to which we shall return later, at some length. As in the case of Chinese culture, it is impossible, in any study of Indian thought, to dispense with a consideration of the vocabulary and semantics of temporality. Indian thought enables us, however, to go one step further in our analysis of the diversity of temporal institutions. It is the grammarians themselves who initiate this meditation upon time. It appears that the study of Sanskrit grammar and its system of verbal tenses is even more instructive than that of the vocabulary of time. The very act of measuring time requires the construction of a semantic grid in which terminological differences reflect fine distinctions in meaning. The establishment of the calendar and the division of time into longer spans are based upon a similar linguistic and semantic operation. It is a remarkable fact, however, that the grammarians of India were the first—at the end of the fifth and the beginning of the sixth centuries, according to Panikkar—to turn to account the self-reflective nature of language, using grammar in order to initiate an analysis of time and its breakdown into discrete moments on the basis of verbal tenses. However, the second-order language in which this analysis is carried out reflects, in turn, certain semantic choices—for example, the distinction between 'permissive force' and 'restraining force'—that go to make up the distinctive system of language and thought which characterizes the culture in question. The philosopher-grammarian bases his analyses on the grammar which serves as his medium of thought. Panikkar stresses the point when he writes that the examples which he adduces 'are sufficient to show that empirical and phenomenological analyses are indeed to be found in the Indian tradition. Yet the fact remains, significantly, that language is the starting-point of these reflections' (p. 71).

I am not, however, wishing to suggest that language—understood strictly in the sense of a vocabulary and a syntax—is the sole basis of the diversity of cultures, as though the different tongues were in themselves so many different views of the world. An obvious objection to any such suggestion is that the *things said* in a given language transform the straitjacket of grammar into a means of expression and compound it with a spontaneity and freedom of conception which is that of human discourse. It is at this level, therefore, that the discussion must be carried on.

Diversity of the forms of discourse

The monographs on time and history as reflected in different cultures provide us here with a second level on which to analyse this diversity, one which I intend to relate to the *forms of discourse*. I shall refer briefly to the two studies mentioned above, dwelling at greater length on the other cultural arenas described in this work.

The author of the study on the Chinese conception of time is able to adduce, in addition to the Chinese lexicon (Chinese grammar affording for this purpose no formal codification of temporal dimensions—past, present, future—in a system of verbal tenses), a category of texts, namely the *Chronicles* and *Archives*, which enable a people to constitute its history by expressing it in story form. At this level, further constraints, not specifically linguistic ones, emerge, which serve to make this culture unique and comparable to none other. Our author proceeds to list the features which distinguish the Chinese form of story-telling: the heavenly mandate of the supreme authority, the seasonal distribution, the annalistic style, then, later, in the so-called classical era, the introduction of a hortatory tone and polemical themes, together with a calculated laconicism. All these features have a 'distancing effect' and prevent us from identifying with the protagonists.

This does not mean we are barred from all understanding. Far from it, indeed; otherwise there could be no question of our even assessing 'the traits distinguishing the Chinese historiographers' conception of history' (p. 53). We understand, but as from afar, without being able to relate this peculiarly exotic insight to the system of meanings by which we know ourselves. A case in point is the cosmic 'centrality' of China. For what we cannot do is to displace the centre to any number of different points. We shall return to this point later. At the very moment, in fact, when the author of this essay succeeds in communicating, in terms which are also our own—democratic trend, anarchy, individualism—the distinctive features which make a culture what it is, he is prudent enough to draw our attention back to its intrinsic uniqueness, which resides in the intimate relationship between the system of writing in ideograms and the ideology of 'correct designations' which he suggests might be better termed 'the rectification of conduct in accordance with correct designations (names, titles)' (p. 55). 'The empirical apperception of time', as the author calls it, is then inseparable from this amalgam of discourse, ethics and politics denoted by the above formula.'

The essay relating to Indian thought takes us somewhat further. Here, the author has warned us that it is not simply reflection on grammar and language, but also 'a spiritual desire to transcend time' (p. 70), which constitutes the distinctive feature of the Indian conception of time and history. This spiritual yearning, however, is expressed in forms of discourse which are markedly related to the message that is being transmitted. The reader finds himself in strange territory with Panikkar's very opening remark: 'Time is born with sacrifice, and it is by sacrifice that it is once again destroyed.' But this statement is itself a transposition, for the reader's benefit, of an original formula: 'If the priest did not offer up the sacrifice of fire every morning, the sun would not rise.' This Vedic intuition could, to be sure, be transcribed as a philosopheme and interpreted conceptually, and I shall return later to this way of understanding. It must, however, first be replaced, as must the other fundamental intuitions of time considered in the remainder of this essay, in the specifically *hymnic* context from which its meaning stems.

The hymn is not, in fact, a form of discourse external to discourse itself and to what is said through and in that discourse—as the expression 'literary genre' might lead one to suppose. The mode of utterance and the way of thinking here intermesh. What is being said in hymnic form could not be expressed otherwise. And no philosophical prose could exhaust the poetical meaning of the texts translated by L. Renou under the title *Hymnes Spéculatifs du Véda*. To speak of transcendental time, of time incarnate in the sun, the planets and the empirical divisions, is to be using a different mode of utterance, to say something inherently different. Would we speak of time as a force that 'works', that 'ripens beings', encompasses all creatures and 'keeps watch when all are asleep' in any mode other than the hymnic? Can the affirmation of Time as something indivisible and all-powerful, transcending divisible, measured time, be voiced otherwise than in hymns, through a mode of utterance which in its form as in its substance is wholly celebration? Even the 'radical transformation', which brought into the foreground, in the period of the Upanishads and the Vedas, that side of Indian thought given to cosmological speculation, did not eliminate the declaratory, proclamatory aspect which is part and parcel of a mode of thought that remains religious throughout, even though the specifically speculative element gives rise to particular problems which are not exhausted by consideration of the hymnic mode of discourse, and to which we shall have to return later.

I should like, however, to broaden my analysis to include some of the other cultural areas covered in this work, though still speaking only of the impact of the *modes of discourse* upon what is given utterance in a particular culture.

I have already referred, in connexion with the genesis of the Chinese and Indian conceptions of time and history discussed in the two above-mentioned essays, to the part played therein by the chronicle and the hymn. The 'pre-and non-philosophical views on time' in Greek thought furnish other examples of the various modes of discourse in which such conceptions are rooted. Lloyd stresses from the outset the 'literary character' (p. 117) of the evidence adduced: 'almost all our evidence comes from texts designed as literary productions, whether prose or verse, of one kind or another' (p. 117). This is precisely what interests us at this point in our analysis. It is not irrelevant that a particular conception stems from the *Iliad* or the *Odyssey*, that is, from epic works, or is to be found in the works of lyric poets or dramatists. Matters of vocabulary (which are undoubtedly interesting and no less instructive than those discussed above in connexion with the Chinese glossary and the Indian lexicon) pertain to an abstract and, to some extent, molecular approach when considered in terms of an investigation focused upon epic time itself. In this connexion, it is to be noted that such expressions as 'day of return' or 'day of enslavement' appear in an epic poem in which 'for each man the day itself possesses the quality of the events it contains' (p. 119). 'Man's dependence on his "days"' (p. 119) would indeed appear to be a theme suited to the whole of the *Odyssey*, considered as a poem. And surely the heroic theme could not but be consonant with the sadness of what is finite, as reflected in the transitoriness and fatefulness of human life. It is the epic chronicle of Achilles' exploits which gives poignancy to his bitter cry that he would prefer to be a bondsman on earth than king of all the dead.

The literary genre exemplified by Hesiod's *Works and Days* is no less illuminating in connexion with problems of time. The main purpose of the poem, Lloyd suggests, is 'to offer advice concerning the regulation of the activities of the year' (p. 120). This mode of didactic poetry requires that the 'days' be qualified in terms of what should or should not be done, according to circumstance. Time thus becomes the pattern of days of good, or evil, omen, of lucky and unlucky days. Hesiod's *Theogony*, with its vision of the successive ages of man, also evinces this concern with the 'works' which characterize each age—for example, the insolent excess (*hubris*) of the 'silver race'. Even the myth, then, in this subtly didactic context, contains a message, namely 'a warning against disproportion of any kind' (p. 121). In this sense, there is a time which is that of 'works and days', in which 'the temporal and the moral order are indissolubly linked' (p. 121). Justice itself is 'conceived, in part, as a matter of the orderly temporal regulation of man's life', while time is 'an aspect of the moral ordering of the universe' (p. 121-22).

Similarly, is it not the very genius of lyricism, that of Pindar and of the tragic chorus, not exactly to celebrate, as the hymn celebrates, but to sing—which can mean to lament—time's 'treachery', the fluctuations of fortune, the

2

ups and downs of human affairs before time 'the judge'? (But does not Paul Valéry also sing of '*Midi le Juste*', the justice of noon?) Time is a 'god that brings ease' only when considered from the vantage-point of a certain tragic wisdom, that of Aeschylus, after being subjected to the hard schooling sung by the chorus in the *Agamemnon*, that of 'understanding through suffering'. And it may be that time is the unrelenting destroyer only in another tragic vision, that of Sophocles, in which all hope of reconciliation is apparently dispelled.

We must, to be sure, be careful not to lapse into a new kind of determinism, that of the literary 'genres', which would be no less naïve than a determinism based upon linguistic structures. The author of the study on Greek thought himself cautions us against such a mechanical conception by showing how certain motifs, themes, concepts forge their way forward, emerge and take shape, as it were sloughing off the literary forms that moulded them and lending themselves to philosophical conceptualization. Illustrative of this process is the realization of the depth and continuity of the past, the speculation on the transition from barbarity to civilization and the awareness gained of the difference between history and myth. The forms of discourse must, therefore, be seen as a springboard rather than a straitjacket. They are, in my view, not so much systems of rigid constraints as sets of rules for the production of discourse of a certain kind, in the same way that grammar regulates our ability to produce fully formed sentences. The generative function of these rules is such that the *things said* are apt to slough off, in their underlying significance, the forms of discourse which assisted in bringing them into being.

Diversity of utterances or 'word events'

The diversity of cultures derives from the diversity of tongues in a wider, but possibly deeper, sense than that of the mere variety of vocabularies and syntaxes, or even the—more 'literary'—variety of the forms of discourse (hymn, chronicle, epic, didactic poem, tragedy and lyric). In several of the cultures studied in this work, the implicit or explicit conception of time is linked with an emergence of Word—or Writing—which situates, with reference to some grounding event of discourse, the whole complex of experiences, forms of behaviour and interpretations which in their turn constitute the peculiarly characteristic body of experience of the culture concerned. This is true, albeit in different senses, of 'the view of time and history in Jewish culture', 'the Christian conception of time' and 'Moslem views of time and history'. If it is true that here once again it is language which diversifies, it is basically in the sense that these conceptions draw their peculiarity from the event of discourse in which they are grounded. The things *said* are here those which are expressed in their *writings*. At this point a new kind of peculiarity and, hence, diversity becomes apparent.

The manner in which André Neher presents the 'conception of historical time in Jewish culture' might, at first sight, seem to conceal the peculiarity of the situation. The author brings this conception closer to us by seeing in it the very source of the 'historical dimension'. In this way it becomes to some extent the fountainhead of one of our modern categories. This conceptual descent is made even more accessible to our understanding if, as Neher does, we see this conquest of historical reality as the antithesis of myth. For the Semites in their migrations and conquests (from the Sumerians to the Egyptians and the Canaanites) myth is haunted by a space that defies all attempts to tie it down—the same space that the Greeks (who thus find themselves in this respect in the same camp) seek to master by means of geometry and cosmology. How close, then, the Hebrews feel to us if it is true that 'alone among the systems of thought of antiquity, Hebraic thought thoroughly dominated space, raising human time to the level of a history that was unique, fertile, bursting with meaning and a challenge to the very destiny of man' (p. 151). Nothing appears to remain of the gulf separating the West from the conceptions of Chinese and Indian cultures.

The peculiarity derives here from the manner in which this 'historical dimension' itself entered into language. It is of crucial importance that, in order to grasp its significance, the author proceeds by way of the exegesis of a *narrative*, 'the biblical narrative of the creation, which simultaneously relates two births, that of the cosmos and that of time' (p. 149). However fundamental may be the antithesis between this story and myth—and I willingly grant that it is fundamental—the fact remains that the unique feature of the story is that it concerns the beginning: 'In a beginning, time was set in motion, and ever since then history has been moving forward irresistibly' (p. 152). To be sure, the significance of this event, which opens the way in all directions, reverberates in that of the stories which relate 'the lives of men whose chief function was to keep the highway open' (p. 152). It also reverberates in the ethic of the Torah and in the structure of the Covenant, the significance of which is historical throughout and in no sense spatial. By the same token, the great biblical narrative of the beginnings finds its interpretation at the very core of our historical experience. An echo is struck within us by the terms in which Neher evokes the teleological significance of history, the way in which it shuttles between the two partners to the Covenant, God and man, the eternal 'improvisation' which is the result, the threat of Chaos and even the possibility of final failure, the absence of any ultimate point or Omega, the profound cleavage introduced by freedom and the tremendous risk which it entails with its uncertainty—'it may be. . . nothing' (p. 157)—necessarily involved in the 'potential existence of Jerusalem' (p. 158).

The unique feature of this vision is that its latent universality derives from utterance entering the stage in a manner which subtends the entire biblical structure. To understand this structure is to understand and interpret a saying such as 'Let us make man . . .' in the sense in which it is understood by the Wisdom writers, and by André Neher himself, namely: 'Let us make man, together you as man, I as God, and this covenant founds for ever the freedom of man whom it has made for ever the partner of God' (p. 157).

But if this is so, then such an utterance or word-event finds its necessary corollary in a diversity of exegesis, by virtue of which an all but universal experience enters into language.

It is, in fact, purely in a spirit of exegesis, at least as far as the initial stages are concerned, that the author of the study on the Christian conception of time approaches his task. In order to identify the basic conception from which the various trends of Christianity later issued forth, we must 'start from the New Testament' (p. 169), that is, start from the document in which the evangelists proclaim their faith in order to discover there the norm for interpretation of Christian experience itself. Now, this document says something concerning time in so far as it says something concerning history, and what it has to say about history is that its entire course is hinged to the time of Christ. The considerable interest of Germano Pàttaro's study resides in the fact that it says nothing about time and history in Christian thought which is not documented solely from New Testament sources and which does not describe the gravitational space centred upon the lifetime of Christ. Not only, then, does the interpretation of history here precede that of time, not only is history considered to be imbued with meaning, but 'there is a reciprocal relation between time and history that begins with Christ who, in the history which he fulfils and inaugurates at one and the same time, appears at a particular moment defined as the "fullness of time", in accordance with a plan that God has laid down in advance, "to be put into effect when the time was ripe"'.

The unique feature of this conception clearly derives from its Christ-centred character, and in order to make it understood its interpreter feels logically compelled to contrast it both with a putative Hellenistic vision and with the temporal conception of Judaism.

Assuming that time for the Greeks was circular—an assumption which is disputed in this present collection of essays itself—and that Hellenism produced a concept of eternity as diametrically opposed to time, the New Testament concept of time is lacking all timeless 'elsewhere', time being fully potentialized along its linear dimension. The historical event represented by the advent of Christ cannot abolish time, but orients all past and all future experience, in so far as 'Christ is both the end-point and the goal of history' (p. 172). It is the gnostic view which empties time of its original density and, in doing so, returns to Hellenism. The Greek world and the New Testament world are thus mutually exclusive. Even God's time can be only unlimited duration, never absence of time. What precedes time is merely without limit or determination and the end of time means only that 'with Christ, the time devoted to awaiting him is ended' (p. 174).

However, though the New Testament gives its full value to time, in contrast to what the author takes to be the Hellenic view, its manner of articulating the 'privileged' moments within time itself distinguishes it from Judaism. There are thus two aspects to the uniqueness of its conception. Once again, it is Christ's time on earth which is the hinge on which all other times hang. His 'hour' (St John), his *kairos* (synoptic gospels and epistles), is the event that furnishes the key to death and resurrection. And the hour at which he came was that appointed by God. All the other *kairoi* are marked by this one, both those which precede it and those which come after it, the Church's present time and the Day of Judgement. Biblical history is the concatenation of these *kairoi*, converging on and inspired by Christ. The tension of this history derives from the fact that the central *kairos* is accomplished, but that its full manifestation is still to come. Here is the point of rupture with Judaism: 'The situation thus established is wholly different from that contemplated by Hebraic tradition, in that the Messianic era can no longer be situated in the future; it lies now and for ever in the past, which is the past of Christ for all the future that comes after him' (p. 180). It is true that the notion of a tension between what has already, and what has not yet, come to pass, a tension which prevents the future from being reduced to a mere continuing memory of the 'moment-event' that was Christ, somewhat attenuates, though it does not eliminate, this difference between Christianity and Judaism. What distinguishes Christianity from Judaism and Hellenism alike stems wholly from the fact that 'it is Christ himself who makes his time the yardstick for this dialectical, tension-generating division' (p. 180-1). In him the past is wholly fulfilled and the future wholly foreshadowed.

A purely exegetic approach such as that adopted by Germano Pàttaro was necessary in order to show how the vision of time and history is here geared to the *level of utterance*. We are no longer dealing with vocabulary or grammar, nor even the forms of discourse—although a closer look should be taken at the 'forms' of discourse characteristic of the New Testament, namely the parable, the proverb, the eschatological statement, the letter and above all the 'form' of the Gospel itself. The level here is that of the word-event, in the twofold sense of the Word become flesh and of what is actually said in the linguistic and hermeneutic context afforded by the New Testament writings. To this level is keyed not only the interpretation of Christ's time and all other 'times' but also, as Pàttaro shows, liturgical time, with its first day, the 'Lord's day'—its annual cycle centred upon Easter and 'Holy Week' and its other special seasons. Time is thus not merely interpreted, but given meaning through ritual. The originality of this conception of time is reflected in the rhythm of our weeks and our years, upon which the Christian community as a whole has stamped its unique imprint.

A similar reflection is prompted by the study on Moslem views of time and history, although I hesitate to speak of utterance or word-event in describing the source of diversity which is laid bare to us in Louis Gardet's study. It is upon the *Book*, as the principle conferring order on a lived experience, at all levels of social and personal existence, that our thinking must here be focused. 'It is from an Arabic book, the Koran', Louis Gardet writes, 'that they

[Moslem values] ultimately derive' (p. 197). This ability of the book to generate and substantiate meaning prevails over the atomizing tendency of Arabic vocabulary concerning time. Vocabulary and grammar, the measurement and scansion of time are in fact as it were magnetized by 'the specific nature of the Moslem vision or visions of time and its evolution' (p. 197). In this respect, Islam affords an exemplary demonstration of the limitations of an unduly one-sided conception such as would make languages *per se* the constitutive principle of the different world-views. It is what is said in a particular language which determines what meaning is attached to the various categories of human experience. And it is Islam as such which imposes, as Gardet shows, 'a piecemeal vision of the succession of things, a sequence of "instants" (*waqt*, pl. *awqāt*), which are the signs and spaces of God's intervention' (p. 201). If 'the sense of time as actually experienced' has taken the particular form it has taken throughout the entire Moslem world, Arab and non-Arab alike, this is because the Koran refers to a 'divine time' which has nothing in common with earthly time, measured by reference to the heavenly bodies.

If such is the 'impact of Islam'—that is to say, of the preaching of the Koran and the 'tradition of the Prophet'—everything which in Islam is directly governed by these is also constitutive of lived time: commemorations and festivals, fasting and the breaking of fasts, sacrifices and pilgrimages. Lived time is thus marked out by 'fixed points of time', indicating the 'period', 'delay' when something has to be done, and by when completed.

As regards the conceptual formulations, these inevitably bear the imprint of this lived time ordered in terms of the preaching and of the practice which is based on it. This being so, it is in no way surprising that the discontinuous apprehension of isolated moments should triumph over the apperception of continuous duration, and that this 'milky way of instants', as Massignon put it, 'is represented as a number of tangential points—points of contact rather than intersection—between human time and the eternity of the Most High' (p. 204). Nor is it at all surprising that the conception of history engendered by this sense of time should be as markedly opposed to a progressive as to a cyclical conception of history. 'In broad terms, it would be correct to say that, in the specifically Moslem view of the world, there are "histories" but there is no such thing as history' (p. 209). The missions of the annunciators and the envoys are so many isolated flashes, whose effulgence corresponds at the historical level to the discrete moments of which time is composed.

Once again, the unique character of the principle as it is uttered and written in the very infancy of Islam is what distinguishes Moslem culture from Greek and Judeo-Christian culture. In confirmation of this it is enough to reflect upon such expressions as the 'Nation of the Prophet' or the 'waiting for the Mahdi' and, even more instructive perhaps, the referential significance of the 'State of Medina'—that group of companions accompanying the Prophet—'conceived not as the immutable prototype of all earthly cities but as the point of refraction in which every earthly city should be rooted' (p. 211). 'The only true "history", that inscribed by God, for those who have eyes to see it, in the "fissures of time"' (p. 212).

It is true that the philosophical, theological and mystical constructions do not entirely square with this distinctive aspect of Moslem cultures. And this relative transcendance of speculative activity raises a problem which we shall not attempt to evade. Here again, the case of Islam is exemplary. The interplay of Moslem, Persian and Greek thought is so complex at a certain level of systematic elaboration that Moslem thought merges in a general ground swell of speculation, and in the process loses its distinctive character. Westerners for their part are well aware that Moslem thought is as it were woven into the fabric of their own Middle Ages: Kindi, Farabi, Avicenna, Averroes, Ibn Khaldun have their place in the universal history of thought. For this very reason, however, the author of the study on Islam feels himself obliged, when referring to these thinkers nurtured on the works of Aristotle, the Stoics and Plotinus, to place them on what he calls its 'divergent lines' (p. 205). He does the same in his account of Shiite esoterics and their scholarly gnoses, particularly those concerned with time, reinterpreted in the light of the emanationist view of the creation of beings. No doubt Gardet is right to refer in this respect from the analyses of philosophers and scholars to the everyday experience of the common run of men in order to affirm that this experience is deeply imbued with the discontinuous, relativist conception of time which reflects the true impact of Islam.

If this is indeed true, then the reader's abiding impression must be not so much of the interplay of speculative thought at a lofty level as of the persistence of an initial vision projected into the world through what the Koran has to tell us of the prophet. This is the key feature in a conception of time as a succession of discrete moments tangential with eternity. According to this conception, 'time is less the measurement of movement than an indisputable sign of the impermanence of created things' (p. 205).

For our own analysis of the diversity of cultures, the most significant feature is 'this Moslem sense of the fleeting instant in its tangential relationship with the divine *sarmad*' (p. 208-9).

Diversity of categories

We have still not got rid of the enigma, the aporia created by the diversity of conceptions, even when we think we can rise above considerations of language, in the narrow sense of vocabulary and grammar, the broader sense of the forms of discourse, or even the deeper sense of a creative Word at the very basis of things. Are there not certain 'conceptions' of time and history which it is possible to translate, transcribe and expound in terms of a 'conceptual' order which renders all modes of expression secondary?

That concepts do operate on a higher level than that of the linguistic modes in which they find expression is not to be disputed—if it were not so, then nothing could be translated from one language to another, nor indeed from one mode of expression to another within the same language—but it is precisely at this level of concepts that there exists a fundamental, specific diversity, perhaps the most entrenched and impregnable of all. Human thought has not produced a universal system of categories capable of embodying a personal experience of time and history itself having universal validity.

This limitation under which all transcriptions from the key categories of one conception into those of another labour is well illustrated, in this work, by Alexis Kagame's attempt to work out in conceptual terms, using the resources of Western metaphysics, 'the empirical apperception of time and the conception of history in Bantu thought'. From the very outset, the author situates this conception of time 'at the metaphysical level' (p. 89). He begins his analysis by establishing the categorial frame of reference wherewith the Bantu conception of time is to be identified: 'Ontologically speaking, Bantu culture regards everything which can be conceived or formulated as falling in the following categories: 1. Being endowed with intelligence (man); 2. Being without intelligence (things); 3. localizing Being (Place-Time); 4. Modal Being (accidentality or modification of Being)' (p. 89-92). Bantu terms can, therefore, be translated direct into metaphysical categories. This is the major presupposition of the study: 'I have therefore translated Hantu as "localizing being" and stated that it expresses the place-time entity' (p. 91). This is a perfectly legitimate assumption. All our other authors have resorted, to varying degrees (albeit in a less systematic way than Kagame), to such transcription or rather 'transcategorization': thus, Claude Larre, in his study of Chinese thought speaks, employing the language of Malebranche, of Chinese occasionalism,[1] and of democracy, anarchy and individualism. Raimundo Panikkar endeavours to make particular subjects of the Upanishads or of Buddhist literature comprehensible by mediating them through their counterparts in the speculative or critical philosophy of the West. André Neher does not hesitate to draw upon the resources of the 'philosophy of history' in order to convey something of the Jewish conception of history. Kagame is not, therefore, alone in his approach; he is simply bolder and more systematic. Not content merely to mention, for purely didactic purposes, the similarities between the concepts held in different cultures, he establishes the conditions under which a Bantu notion or expression becomes intelligible by setting forth the explicit system of categories in which Bantu thought is founded. For example, having found a Bantu term signifying both 'there' and 'then', he endeavours to account for the existence of an undivided 'localizer' which is both spatial and temporal. The 'metaphysical justification' (p. 92) thus brings into play the entire conceptual apparatus which was forged, chiefly by Arab, Christian and Jewish thinkers of the Middle Ages, on the basis of the Greek heritage: being and non-being, existence and the what-is, the same and the other, the necessarily existing and the pre-existing, entity and motion, etc. By this means, it is possible to conceive how to 'individualize the movement of each existent' existing (entity) (p. 94). Now, the conjunction of the point in time and the point in space ceases to be a confused idea once 'the "individualizing co-ordinate" of all movements' proves to involve a single localizer as a point common to time and to space.

But what, it may be wondered, is this 'underlying level of thought processes' (p. 94) at which time and place ultimately become one? Alexis Kagame's answer to this question is most interesting: this conception, he writes, is 'as old as Bantu language' (p. 94). Thus it is the linguistic system which is the storehouse of Bantu philosophy. This being so, we are not guilty of any abuse in employing an explicit system of categories in order to develop—in the photographic sense of the term—the system of categories implicit in language, for, to quote Kagame once more, 'everyday language cannot be separated from its underlying basis, which is the structure of the linguistic system' (p. 99).

Is the difference between this and other conceptions thereby banished? By no means. By conceptually assimilating the underlying linguistic structures, we provide a backcloth against which what the author terms the 'empirical apperceptions of time in Bantu culture' (p. 98) stand out clearly. Let us take as our starting point the observation, seemingly incidental, 'that there is no abstract substantive in Bantu to denote time as there is in European and American culture . . . the Bantu think only of the time *of* this or that, the time *for* this or that'. The conceptual reconstruction of time, having previously proceeded by assimilation, now proceeds by differentiation. Whereas Greek thought generated the concept of abstract time, as the 'number of movement' (Aristotle), in Bantu thinking time is seen as being stamped by particular events; and this notion of time as being 'marked', contrasting with our notion of 'empty time', leads on logically from that of the individualizing co-ordinate. This differential approach continues in the determination of the ideas of past, present and future, since it is always this 'marking' of time by particular events which governs the play of temporal significations. The inability of Bantu thought to assimilate the notion of eternity considered as the totality of duration confirms its difference from the conceptual model which was used to reconstruct it. This difference is evidenced even more tangibly by the linguistic system and by all the other marks of civilization: laws and political customs, social behaviour patterns, knowledge and skills, philosophical and religious systems. It is all these ways of *making history* which 'mark' or 'stamp' time. Here again, conceptual reconstruction, just as it appears to be establishing equivalences between one way of thinking and another, serves finally to emphasize unfamiliarity. Thus the—extremely rational—account given of the basic concerns which govern the survival of the group suddenly make one realize the singular role of the ancestors, the dead, in the very make-up of historical time; their 'intervention' (p. 113) in history in fact entails, at the social level, a whole series of practices and roles (that of the soothsayer, for example), and in the realm of thought causes a supernatural subject-matter and a 'magical logic'

(p. 114) to develop. The expression 'magical logic' does not, to be sure, imply a return to the pre-logical category employed by earlier sociologists: 'what we have termed "magical logic" is not a stage of thinking which is advancing towards Cartesian logic' (p. 114). It is nevertheless a fact that patient conceptual reconstruction, which had seemed to be using only categories familiar to us, ends up by identifying, under the name of 'magical logic', 'a system of thought which is complete in itself but of a different kind' (p. 114).

Are we justified in concluding from this examination that a culture possesses a finite capacity for conception and expression, and that it is interpretation itself which, using the resources of our 'own' categories, enables us to understand, by contrast, the 'other' categories? It may be that this tension between 'own' and 'other' opens the way towards an important discovery which it will be necessary to elucidate later.

I should like, however, to substantiate my present argument by adducing certain illustrations taken from the two areas where the elaboration of systems of thought has been carried furthest, namely, India and Greece. It is at this specifically speculative level that the diversity of cultures proves to be most deep-rooted.

We broke off our analysis of Indian conceptions of time at the point where the hymn emerged as the matrix of speculative thought itself. Now, what Panikkar describes as the 'interiorization and transcending of time' as seen mainly in the Upanishads, is based upon themes of which Western thought offers certain equivalents: Neo-Platonism too sought the living, spiritual continuity of time 'internally, within man, or more exactly within the Self' (p. 71)—which in India is termed the *ātman*, and even the symbol of the full vessel which is never drained and which never overflows has its counterpart in Plotinus' images of the brimming spring. It is, however, precisely at the point of greatest similarity that the difference re-emerges. We are suddenly reminded that mastery of the inner rhythm is inseparably bound up with exercises which are not merely spiritual but also—so to say in the same breath—exercises in breath control, and hence we are led to ponder the indissoluble unity of what is separated in so many Western systems of thought, namely, the breath of life (*prāna*) and the spiritual act (karma).

This is why the concept of karma defies transcription in terms of Western thought; the only way to speak of it is by linking together the disparate elements of a transposed discourse. For example, it is said to be 'in the first place action, then the residuum of the action which produces good or bad results and which lives on after the person, and lastly, the law that governs the retribution of actions and the network of interconnexions between the karmas of beings' (p. 74). This is tantamount to saying that this concept cuts across the very distinctions upon which the terms used to translate it are based.

Does the translation, conceptual as well as linguistic, then refer us back to an experience of time and history to which anybody can have access by means of a sort of short-cut from direct experience to direct experience, not passing through the cultural expressions of that experience? The author assures us that this is by no means so in the following sentence: 'India has experienced its past much more through its myths than by interpreting its history as a recollection of past events' (p. 76). It is here, indeed, that the difficulty of understanding and the possibility of misunderstanding reside: 'What the Westerner considers as history in the West, he would regard as myth in India. In other words, what he calls history in his own world is experienced by Indians as myth (p. 76).

This conceptual boxing and coxing gives some indication of the difficulty of communication which typifies the present venture in cultural typology.

The reader may object that the commentary does not give due weight to the difference made by the introduction of Buddhism to the 'regimen' of Indian thought, by which I mean not only the subject-matter but the speculative mode itself.

But this does not in the least detract from our argument. On the contrary, the spiritual gap widens when we come to consider those themes of certain Buddhist schools which are, both in their form and in their substance, more specifically philosophical: the unreality of instants and cosmic ages, the instant without past or future, the eternal present, intemporality. To be sure, all these words can be fairly well expressed in a philosophical language forged by Aristotle, Plotinus, Hegel, Kierkegaard and Nietzsche. And yet . . . and yet awakening and deliverance—pre-eminently Buddhist themes—appear to denote something quite different from categories of thought which can be isolated and transcribed. These approximate terms obliquely designate a total spiritual regimen which cannot be apprehended without also adopting the spiritual techniques, the exercises, ways of life, institutions, and social roles which constitute the concrete expression of a living spirituality.

Inherent limitations of philosophical 'inquiry'

When we come to consider Greek philosophy, it might be thought that we have finally entered a universal mode of thought in which the diversity of cultures has no place. The second part of the study by G. E. R. Lloyd (p. 127) provides a precise account—albeit, as was inevitable under the rules of the present work of cultural typology, a very brief one—of the conceptions which bear testimony to what for the West is a philosophical problem, the scrutinizing of a hypothesis, the evaluation of an argument and the discussion of a thesis. In the technical sense, there is in the Western context no 'inquiry', i.e. philosophical discussion, which does not derive from the reading and interpretation of the writings of Greek philosophers.

Why then include an account of Greek philosophy in a volume which takes the diversity of cultures as its theme? The first effect of including it is a retro-effect upon the account itself, revealing philosophical inquiry to be itself a distinctively Western feature: 'So far as the West is concerned', Lloyd writes, 'philosophical debate in general originates with the Greeks . . .' (p. 144). We should not write 'in the West' were we not conscious of systems of thought outside of Greek thought by reference to which it may be identified as specifically Greek; it is this reference to other cultures which makes the very notion of the universality of philosophical discussion a relative and specifically Western one. This impingement of the external world is inconceivable from within; the Greeks thought only in terms of the contradiction between Greek and barbarian. We, however, being familiar with the diversity of cultures, know that the speculative thought of India—to take an example which the present volume makes irrefutable—is certainly not barbarian.

The distancing effect thus produced by an outlook in which the teachings of India, of China, of the Hebrews and all the other 'outsiders' are taken into consideration continues to be felt within Professor Lloyd's study, which is thereby diversified in several ways: 'First there is, we must repeat, no such thing as the Greek view of time. The very variety of ideas and approaches, both within and outside philosophy, must be not only given due weight in itself, but also acknowledged to be one of the essential features of the Greek contribution' (p. 144).

The very expression 'outside philosophy'—within the Greek sphere—must give us pause. An account of Greek thought cannot begin with Parmenides (or even with Anaximander) and end with Plotinus (or even with Augustine, (p. 127-43). It requires that non-philosophy—or pre-philosophy (p. 118) and philosophy be confronted one with another, in other words, that we should think of philosophy and non-philosophy as it were together. To consider them together, however, does not only involve listing those themes of the epic, the lyric and the tragedy which can be given the status of philosophemes nor is it simply a matter of tracing the history of the victory of *logos* over *mythos*, for this transition is highly complex and does not exclude the possibility of myth being perpetuated in philosophical reasoning, for example in the work of Pythagoras and Empedocles, and even in Greek political philosophy (p. 123, 130), as is apparent whenever the theme of the Great Year resurfaces. The transition from *mythos* to *logos* does not even exclude the possibility of the deliberate reintroduction of myth into philosophical discourse, as in Plato. These complex relationships between myth and reason constitute in point of fact a model of the transition from non-philosophy to philosophy, a model which itself contains a certain inner diversity. However complex it may be, being a totality this model constitutes a finite configuration, a limited space of variations which distinguishes Greek thought from that of India, including that expressed in the Upanishads and in Buddhism.

There is more to it than this: Professor Lloyd's essay prompts the reader to ponder other forms of inner diversity in Greek thought than that in which philosophy and myth are held up for comparison. Let us consider the expression 'pre-Socratic philosophy'. All students of Greek literature are aware of the fact that the fragmentary writings of Anaximander, Parmenides, Heraclitus, Empedocles and Zeno of Elea have quite a different ring to them as compared with Plato's dialogues or Aristotle's treatises. Nietzsche and Heidegger have accustomed us to regard these authors not as pre-Socratic, that is, as mere precursors, but rather as thinkers in their own right, as it were eclipsed and forgotten by Socratic thought. Greek philosophy is thus not only that thinking which accomplishes the transition from *mythos* to *logos*, but also that which contains within itself the difference between pre-Socratic and Socratic thought and the obliteration of the former by the latter. This observation is particularly significant with regard to time. The 'cosmic justice' (p. 127) mentioned in the celebrated fragment of Anaximander's writings transmitted by Simplicius, Parmenides' statement that 'day and night are one' and even his assertion 'it is' and his rejection of 'it is not' are not situated in exactly the same universe of discourse as that of the Socratics, even though we have here left behind the poetry of Hesiod. This is why the exegesis of Parmenides' statement 'it is now' cannot be wholly undertaken with the resources of reasoning deployed by Aristotle in Book IV of the *Physics* on the apparently similar theme of the 'now'. It is only when we adopt the latter's precise definitions as our yardstick that it becomes perfectly legitimate to say, as Lloyd says, that Parmenides' 'now' is unclear. We are here somewhere between myth and discursive reasoning, in fact—not, however, that this intermediary stage can be thought of merely as a confused form of transition. A system of thought which does not yet draw a contrast between the ethico-political sphere and the cosmological and between the human order and nature, cannot simply be reduced to those foreshadowings of Socratic reasoning which, with benefit of hindsight, the history of philosophy discerns therein. This stage of thought is extremely complex, since certain contradictions, as for example that between Parmenides and Heraclitus, can be discerned within the same mode of thought, while the arguments of Zeno of Elea are themselves a sort of transition between the pre-Socratic mode of thought and post-Socratic philosophical inquiry. It is not, therefore, surprising that Zeno's famous arguments provide Aristotle with a worthy interlocutor, even though his 'confusion of two senses of "now"' (p. 135)—instant and interval —once again shows a lack of clarity. For the same reason, modern thinkers— among them Cantor (Lloyd, p. 134) do not disdain to tackle these redoubtable paradoxes, at the risk of themselves coming to grief thereon (p. 133-6). It is against this non-philosophical and philosophical background that Plato's and Aristotle's doctrines, which are for us the very model of what we call philosophy, stand out. We now know that Plato cannot be understood except against this background. In his *Politicus* and elsewhere, Professor Lloyd (p. 137) remarks, Plato 'uses and modifies traditional ideas connected with time'. His eternal, even though it is distinct from everlasting, cannot be separated, from the philosophical anabasis which retains something of the catharsis and ascesis upon which the Greeks had already been meditating, albeit in a non-philosophical mode. In this connexion, neo-Platonism has a decisive clarifying effect, even though it adds much to Plato, particularly on this very question of time.

It will be objected that in the case of Aristotle discursive inquiry ceases to owe anything to other modes of thought. 'We have to wait until Aristotle', Lloyd writes, 'for the first comprehensive, systematic philosophical analysis of time' (p. 138). The well-known formula in *Physics IV*, that 'time is the number of movement in respect of before and after' the distinction between the now as limit and the now considered as an infinitesimal part of time, and the relating of the measurement of time to the movement of the heavens—all these are on a level of discourse which was to cause the Middle Ages to regard Aristotle as *the* philosopher.

How is it, then, that the universal nature of this level of discourse fails to cancel out the diversity of cultures?

There are two possible answers to this question which refer back to previous observations but do not correspond exactly to the nature of the question. We might go along with André Neher and use the contrast with the essentially historical tenor of Hebraic thought to bring out a certain limitation inherent in the essentially spatializing, 'cosmologizing' conception of time held by the Greeks and, by the same token, the limitation inherent in their model of a temporal and moral order, which Lloyd himself discusses *in fine* in his essay (p. 145). The revelation of these inherent limitations is not without interest, but has no bearing upon the point at issue, namely, not so much the themes as the level of discourse. The Hebrews have nothing comparable to *Physics IV* on time and movement, time and number, continuous and discontinuous, the now as limit or boundary and the now as part of time. The point at issue, in fact, is the style of discourse, the level of analysis, the degree of conceptualization.

For the same reason, it would not be a decisive argument were one able to show—as would undoubtedly be possible—that Greek philosophy, for all its qualities, continues to bear the stamp of myth and of the so called pre-Socratic modes of thought, for we should still be comparing philosophy with what is external to philosophy. What is at issue, however, are the inherent limitations of the Greeks' philosophical approach to time.

These inherent limitations are to be sought in the concepts of nature and motion, upon which the Aristotelian concept of time depends. As we know, for Aristotle, time is 'something of motion'. However, motion is conceivable only in relation to the ontological structures of being and non-being, of becoming and privation, act and potentiality. The question is, do we still think, in these categories?

The level of the purest Greek philosopheme had first to be reached before it was possible to discover the decisive distancing factor that constitutes the Galilean revolution, which, as Koyré has demonstrated, undermines the notion of potentiality and rest, and, later, for Descartes to discover the force of inertia, which puts an end to the concept of a motion which gradually runs down, to peter out completely when the moving object reaches its 'natural place'. In the last analysis, it is the development of the modern science of motion which distances us in every respect from the Greek ontology of time. A number of consequences follow, chief among them being that all other relationships between man and nature are, in the modern age, subordinate to that relationship in which technology is the intermediary. The time which is the medium of our scientific thought and our technological activity has set a vast distance between us and the Greek conception of time.

Towards a new relationship with the cultures of the past

The terminal point of this meditation upon the many meanings inherent in the diversity of conceptions of time can become the starting point for a new kind of effort to *make something* of such a discovery.

It may, however, seem that nothing can be made of it. I can well imagine a reader who, having been unable to find his bearings on this strange voyage of discovery, is left completely unaffected.

He may find himself inhibited by two kinds of consideration. He may, firstly, consider that there is no 'viewpoint' from which he can survey the entire battlefields and this absence of viewpoint appears to put him in a quandary: either he may identify wholly with one of the traditions described and decide to disregard all the others, in which case he lacks that lofty impartiality familiar to the dramatist, who has an emphathic understanding of the arguments advanced by all his characters, or else he attempts to exercise this higher impartiality, but succeeds in doing so only as an aesthetic exercise, and thereby does less than justice to the claim to truth which each of those different visions makes.

On the other hand, the reader may consider that he does in fact have a viewpoint, but that it is not referred to in the present volume (for the very good reason, incidentally, that it will be dealt with in a later survey). We already designated this viewpoint in the course of our discussion of the inherent limitations of the philosophical inquiry characteristic of Greek philosophy: the viewpoint of modern science. It is because our culture has made science and technology the predominant modality of its relationship with reality that we now stand at such a remove from Greek origins of the scientific approach itself. Where, in fact, does the average reader of this study of cultural typologies stand? He is, truth to tell, placed in an orbit quite outside this entire area by the fact of his involvement with the problems of physical time, the time with which rational forecasting, economic calculations and scientific—or purportedly scientific—futurology operate. If his view cannot encompass all past cultures as a totality, this is not only because they are in themselves so many and varied and cannot be fitted into any all-embracing pattern, but also because we have moved on out of the area in which those cultures have their being.

Reflections of this nature upon our dilemma can indeed have an inhibiting effect but the question is whether we should not take the very things by which we are now inhibited as the basis for an attempt to *make sense* of this very discovery of diversity.

Basing myself on the second or the considerations outlined above, I would suggest that we should pursue our voyage of discovery to the very end. That which estranges us from the Greek origins is also that which estranges us from the Hebraic and the Indian origins. We are today as far removed from those cultures in which our roots were as from those which have always been alien to us. Even if, as Neher suggests, Hebraic thought has inculcated in us a sense of history, we are no less far removed from that historical perspective, inasmuch as science and technology have estranged us from the problems of the 'beginning' and the 'creation through the Word'. Even if the articulation of 'days' and 'generations' is a very meaningful one—and indeed without mystery—in the biblical scheme of things, it is from the entire biblical scheme of things that the scientific vision of the world has estranged us.

Is not the remedy, however, implicit in the ill? Was it not necessary that modernity would estrange us from our very roots in order that, transcending the rift created by critical scrutiny, we might once again draw near, in a second, post-critical 'innocence', both to what was farthest from us and to what was nearest to us? Equally estranged from things near and far, can we not find our way back to both thanks to the fact that the scientific revolution has created this equal distance between us and *all* traditional cultures?

How could this come about?

What can bring us closer back to that from which we have become separated is, in my view, our dawning realization that it is wrong to identify science and technology with the relationship of truth which we can have with all things. It is on the basis of criticism from within of this pretension by objective knowledge to be equivalent to truth that we can today essay a post-critical re-reading of the cultural evidence investigated in this volume. Seen thus, the distance which separates us from the cultures of the past becomes productive, enabling them to speak to us across the divide. The task today is to discover what, in the cultures of the past, is more than merely pre-scientific and hence has not been cancelled out by the scientific revolution and can speak to us from the far side of the Galilean and Newtonian revolutions.

Distance in proximity, proximity in distance, this is the paradox which governs all our present efforts to approach the cultural legacies of the past anew and to reactivate them in present-day terms.

The same paradox may govern not only our relationship to past cultures as a whole but also the relationship of one culture to another. Let us go back to the first of the two inhibiting considerations which we mentioned. We spoke of the feeling that there was no 'position' from which the entire field of cultures could be taken in. This is indeed true; but it does not mean we are doomed to oscillate between fanaticism and aestheticism. On the one hand, our over-view of the entire cultural field is always obtained from a certain position, and it is by degrees that we grasp its diversity. Any effort to understand is an effort situated in a particular context. On the other hand, however, we can no longer adhere to one tradition without a critical awareness of its relativity in relation to other traditions insinuating itself into the very heart of our allegiance. Any effort to approach anew, in a critical spirit, a particular legacy from the past is today accompanied by a sense of the difference between that and other world-views. Receptiveness to other cultures is today the precondition of our allegiance to any viewpoint; the tension between what is 'our own' and what is 'alien' is all part of the interpretation by which we endeavour to apply to ourselves the distinctive significance of a particular tradition. This tension between 'own' and 'alien' implies no over-view, no all-embracing vision.

Thus, the same dialectic of distance and proximity which underlies the relationship between the post-critical awareness and the world's cultures in the aggregate may also provide a basis for the relationship between one cultural heritage and another.

NOTES

1. Mr Gurevich's essay can be considered as a symmetrical counterpart to this introduction; there is, in fact, no such thing as a Marxist conception of time and history as there is a Hebraic conception, a Moslem conception, a Bantu conception, and so forth. Focusing his attention upon the same cultural diversity as I myself have been concerned with, Mr Gurevich has attempted to provide a Marxist solution to the enigma stemming from this diversity. His analysis does not constitute a further element in the series of essays devoted to individual cultures.
2. Claude Larre adds, it is true, that 'this is quite well understood in China without the aid of philosophers' (p. 44).

THE EMPIRICAL APPERCEPTION OF TIME AND THE CONCEPTION OF HISTORY IN CHINESE THOUGHT

Claude Larre

Empirical apperception of time

The way in which a people experiences the conditions and limitations affecting its life is reflected in its language and in its behaviour. This distinction between speech (*yen*) and behaviour (*hsing*) is commonly drawn in Chinese. The biography of an emperor, a minister or a scholar will record the words attributed to him and the acts he performed, invested with all the authority deriving from his rank and his 'virtue'.

Chinese people's conception of time is therefore reflected in their language and in their way of life; they have a wealth of expressions relating to time and a certain logic regarding the conception and organization of time running through their speech and the whole of their life. This is what we have to investigate. Before we begin, however, the reader should be warned that the information we present should as far as possible be dissociated from the English form in which it is cast. A distinction should also be drawn between measurement of time and the way in which it is experienced. The Chinese themselves have, of course, also been aware of this distinction. Up to the recent past, time was measured, in China as elsewhere, by observation of the heavens combined with mathematical calculations. The movements of the Sun, the Moon and Jupiter were closely followed and used as a basis for various calendars. The passage of time was measured by water (clepsydras) until 1601, when a Jesuit father named Matteo Ricci introduced ingenious devices for measuring time in the shape of Western clocks. Another method used was the slow-burning graduated incense stick while the use of the sun-dial had been familiar for centuries. A work dating from 150 B.C. contains the statement that the saint values an inch of shade (unit of time) more than a length of jade.

THE SAVOUR OF TIME

The arts of China, poetry, painting and pottery, are marked by a strong yet delicate impressionism which in itself denotes a way of savouring time. Chinese sensitivity being wholly attuned to the changing states of nature, fleeting variations of delight and the most exquisite moments of harmony were always illuminating not only the lives of noblemen, scholars and the monks of the great monasteries, but those of the uneducated poor as well. The quality of time was appreciated in the same way as that of tea, paper, silk or any other of the thousand and one things which lend charm to life. Time came, went and returned: the time of the plum branch, of the bamboo stalk, of the maple leaf, and of pine branches, the time of the grey lags harsh cry, the sweet song of the oriole, the call of the quail. So many different savours and scents impinging upon the consciousness stamped the quality of passing time. Poems and paintings were placed and dated and the solar period (twenty-four in a year) of their composition noted. The celebrated *haiku* (seventeen characters written in three lines of five, seven, five characters), at which the Japanese excel, is of Chinese origin. This is an improvisation composed under the impact of strong emotion to perpetuate and communicate the experience, a black-and-white or colour photograph of time, in an age before photography existed.

THE CHARACTER *SHIH* [1][1] AND SOME NOTEWORTHY COMPOUNDS

Shih [1] refers to time in general, indicating qualitative duration. The state of consciousness, as duration, whether permanent or successive, is '*shih*'.

Etymologically this character, in which the sun radical is clearly apparent, was associated with an arrangement of strokes which is typical of characters relating to vegetation [2]. The seeds of life lying in the earth begin to sprout in the warmth of the sun. Time may therefore be thought of as a union of 'vital principles', *ch'i* [3][2], producing life. This character has been found on the shells of giant tortoises and on oracle bones used for divination by fire, on stone drums and funerary bronzes, dating from before the middle of the second millennium B.C. The character is pronounced as 'she(r)' in English, and it seems appropriate for duration to be expressed by a sibilant. Other characters pronounced 'she(r)' signify beginning, initiative, putting into action, and development [4].

In an ancient agrarian civilization, the concept of time is merged with the more concrete and diversified concept of 'seasons'. Everywhere in China, the year is divided into four seasons, the definition of which is remarkably consistent. From the 'season' it is an easy step to the concept of epoch, period, era. What is meant is sometimes longer and sometimes shorter than a 'calendar season' but it is, of course, a qualified period of time. The concept of 'season' also indicates a succession in time, as seasons, by definition, follow one after the other; months and days then also follow one after the other. When the idea of a point of time is dominant, *shih* [5] means 'moment' or hour, either the double hour of Latin cultures or the twenty-fourth part of a day, as in modern times. In the latter case, the term *hsiao shih* [6], small hour (of 60 minutes) is often used. The same *shih* also means 'frequently'. The accumulation of energy represented by time and its qualitative value in the seasons turns attention to duration, the division of time and the repetition of moments, which is one aspect of duration.

So far we have been very much concerned with 'nature', rather neglecting the more human aspect of time. Time is, however, relevant to human activity. There are always 'works' for 'days'. From this point of view, *shih* involves the idea of a situation, of a combination of circumstances which, if favourable, constitutes an opportunity to do something. Used as a verb, *shih* means to adapt oneself to circumstances, to come at the right moment, to fuse with a particular 'state' of affairs, to be in harmony with things at the right moment.

Let us now consider some compounds of *shih*. Often they merely define one of the possible meanings of the single character:

Shih an (or *ngan*) [7] is used in a formal phrase of greeting approximating to our 'compliments of the season'. Peace and tranquillity have a different savour at different seasons.

Shih chi [8]: opportune moment. *Chi* emphasizes the infinitesimal aspect of the opportune moment.

Shih ch'i ping [9]: epidemic disease, links together 'time' and 'vital principle' an epidemic being the result of the untoward quality of vital principles of the time (but this is tautologous in Chinese).

Shih chieh [10] and *Shih ling* [11]: seasonal ordinances or 'proceedings of government in the different months'. Strict rules regarding what is to be done are laid down for each season and for each month of the season. Heaven and earth observe the rules laid down for them in each season and the emperor, with his ministers and court officials, is just as much subject to the 'vital principle' or the spirit of the season. Food, clothing, mode of travel and work all vary according to the season. A system of correspondences, which, although originally based on nature, was made more artificial for the purposes of sympathetic magic, bound all the elements of life together in a complex network of interrelationships. Thus the five colours, the five sounds, the five smells and the five tastes were all linked and each of the sense organs corresponded to an internal organ. The emperor and his ministers worked together as interlocking parts driving the State machine, ensuring that the relationship between heaven and earth, for which they were responsible, was shielded from all harmful influences and always suited to the quality required by the particular time of year, season, month or solar period. That is the significance of

1 時

2 㞢

3 乞

4 始施使設

5 時

6 小時

7 時安

8 時機

9 時氣病

10 時節

11 時令

12 時間

13 時候

14 時辰

15 時刻

16 時歷

17 歷

18 歷史

19 時律

20 時女

21 時牌

22 時病

23 時代

24 時代觀

25 時代精神

26 時夜

27 時雨

28 世

29 二世

30 世紀

31 世家

32 世界

33 世人

34 世代

35 時代

36 末世之光

37 始

38 古

39 始

40 時

41 年

42 歲

43 年歲

44 年 歲

45 年 齡

46 旦

47 月

48 陽

49 陰

50 東

51 西

52 夕

53 動

54 息

55 八 字

56 來

57 曾

58 過

59 史

60 太 史

61 太 史 公

62 堯

63 尚書

64 詩經

65 史記

66 春 秋

67 春秋繁露

68 子

69 甲

70 乙

71 元

72 孟

73 仲

74 季

75 營 室

the seasonal ordinances (cf. Appendix 1). The character *chieh* denotes division or feast day, a particular section of time, whereas the character *ling* denotes the cosmic ordinance which must be observed. This is one of the most deeply rooted aspects of the approach to time in Chinese civilization. It is essential to it but probably not peculiar to it.

Shih chien [12]: modern term for time. The character *chien* indicates that this time is divided into sections and thus introduces a notion of quantity, which also requires some attention.

Shih hou [13]: a very old term which originally related to the idea of the seasons and their division into periods of five days. Now used to mean 'time', 'moment'.

Shih ch'en [14]: designates the division of time according to the motion of the sun and moon and the signs of the zodiac in which they come into conjunction.

Shih k'o [15] is the gradation of time as shown on the clepsydra.

Shih li [16] is the imperial almanach. The meaning appears to be 'that which enables the sun's apparent revolution to be followed'. The same character, *li* [17], is also found in the term normally used for 'history', *li shih* [18].

Shih lü [19] is the note corresponding to the month. The quality of energy, or the complex of vital principles, varies with the season and can be translated into musical terms. The vibration of a column of air in a pipe is an epitome of the universe. The air moving in the cavity of the earth, here represented by the pitch-pipe, reveals a celestial note and gives forth an earthly sound. As the relationship between heaven and earth varies from one season to another, the note characteristic of the season and the length of the pitch-pipe also vary. Seasons, music and lengths are different elements of a single reality.

Number expresses quality

This idea makes it easy to understand the importance of musicians (generally blind ones) in revealing the secrets of the heavens. To play certain types of music or certain notes at certain moments may disturb the balance of the universe. But for this to be possible, there must, of course, be a purity of heart, an excellence in 'virtue' which opens the way to what is most secret in the world, the essence of the universe:

Shih nü [20]: maiden, virgin. Curiously enough, there is a parallel expression referring not to time but to place. The meaning would seem to be: a woman who, for the present, because the time of her marriage has not yet arrived, is a virgin. She is, for the present, in the state of virginity.

Shih p'ai [21]: from the hour of Mao (5-7 a.m.) to the hour of Yeou (5-7 p.m.), the hour was posted up on a board at court. There were only seven postings a day.

Shih ping [22]: same meaning as *Shih chi'ping* [9] above; epidemic, but also illness due to disturbance of the seasons or to difficulty experienced by the organism in adapting to regular seasonal changes.

Shih tai [23]: the succession of the ages, the following of one epoch after another. Used in compound: such as *shih tai kuan* [24] or *shih tai ching shen* [25]: mentality of the time, up-to-dateness: the variability of the collective consciousness can be seen. But ideas of this sort are modern developments.

Shih yeh [26]: the cock. Literally: announcement of time at night.

Shih yü [27]: rain falling at exactly the time expected. This expression was naturally to be found in an agricultural society, subject to the twin scourges of drought and flooding.

ANOTHER *SHIH* CHARACTER [28]

Mankind is one section of the realm of nature borne by the earth and roofed by the heavens. The successive strata of men are distinguished by different generations, by the reigns of sovereigns, epochs or eras. This is the idea expressed by the character *shih* [28].

Its meanings are:

Time span between two generations (usually thirty years).

Position of a sovereign in the order of succession (within the same dynasty).

Thus the son of Chin Shih Huang Ti was called Erh Shih [29]: the second emperor.

Hereditary transmission.

Epoch, dynasty.

This world, 'here below', the world as it is now.

Year (very rare usage).

The following are some more significant expressions.

Shih chi [30]: cycle or period of one hundred years, century.

Shih chia [31]: hereditary houses (great feudal lords).

Shih chieh [32]: the world: the time of the generations also combined with space expressed within limits.

Shih jen [33]: the human race.

Shih tai [34]: epoch. Fairly close in meaning to *Shih tai* [35] but perhaps laying more stress on the social aspect of the epoch. The expression *mo shih chih kuang* [36] refers to the 'last' age, in contradistinction to the Golden Age.

YET ANOTHER *SHIH* CHARACTER [37]

In both ancient and modern Chinese, the idea of an imperceptible beginning is felt to be most clearly exemplified by human conception. Only after a certain time does the fact of a beginning become perceptible. It is commonly to be seen that nothing is more important, in life, in health, in politics, in trade or in war, than to be aware of the beginning of a change. And this, of course, applies even more to agriculture.

Beginnings are most often thought of in terms of the germination of a seed or the exhalation of a vapour: *yi* [38].

Before time could be spoken of, there was a period of indistinctness. When, in the primaeval chaos, there was as yet no beginning [39]; neither was there any time [40]. Time and beginning begin and end together: when a being disappears, what he was returns to indistinctness, he ends and with him his time, too, ends.

Above the time which begins and ends, and whose beginning and end are determined by the individual quality of life (varying slightly between the limits laid down for each species), there is something which has neither beginning nor end, from which everything proceeds and to which everything returns. Individual creatures enter into and issue from the cosmic loom, but the loom itself describes a circle, which by definition has no beginning and no end.

Time can be abolished only by identifying the self with that which keeps the principle of life endlessly turning between heaven, which fertilizes, and the earth, which bears. The regular motion of the sun, the moon and the stars seems to be less important than the union of the vital principles circulating throughout the year and distributed by the mechanism of the seasons. More precisely, and ever more clearly, although it is impossible to date, even approximately, this empirical perception of life, the interplay of the influences of *Yin* and *Yang* (cf. Appendix 2) emerges as the reason for the production of corporeal beings in springtime, their growth in summer, their decline in autumn and their disappearance in winter. This scheme applying to the annual crops explains the development of all other living creatures. Here again, we have energy 'beginning' and 'ending'. The aspects of *Yang* in *Yin* and of *Yin* in *Yang* characterize the beginning and the end respectively. There is no question of measurement in all this; the idea is to show due reverence to the august heavens and to establish good relations with the whole celestial bureaucracy of spirits guarding the cardinal points, the stars, etc. The life of the people depends on the proper observance of rites, and the rites in turn on accurate measurement of the flow of the four seasons. In order to carry out this crucial task, some very important personages, the astronomers Hi and Huo (and all their retinue) were sent by Yao, the first legendary emperor (the *Classic of History*, Canon of Yao, third paragraph) with instructions to greet the sun and make an exact record of its rising and setting. The description of the four seasons given in the third paragraph of the Canon of Yao shows that in spring, with *Yang* ascendant and the life force expanding through the universe, animals mate and men emerge from their winter retreats (maybe to conclude their own matrimonial alliances at rustic festivals by the riverside, but the version we have, which is no doubt censored, makes no explicit statement; others can be found and, in all poetic writings, spring is taken to be the season for love). In summer, when the effect of *Yang* on behaviour is more marked, birds and beasts lose their feathers and fur. In autumn, men work in a more leisurely way and take their ease and the animals' coats are in good condition. Then *Yang* withdraws, winter comes and *Yin* becomes more influential; men make themselves snug in their houses and the coats of birds and beasts are downy and thick. The notion of time thus merges with that of the alternation between *Yin* and *Yang*, as has been so clearly illustrated by Granet.[3]

THE CHARACTER *NIEN* [41] AND THE CHARACTER *SUI* [42]

Nien [41: year, harvest. The old form of the character shows an ear of corn bending over with its weight, an indication of harvest-time. *Sui* [42]: year, harvest, Jupiter. In both cases, year is equated with harvest: abundance resulting from the mingling of the vital principles of heaven and earth. The year and its produce together give the idea of work continuing from day to day. People are sometimes conscious of one aspect and sometimes of the other, but more often of both. Is not this typical of an empirical perception of time? The compound *Nien sui* [43] means age, the number of years, but also year, harvest. The compounds *nien ch'ih* [44] and *nien ling* [45] introduce dentition, a very empirical way of calculating age. The age of men, horses, cocks and so forth could be quite accurately appraised by eye.

At this point, we must revert to a matter which has so far only been mentioned in passing: the sacred opportunism of the Chinese, their radical occasionalism.

THE CHARACTERS *JIH* [46] AND *YÜEH* [47]

Jih [46]: sun, day. The old form was a circle, in the middle of which a short stroke was drawn. This stroke particularizes the circle, indicating that the round object contains an important element, solar energy. *Yüeh* [47]: moon, month. The old form was crescent-shaped with two strokes in the middle of the crescent. They particularize the crescent and indicate the presence of another important element, lunar energy.

Several characters having the sun as one of their components indicate different times of day, as determined by the position of the sun: dawn, dusk, etc. The sun is clearly identified with the *Yang* principle, both character and phoneme appropriately expressing the idea of expansion which is the very nature of *Yang*. The *Yin* principle is not (normally) represented by the moon. The character shows a mass of clouds.

YANG [48]; *YIN* [49]

The expression in characters of the five directions, east, west, south, north and centre, quite logically stresses the representation of the sun in the expression of east. It is in the east that the sun can be seen rising behind the branches of the trees. The west is represented by birds (creatures of heaven) at rest. And the moon's crescent which appears in the evening is used, logically enough, to denote evening as well.

TUNG [50]: EAST. *HSI* [51]: WEST. *HSI* [52]: EVENING

It may be interesting to note that the phoneme *tung*, used for the character meaning east, is also used to mean movement, or activity; and that the phoneme *hsi*, used for the character meaning west, is used to mean rest, cessation of activity; *tung* [53]: activity; *hsi* [54]: cessation of activity.

CHINESE OCCASIONALISM

Malebranche has spoken of occasionalism and of the sacred nature of the power at work in the universe. Creatures can only try to put themselves in a position to benefit from the effects of this power. This is quite well understood in China without the aid of philosophers. The livelihood of both peasants and merchants depends on the agricultural or financial circumstances of the time. Doctors' work depends, too, on the 'turn of events'. Diviners would not be able to make a living were it not for the general belief in this universal conjunction of the states of the vital principles, represented by ephemeral beings, each reacting with the others and all following the same general trend. Time is the universal mediator of all that involves agreement: care is taken to see that things are properly started: betrothals and marriages, conception and birth, first and second burials, the opening of shops. Hence the use of *pa tzu* [55]: the eight cyclic characters—two for the year, two for the month, two for the day, two for the hour of birth—which must be in harmony (eight for the boy and eight for the girl) for marriage to be considered. As qualitative Time relates to orientated Space, a very subtle science (or art) adaptable to all sorts of circumstances—geomancy—was universally practised on Chinese territory, in order to determine the right time and place to bury the dead in their final resting place or to build houses for the living.

Determination of the most auspicious moment in time is of prime importance, but is also a very delicate operation requiring great care. In early times, many methods were used for divination: the official method using fire and tortoise shell (celestial) and the formation of a hexagram by drawing and counting fifty sprigs of milfoil (earthly), not to mention inspection of the entrails of sacrificial animals, the tossing of coins, bones, etc., and the various ways of casting a horoscope. The aim is always to ascertain the general 'trend' governing a given situation at a given moment in time. Partly from caution, but partly also from inward conviction, a responsible diviner will never predict a definite result. All he will do is to determine, by methods of his own, which may, of coseur, be challenged, what is the exact balance of forces connected with the individual or affair on which he is being consulted. The indications contained in the commentary on the figure (hexagram) and on each of the six lines of which it is formed regarding the 'trend' are full of a lively logic which transports the mind, stimulating and guiding it by subtle paths in the analysis of a personal situation which can in fact only be made by it. The wisdom of *Yin* and *Yang* can bear comparison with the deductions and calculations of Western-style formal logic and proves that the empirical notion of time has, from the beginning of life in China up to the present day—and indeed in the highest degree through the operation of Maoist dialectical historical materialism—represented a constant analysis of gradual development. In what way? By consideration of the infinitesimal forces which are at work in processes of change. Heaven and earth, the one by its *Hua* (initiating changes) and the other by its *Pian* (effecting changes), are together responsible for transformations. These affect all that is created between heaven and earth: the Ten Thousand ephemeral existences of the Ten Thousand beings, which include man among their number. He submits and co-operates because he is endowed with reason and is existentially situated at the centre of the vortex. And time, practical time, the different aspects of the 'vital principles' of the universe, is in fact the succession of the qualitative states of time. To act is therefore, by close observation of nature and history, to perceive at the earliest possible stage the beginning of a 'trend' which at any moment will give rise to a new form among the vital principles and, by a slight movement, to put oneself in a position to take advantage of it. There is something sound in this sort of sacred opportunism, this way of feeling the wind. It might also be said that the sole purpose of Chinese 'natural' medicine, of which acupuncture is one of the most remarkable aspects, is to restore the life of an individual to order. It achieves this object by making time part of the treatment. Time is the aspect of energy in a human being which defines its place or its duration and indicates the ascendancy or decline of particular energies, which are at the same time linked to particular organs and particular moments. The discreet action of the doctor and the ready collaboration of the patient are aimed solely at making the vital principles of life circulate once more, using theoretical and practical knowledge (semiology) of the signs of life. This is based on a purely qualitative appreciation of time.

THE GRAMMAR OF TIME (TENSE)

European languages, which are in general highly formalized, cannot do without some way of expressing time by tense. All verbs are used in the present, the past and the future with the additional refinements of past perfect, present continuous or future perfect, etc. The same is not true of classical Chinese or of the modern language, at least in the main; although contact with the Western mentality has recently introduced into Chinese a growing trend towards formalization.

The fact that tense is not indicated by form does not mean that the Chinese language is in any way inferior, but is on the contrary a factor which confers great flexibility and ambiguity, the ambiguity being all the greater when it is sought to put Chinese matter into a set of Western logical moulds.

Chinese thought takes intelligence for granted. Where the context makes clear a point which in itself may appear ambiguous, there will be no indication of past, present or future tense, on the principle that there is no need to state what is already understood. In the following case for example, 'He came, but on seeing that all was not ready, decided that it would be better to go away and come back later', English uses the past, the present participle and the future conditional. In classical Chinese, none of these aspects would be indicated. The sentence would read simply: 'He come, he see all not ready, he think leave now, come back, that be best course.' Chinese has not cultivated formalism of expression for its own sake.

The formal expression of the present introduces the notion of stability—*Tang*. The character indicates stability both in place and in time, presence and even, to some extent, obligation, the latter probably on account of the compelling element in the reality of the moment, when recognized for what it is. There is a vital intensity and an instinctive realism in apperception and behaviour which give an intensive value to the present. The past merges with what has been left behind, because life flows onwards, the universe is in motion, action is a proceeding, and conduct a road which must be travelled. In the same way, the future is what is to come: *lai* [56].

The past may also be indicated by *ts'eng* [57], which is more static than *kuo* [58].

The conception of history

China, vast as an ocean, spreads over Asia and stretches through the centuries. Its origins are lost in the mists of time so that it is impossible to say how or when it began to combine the features that distinguish the Chinese from other nations. What races, what ethnic groups little by little submitted one to the other on the banks of the Yellow River or of the Yang tze Kiang, slowly but surely raising up a nation which is now so old and yet so young, so steeped in its traditions and yet so determined in creating a new 'image' of itself?

In such circumstances, is it reasonable even to attempt to estimtae what a 'Chines' conception of history is? Which formative period are we going to take? The twenty-three Marx-Lenin-Maoist years and the effort made wholly to reinterpret the past? Or should we, rather, leap back forty centuries in time to try to understand life, the conception of life and its reflection in men's minds at that time, taking as our history the history of the agricultural people of the Hsia period as they tried, without great success, to protect their crops from raiding parties of nomads from the north? Or should we take the mean between these two extremes, the periods when the Sung or Ch'ing dynasties flourished, producing the Great Mirrors of History and their summaries, which were the source of all the *Descriptions of China* published in Europe on the basis of the 'Annual Letters' or 'Edifying Letters' sent from Macao, Canton or Peking, by learned missionaries[4] and navigators, from Marco Polo to MacCartney?

There is no decisive answer to these questions. It would be more reasonable perhaps to work through from the twentieh century B.C. to the present day, taking one major period at a time. This would be more honest and also more interesting than an attempt to give a general bird's eye view of such a great span of history. Or it may be found preferable—and this is the course to which we shall resign ourselves—to single out reliable, significant data to be used as the basis for an independent appraisal of the Chinese conception of history.

SOME SIGNIFICANT FACTS COLLECTED

From 841 B.C., chronology is well established, and continuous and extremely detailed historical accounts survive. A good deal is known also about the period from approximately 1050 to 841 B.C.

The most ancient historical records in existence today, which were discovered fairly recently and have been used for research since 1928, seem to date from between 1384 and 1111 B.C. They are oracular inscriptions incised on tortoise shell or flat bones. These inscriptions mark the beginning of writing in China, but probably not the beginning of divination. But what of history? It may be argued—but purely as an hypothesis—that in a well-organized, and already sophisticated, society such as that of the Shang, the administrative organization was probably of the type described by tradition. The king was served by six 'celestial' officials, so called because their functions were directly concerned with communication with heaven. The father of historians (*Shih* [59]) and historiographers (*Dai Shih* [61)], was one of their number. This *Dai Shih*, later known as *Dai Shih Kung* [60], the Lord Grand Astrologer (or recorder), was responsible for all records. History consisted of the official archives of the principality holding supreme power and, as long as vassal kingdoms existed, those of their vassal principalities.

History is a set of written records used by the king's officials.

It is the responsibility of a 'celestial' official of high rank; it is therefore religious in essence and contributes, like all the other functions of the celestial ministry, to governing the empire and keeping it dependent upon heaven.

It is written in the form of annals. As the most important periods of the calendar year are spring and autumn, historical chronicles are often entitled 'Spring and Autumn Annals', the best known being the 'Spring and Autumn Annals' of the Principality of Lu, covering the period 722–481. Kung tzu

(Confucius, 551–479), a teacher in the Principality of Lu where he was born, is said to have been responsible for the revision of these annals (*Ch'un Ch'iu*) and there is some reason to believe that this was indeed the case. This extremely concise, indeed elliptical, chronicle has been rendered intelligible by various commentators, the most important being Tso Ch'iu Ming, himself Grand Astrologer of the Principality of Lu. His commentary raises the annal to what may be called the level of history, as it provides an explicit interpretation of the facts.

The following are some extracts from the *Text* of the 'Spring and Autumn Annals' followed by a *Commentary*. The text makes statements which are explained in the commentary. The commentary assumes the terseness of the text to be deliberate and sets out to throw light on its intentional obscurities. In doing so, it is obliged to select one interpretation of the recorded event—in short, to write a history. But a commentary is bound by the text and it is only when the commentator starts to depart from the text and to re-organize the factual material that what we call history can be said to take shape.

Text. In the third month of the year, In Kung and I Fu of Chu concluded a treaty at Mie.

Commentary. The commentary explains the limits applying to the title of I Fu and gives a political reason for the Treaty of Mie. In the first case, the commentator draws on his knowledge of heraldry and, in the second, on his sense of history.

Text. In summer, in the fifth month of the year, the prince of Cheng conquered Tuan at Ien.

Commentary. The commentary on a text comprising nine characters runs to 647. The circumstances of the birth of Prince Tuan are related in detail: as he emerged from his mother's womb, he wakened her and startled her: she took an instant dislike to him. This information gives an interesting insight into contemporary attitudes to birth. This is not peculiar to the Chinese but is characteristic of their mentality. A proper understanding of history presupposes an acquaintance with such circumstances. It is therefore not surprising that commentators give a meticulous account of them as long as they themselves are living in an atmosphere saturated with magic, where in signs and symbols foretell the fate to come.

The commentator habitually notes the peculiar features of the annalists' choice of words. For example, 'The Ch'un Ch'iu uses the word *k'o* [62], to conquer, as two brothers are making war on each other'. The intelligence (and the knowledge) of disciples of Confucius or the genius and the culture of a Ssu-ma Ch'ien are needed to discern aright so many hidden allusions in such laconic statements. And the historiographers themselves must have been men of great independence of mind, exemplary honesty and dauntless courage to record in the appropriate terms events occuring through the actions of the prince, his entourage or his adversaries.

This middle period of Chinese history shows a marked tendency to moralization, presupposing a knowledge of psychology, which was a striking feature of the writing of Mencius (372–289) but certainly already well developed even at the time of the *Classic of Poetry* (or *Book of Songs*), the oldest parts of which were written in the seventh century B.C.

A political trend also emerges, as ministers expatiate on the reasons which led them to recommend certain decisions or to draw the sovereign's attention to certain dangers. As one reign follows another, the further details provided by the commentaries begin to build up a picture of many aspects of life at court. Genealogical and astrological data form the basis for a monotonous history of court rivalries strictly confined within the frame of feudal ceremonial.

HISTORY IN THE PERIOD OF THE CLASSICS

We have just given a first brief idea of history as understood at the time of Confucius and of the learned commentators who interpreted the authentic text, ritually established by the annalists of the Principality of Lu. But history appears in rather a different light in another work said to have been revised by Confucius and graced with a preface by the master. This book is also a classic, one of the canonical books, a *Ching*. It is known to the Chinese as the *Shang Shu* [63]: the *Great Book*, or *Documents of Former Generations*.[5] The contents of the four parts of the book may be briefly summarized as follows:

First part. Annals of the first sovereigns (the term 'annals' is not to be taken literally). This is a collection of sayings and deeds attributed in the first chapter to Emperor Yao, in the second to Emperor Shun, and in the third to Emperor Yü, the legendary founder of the traditional First dynasty, the Hsia dynasty. As the ministers acted as advisers to the emperor, their opinions are regularly noted alongside the 'sayings' of the emperors; this part therefore contains two further chapters, consisting of two 'counsels' of Kao Yao, a minister of Emperor Yü.

Second part. It contains the Yü Kung, an important treatise on historical geography, in which the location, population and value of the various estates and their produce are described in detail. This was no doubt used as a basis for assessment of the 'Tribute', the ancient feudal tax which was accepted as recognition of vassalage. The 'Tribute' is followed by the Speech of Ki, second emperor of the Hsia dynasty, before the battle of Kan, the Imprecations of the five brothers of Tai Kang, the former's son and successor, during a revolt of the aristocracy, and a fierce speech made by the Prince of Yin before meting out their deserts to the lords Hi and Huo, two of the emperor's astronomers, who had taken to a life of debauchery 'and by their unprecedented disorderliness had thrown the laws of astronomy into confusion and grossly neglected their duties'.

This second part seems to contain, in conventional guise, material which is historically more authentic than that of the first, alluding to actual events which appear to have disturbed the political life of the otherwise nebulous Hsia dynasty.

Third part. The account now begins to give more reliable dates for events of much greater historicity.[6] The first speech in this part is that of Emperor Tang, the founder of the dynasty, followed by a laudatory address delivered by Chung Hue in the form of a ministerial counsel and a very fine speech by the same Tang after his decisive victory over the previous dynasty. On the death of the emperor, the minister of Tang the Victorious was obliged on several occasions to remind him of what he owed to his father's 'virtue' and to set him sharply right. A little later, a wise and courageous emperor, P'an Keng, ascended the throne. He decided to establish the capital on a different site, this change coinciding with the dynasty's change of name: from now on it was to be known as the Yin dynasty. P'an Keng experienced some difficulty in getting this transfer accepted. He makes several appeals to the officials of his administration and to the people. His successor delivers an address which is answered by the counsels of his minister, Yue. This part concludes, naturally, with a remonstrance addressed to the last of the Shang-Yin emperors who, in the nature of things, was bound to be thoroughly wicked. The stage is thus set for the entrance of the hero of the next dynasty, Wen Wang, who has a network of agents already working for him. He is a very distinguished figure whose praises are the constant theme of another classic—*The Classic of Poetry*, *Shih Ching* [64].

Fourth part. This is a panegyric of Wen Wang and Wu Wang: address to the confederate princes, followed by five speeches, four announcements explaining to the army the reasons for the action taken against the last of the Shang-Yin dynasty, and one address inaugurating the new empire and finally establishing the power of the Chou. These different elements form a very homogeneous whole as regards ideas and style; the speeches themselves are linked by narrative passages, such as the celebrated description of the decisive battle on the plain of Mu. For each event the day, month and year of the reign are given.

This section is followed by a very fine solemn passage setting out the 'Great laws of society and the mutual duties of men'—this representing the formulation of the official ideology. It has marked Confucian overtones but its origins may be much earlier. This section is known as the 'Great Rule', being a (comparatively) long passage of approximately 1,000 characters. The fourth part consists in the main of statements on the suppression of vice, the encouragement of austerity and the 'virtuous' inauguration of the new capital, Lo, south of the Yellow River, together with various more or less threatening admonitions to former officials of the Shang-Yin dynasty, counsels from wise advisers, appeals to the administration to treat the people well, a recapitulation of the Penal Laws of the Prince of Liu and a moving account of the death and funeral of Wen Wang. This last part takes up half of the *Classic of History*. It is in marked contrast to the ritualistic style of the annals, as can be seen by reference to the 'Spring and Autumn Annals'. We are now coming closer to the conception of history found in Livy.

It is impossible in these few lines to convey an understanding of the extent to which these writers of the time of Confucius, in the fifth century B.C., by dint of constant and increasingly reflective remembrance of the past, were able to produce a genuine work of history. But the *Classic of History* is only an anthology. The story of its transmission is hotly disputed and the dating of events which cannot be corroborated from other sources is impossible. Moreover its moralizing tone and the virulence of its diatribes against deposed monarchs seriously compromise the historical veracity of such a work.

It is not until the end of the feudal period and the triumph of the Ch'in, the establishment of the empire by Ch'in Shih Huang Ti and the reigns of Han Kao Tsu and his immediate successors that we find the 'father of Chinese history' appearing, Ssu-ma Ch'ien (145–86 B.C.), Lord Grand Astrologer at the court of Han Wu Ti, who succeeded to the office of his father, Ssu-ma Tan, and carried on his historical work. His *magnum opus*, the *Shih Chi* [65] (*Historical Records*) did not completely disregard the annalistic conception of history of the Classics but remoulded and refined it to such an extent that it in its turn became a model which was imitated by all subsequent official histories, including the *History of the Ch'ing Dynasty* (1644–1911).

HISTORY, A CRITICAL RECORD OF THE PAST

We need only look at the preface and the opening lines of various chapters of his masterpiece, the *Shih Chi* [65] (*Historical Records*) to appreciate that with Ssu-ma Ch'ien a new era has begun. It may be noted in passing that his tribute to Confucius is neither stereotyped nor servile. He praises him for having shown great circumspection in his approach to the dating of ancient events. The preface to the first chronological table,[7] for instance, reads:

> The Grand Astrologer (himself) says: the chronicles of the Five Emperors and the Three Dynasties go back to very ancient times. Neither the Yin dynasty nor the princes reigning before their time were able to keep records of their family histories. This became possible only under the Chous. When Kung Tzu revised the Ch'un Ch'iu with the help of the ancient texts he noted the first year of a reign, the time when the year began, the day and the month for each entry. Such was his exactitude. But his prefaces to the Shang Shu makes only general references, without mentioning month or year. When there was a question of doubt, he recorded it as doubtful. Such was his circumspection. . . . Thus, basing my work on the'Continu ation' and on the Shang Shu anthology, I have drawn up this chronological table of the generations, from Huang Ti to the time of Kung Ho (841 B.C.).

In the second table (Chapter XIII), Ssu-ma Ch'ien lists the sources he used in writing his account of the Histories of the Twelve (twelve or thirteen depending on the method of counting) Feudal States of the Ch'un Ch'iu (722-481, plus the preceding period beginning in 841 which could be reconstructed on the basis of the archives of the Principality of Lu). His main source was of course the *Ch'un Ch'iu* [66] with the commentary of Tso Ch'iu Ming. But each feudal court had its own annals, dependent to a greater or lesser extent on others. Annals were written at Ch'u, Chao, Chin, etc. Ssu-ma Ch'ien was particularly impressed by the *Ch'un Ch'iu Fan Lu* [67] of Tung Chung Shu. But his own conception of history, which was to become that of China after him, is revealed most clearly when he takes strong exception to his predecessors' handling of their material:

Scholars always summarize their opinions. [This is a reference to the studied brevity of the writers.] Careful ordering from beginning to end is not for them. The chronologist concentrates on the years and the months; the caster of horoscopes exalts the sacred course of evolution, while the genealogist merely lists the successive generations and posthumous titles. Each is succinct in his explanations; it is indeed difficult to seek to take in all the essentials at once.

This is nevertheless Ssu-ma Ch'ien's ambition:

To bring together the essentials of what all the most learned scholars who have dealt with the ancient texts have said, I have drawn up this table.

Ssu-ma Ch'ien's firm grasp of essentials is precisely what makes his *Historical Records* so outstanding. He has no peer when it comes to describing the rise of a military power in a few words, outlining the main features of a particular policy, or setting out in one paragraph the reasons for the downfall of a dynasty such as that of the Ch'in (221-207) or the rise of the Liu family which founded the Han dynasty (206 B.C.—A.D. 220 approximately). Combined with this power of reflection, this sureness of judgement and this vigour of thought, he also has the temperament of a philosopher. The *Historical Records*, when judged on the basis of their conclusions, contain a philosophy whose raw material is the series of events leading up to the establishment of a strong and stable empire after the inevitable civil or perhaps foreign wars—it is impossible to be sure which—of the long feudal period of the Spring and Autumn Annals and the Warring States. But the lofty tone of thought has not been achieved at the cost of factual information, criticism and systematic efforts to discover the true story of events, to describe them in detail and to date them with the greatest precision. The *Historical Records* set the science of history in China firmly on the right path. The historiographers who followed Ssu-ma Ch'ien drew up the *Official Dynastic Histories*, of which there were to be twenty-four (or twenty-five counting that of the Manchu usurpers, the Ch'ing dynasty (1644–1911)). The ruler's actions were noted by one annalist in the 'Diary of Action' and his words by another in the 'Diary of Repose'. For a certain period of time there was also a 'grand historiographer' who recorded the events of each year, with another linking them together to form more and more comprehensive surveys, the use of records continuing to be of prime importance. The tradition of scientific integrity and independence of mind was maintained and these historians continued to be distinguished by their care for the public good and their very prudent attitude towards the various emperors and dynasties, whose histories were officially written only during the following dynasty. Although originally compiled on a dynastic basis, countless monographs were also written on collateral subjects, one of the most interesting and detailed of which was always the descriptive catalogue of literary works. These are the monographs of the *Historical Records*, known as *Treatises* when dealing with such subjects as rites, music, pitch-pipes, the calendar, the governors of heaven (astronomy), the sacrifices of Feng and Shan, the Yellow River and canals and the balance of trade, and as memoirs when dealing with famous men such as Confucius or Lao Tzu. They provide a wealth of information in connexion with the 'hereditary houses', stretching back through the generations of a family to the ancestral heavens, a fascinating image of the life flowing through the universe, unified, harmonized and multiplied by the virtue of the sovereign (cf. Appendixes 1 and 2).

SPECIAL FEATURES OF THE CHINESE CONCEPTION OF HISTORY

In speaking of the 'special features of the Chinese conception of history', I have in mind a number of traits distinguishing the Chinese historiographers' conception of history, but have no wish to imply that the same features may not be found elsewhere.

The breadth of the historical panorama. If both historical accounts and the semi-legendary history of the earliest times are included, Chinese history can be said at the present date to cover a period of forty centuries. This time span encourages a broad historical vision not bounded by the slow procession of the years, but apt for considering major trends of profound and lasting significance. If European historians, for example, were to decide no longer to concentrate their attention primarily on one country but to consider the continent of Europe as a whole, a similar approach would evolve. They would begin to interest themselves in the general rather than the particular and their perspective would be corrected. The phenomena considered would be more difficult to analyse but the objective knowledge thus acquired might be more telling and more satisfactory.

The central position given to the Han. No one who has lived in China can fail to be aware of the persistent rivalries between the ethnic groups making up the Chinese nation today. History gives special prominence to the Han, a race of eastern origin established far to the north of the Yang tze Kiang, and the fame of the huge areas around Shanghai (the ancient kingdom of Wu) and north of Canton (kingdom of Yüeh) has undoubtedly suffered as a result.

The inward-looking approach. What is more serious—and accounted for partly by the isolation of the Chinese territories from other parts of Asia, and partly by the relatively late development of maritime communications—Chinese history was written on the assumption that human life was essentially what went on in central China, China itself being the centre of the world, washed by four seas and casting its brilliant light over the less fortunate and inhospitable regions inhabited by barbarians on the borders of earth and heaven.

The dominant rural note. The fact that China has always been a land of farmers has had a marked influence on Chinese life, resulting in the formation of a typically peasant mentality and peasant reactions which are a recurring feature of Chinese history. This is clearly illustrated both in the wisdom of China and in its social organization, which continually interacted with one another, as can be seen in Marcel Granet's detailed, often subtle and always penetrating studies. The innumerable peasant revolts and the physiocratic approach of the never-ending discourses on the prosperity of the people delivered by ministers, masters, *tzu* [68], and sovereigns are clear signs of the same thing. But above all Chinese history is dominated by an empirical apperception of the mystery of life, which merges in one dynamic movement, the progress of human society and the succession of nature, regulated as it is by the immutable alternation of *Yin* and *Yang*, made manifest in the distribution of the energy of the 'vital principles' throughout the seasons. Sociologically speaking, however, this is to be attributed to the dominance of rural life among the Chinese people.

The spirit of democracy. At the highest levels of national and provincial government, power in China has been mainly autocratic, both in the distant past and in recent times. But this has not prevented village life and local institutions all over China from being run on genuinely democratic lines. It would seem that, from the very beginning, those who were given—or who themselves assumed—administrative responsibility thought of the empire as a living reality in which cosmological nature and human society could coexist only in a symbiosis whose basic principle is 'spontaneity'. But in order to ensure that all have due chances in life, the natural order had to be preserved by a power assumed on the strength of the 'virtue' of a central point towards which all would converge and which would, like a sun, radiate its light over the whole of a meticulously organized society. There is a profound wisdom in all this which long sustained the monarchy in China and often moderated its excesses.

A communal type of life, exemplified in the clan and the extended family. Right up to modern times, the individual's sense of security was dependent on his belonging to an 'extended family' or a 'clan'. Not only do inter-clan conflicts form the basis of the official histories, but the whole structure of the country has been determined, in the sphere of economic, demographic and cultural development, by the mutual support and the powerful concentration of material and moral resources that the clans represented. Han Yü-shan, in a useful study published for the United Nations in 1946,[8] rightly emphasizes the formative influence on Chinese mentality and behaviour of the respect, admiration and worship of ancestors, even those long dead. The continuity of the race and remembrance of the past which provide the quasi-biological basis of history are present in the minds both of the humblest citizen and of the emperors, who feel—perhaps more than rulers elsewhere—accountable to their ancestors for the empire committed to their charge. This instinctive feeling for history, the history 'made' by those in power and the history which reflects the road trodden by one's predecessors, thus has a direct influence on the 'compilation' of history itself. While anarchy and individualism may have flourished in China from time to time, it was never for long; here we have a race, a people, a nation whose self-awareness has been heightened by the attention given to history.

Formalism in thought and expression. Historical writings starting from the time of Ssu-ma Ch'ien, whose literary gifts were as outstanding as his gifts as a historian, are always a pleasure to read. The written language is characterized by speed, alertness, concision, a firm grasp of essentials and nobility of expression. The *Twenty-four* (or twenty-five) *Histories*, of course, have the irreproachable elegance and perfection of style characteristic of classical Chinese. But as one reads one cannot but be struck by a somewhat formalistic approach in the judgement of the words and deeds of the *dramatis personae*. To what is this formal tone to be attributed? In all probability to the use of characters for writing. A Chinese character is an abstract image. Corresponding to any form of human conduct there is an expression sufficiently pictorial to reproduce it visually and yet sufficiently abstract to extend its scope and universalize its meaning. When Confucianism, which has had a lasting influence on Chinese life, established the famous doctrine of the 'correct designations', which should rather be called the 'rectification of conduct in accordance with correct designations (names, titles)', the sovereign, his officials and the common people were presented with a complete range of types of behaviour, edifying examples of which will be found in any of the rituals contained in the 'Book of Etiquette and Ceremonial'. This universally accepted formulation of what one must do to be a good emperor, a dutiful son, a loyal minister or a virtuous wife naturally had its effect on history. This moralizing approach, apart from being liable to induce boredom, often confines the view of history within a ready-made framework. In China, people are qualified a little too readily as virtuous or otherwise. There is thus a sort of failure to recognize the reality of human behaviour which often masks the real face of history, just as the stereotyped masks of the theatre made the villain white, the hero red and the sly intriguer multi-coloured. In concluding these few remarks on the trends which have combined to produce a particular conception of history in Chinese thinking and practice, we must come back again to the empirical apperception of time, for time is, after all, the raw material of history.

You must have seen, as I have, a wisp of cloud swirling around a mountainside, endlessly furling and unfurling itself in the wind, releasing the energies hidden within it as the morning sun plays upon it. It is a single, continuous whole and yet perpetually changing. The same is true of life, created by the universe between heaven and earth, continually being made and unmade, with man at its centre. Time is only the succession of unforeseeable and yet inevitable changes which obey the secret impulses of moisture and heat, the unexpected gust of wind and the infinite variations of the earth's terrain. Anyone wishing to write the history of what he beholds should seek in what is deepest and most subtle, in the heart of earth and heaven, the mystery and clarity which combine to produce one single activity or, if you prefer, passivity of man: illumination. The history of the world—resulting from the interplay of celestial and terrestrial influences, in which mankind, by virtue of the gift of reason, represents the region of light—is simply the account of transformations, each ephemeral but together forming an abiding whole, made possible by the existence of a central emptiness, and governed by the law of growth and decline. In the periods when religion and magic clearly dominated all, the will of heaven was easily discernible. The mandate of heaven 'fell' upon obscure sages, exceptional beings of whom Yao and Shun are the immortal examples. What heaven had not willingly revealed was forced from it by means of divination. For good and for ill, for good luck and for bad, one was completely dependent on the will of heaven. The whole history of legendary times and much of history proper serve merely to show how the mandate of heaven was given and received, prospered and declined; and how it rounded on those who had misused it, returning like a boomerang to strike them down, or was conveyed by the hand of the successor who presents himself at the palace gates with the inevitability of retribution and the terrifying aura of a messenger from heaven.

At times when religion and magic were dominant but a need was felt for a more clearly cosmological explanation, a conception of the working of the universe on more sophisticated lines than the simple bipolar dynamics of *Yin* and *Yang*, taking shape rather in a dialectical system based on the dominance and subordination of four poles, each of which in turn and in rotation exerted on overriding influence, we find theories of the mandate of heaven further complicated by the five-element theory.[9]

Confucianism and many other influences, one of which was legalism, added an ethical dimension to these systems which, while not excluding moral considerations, did not perhaps distinguish them so clearly. Confuciansim was to prevail in defining the concept of power as well as presiding over the writing of history in China. But other influences such as Buddhism, cosmopolitanism and Western ideas, by introducing different points of view, were to diversify the Chinese consciousness and, with it, the Chinese conception of history. But, always alert to the subtle changes in the distribution of cosmic forces, Chinese historians have preserved man's share of freedom and activity, for ever operative in that area where the initiatives of heaven are met by the eager and submissive responses of earth.

APPENDIX 1

BOOK IV. THE *YUEHLING*[10] OR PROCEEDINGS OF GOVERNMENT IN THE DIFFERENT MONTHS

Section I. Part I

1. In the first month of spring the sun is in Shih (Pegasus), the star culminating at dusk being Zhan [Orion], and that culminating at dawn Wei (the Tail of Scorpio).

2. Its days are *kiă* [69] and *yī* [70].

3. Its divine ruler is Thai Hāo, and the (attending) spirit is Kāu-mang.

4. Its creatures are the scaly.

5. Its musical note is *kio*, and its pitch-tube is the *rhāi-zhāu.*

6. Its number is eight; its taste is sour; its smell is rank.

7. Its sacrifice is that at the door, and of the parts of the victim the spleen has the foremost place.

8. The east winds resolve the cold. Creatures that have been torpid during the winter begin to move. The fishes rise up to the ice. Otters sacrifice fish. The wild geese make their appearance.

9. The son of Heaven occupies the apartment on the left of the Khing Yang (Fane); rides in the carriage with the phoenix (bells), drawn by the azure-dragon (horses), and carrying the green flag; wears the green robes, and the (pieces of) green jade (on his cap and at his girdle pendant). He eats wheat and mutton. The vessels which he uses are slightly carved, (to resemble) the shooting forth (of plants).

10. In this month there takes place the inauguration of spring. Three days before this ceremony, the Grand recorder informs the son of Heaven, saying, 'On such and such a day is the inauguration of the spring. The energies of the season are fully seen in wood'. On this the son of Heaven devotes himself to self-purification, and on the day he leads in person the three ducal ministers, his nine high ministers, the feudal princes (who are at court), and his Great officers, to meet the spring in the eastern suburb; and on their return, he rewards them all in the court.

11. He charges his assistants (the three ducal ministers) to disseminate (lessons of) virtue, and harmonise the governmental orders, to give effect to the expressions of his satisfaction and bestow his favours; down to the millions of the people. Those expressions and gifts thereupon proceed, every one in proper (degree and direction).

12. He also orders the Grand recorder to guard the statutes and maintain

the laws, and (especially) to observe the motions in the heavens of the sun and moon, and of the zodiacal stars in which the conjunctions of these bodies take place, so that there should be no error as to where they rest and what they pass over; that there should be no failure in the record of all these things, according to the regular practice of early times.

13. In this month the son of Heaven on the first (*yüan* [71]) day prays to God for a good year; and afterwards, the day of the first conjunction of the sun and moon having been chosen, with the handle and share of the plough in the carriage, placed between the man-at-arms who is its third occupant and the driver, he conducts his three ducal ministers, his nine ministers, the feudal princes and his Great officers, all with their own hands to plough the field of God. The son of Heaven turns up three furrows, each of the ducal ministers five, and the other ministers and feudal princes nine. When they return, he takes in his hand a cup in the great chamber, all the others being in attendance on him and the Great officers, and says, 'Drink this cup of comfort after your toil'.

14. In this month the vapours of heaven descend and those of the earth ascend. Heaven and earth are in harmonious co-operation. All plants bud and grow.

15. The king gives orders to set forward the business of husbandry. The inspectors of the fields are ordered to reside in the lands having an eastward exposure, and (see that) all repair the marches and divisions (of the ground), and mark out clearly the paths and ditches. They musy skilfully survey the mounds and rising grounds, the slopes and defiles, the plains and marshes, determining what the different lands are suitable for, and where the different grains will grow best. They must thus instruct and lead on the people, themselves also engaging in the tasks. The business of the fields being thus ordered, the guiding line is first put in requisition, and the husbandry is carried on without error.

16. In this month orders are given to the chief director of Music to enter the college, and practise the dances (with his pupils).

17. The canons of sacrifice are examined and set forth, and orders are given to sacrifice to the hills and forests, the streams and meres, care being taken not to use any female victims.

18. Prohibitions are issued against cutting down trees.

19. Nests should not be thrown down; unformed insects should not be killed, nor creatures in the womb, nor very young creatures, nor birds just taking to the wing, nor fawns, nor should eggs be destroyed.

20. No congregating of multitudes should be allowed, and no setting about the rearing of fortifications and walls.

21. Skeletons should be covered up, and bones with the flesh attached to them buried.

22. In this month no warlike operations should be undertaken; the undertaking of such is sure to be followed by calamities from Heaven. The not

undertaking warlike operations means that they should not commence on our side.

23. No change in the ways of heaven is allowed; nor any extinction of the principles of earth; nor any confounding of the bonds of men.

24. If in the first month of spring the governmental proceedings proper to summer were carried out, the rain would fall unseasonably, plants and trees would decay prematurely, and the states would be kept in continual fear. If the proceedings proper to autumn were carried out, there would be great pestilence among the people; boisterous winds would work their violence; rain would descend in torrents; orach, fescue, darnel, and southernwood would grow up together. If the proceedings proper to winter were carried out, pools of water would produce their destructive effects, snow and frost would prove very injurious, and the first sown seeds would not enter the ground.

APPENDIX 2

SERIES: THE LOGIC OF CHINESE THOUGHT
PERIOD: CH'IN (250 B.C. APPROX.)
WORK: THE *LÜ SHI CH'UN CH'IU*, EDITED BY LÜ PU WEI (DIED IN 235 B.C.)

In this note we deal with a subject which is central to the logic of Chinese thought: the energy cycle contained in the Four Seasons. The Chinese calendar maps out, month by month, the course of the life-giving exchanges between Heaven and Earth, showing how they govern human society, whose life, as it begins and proceeds is borne by Earth and ruled by Heaven.

The year is divided into four seasons: Spring, Summer, Autumn and Winter. Each season consists of three months: in the first month, Yang (or Yin, as the case may be) is in the ascendant. During the second month the same principle continues to be dominant, representing its mean energy, and during the third month its phase of power begins to decline. The first month is called *Meng* [72], the second *Chung* [73] and the third *Chi* [74].

In all the writings of this period and of the following Ch'in and Han dynasties (255 to 209 B.C. and 209 B.C. to A.D. 220), and indeed long afterwards, until the beginning of regular contacts between China and the West, the calendar was considered to be a guide to the life of the Universe, whose rhythm was dictated by the alternating influences of Yin and Yang. It was in order to ensure that their own public and private lives conformed with this rhythm that the Chinese watched with such intense interest the modulation throughout the Four Seasons of the stream of life running through the world of nature and human society alike.

The all-embracing scope of the system, its astronomical accuracy of observation and the clearly apparent structure of both cosmic and social life make of the components of this calendar a system of living logic of such potency that those who wish to penetrate into Chinese thought without doing violence to it muet use it as their key.

To give no more than a brief description of this system, we shall concentrate here on the ideas underlying the organization of the first month of Spring; other months, following the same general pattern, need not be described.

The beginning of the month is determined by the position of the sun, the source of energy in its Yang aspect: in the first month of Spring, the sun is in the constellation *Ying Shih* [10] [75] (Pegasus). The fact that this was the time for building houses is perhaps due to the survival of an ancient custom: in Spring one could move to more flimsy dwellings which were built (or later repaired) at this time of the year. At dusk, the sun has reached the constellation Zhan and at dawn the constellation Wei (the Tail of the Scorpio). Three positions are therefore given for the sun. The days of this month are known as *Kiā Yī*. These names together mean bursting of buds. Attention is thus drawn to the lively, 'blossoming out' quality of the days of Spring.

In the heavens there are concentrations of energy, ranking as 'divine rulers'. The sovereign (Ti) of the Spring is *Thāi Hāo*. An Emperor always has an associate or attending spirit (Chen) in the sky. *Thāi Hāo's* associate is called Kāu Mang. The quality of the air is such that the animals of this season need to be protected: they are scaly.

In Spring vibration of the air produces the note *Kio;* like all notes, it is celestial, but produced in a wooden pipe which is terrestrial; the pitch-pipe for Spring is Thāi Zhāu. Measurement is based on the pitch-pipes; the number of Spring is eight. The 'vital principles' perceptible to the sense of taste, which are flavours, are sour-tasting in Spring; and those perceptible to the sense of smell, which are odours, are rank. A little later the colour peculiar to Spring is said to be blue-green, the hue of the foliage. Domestic sacrifices are directed towards opening: offerings are therefore to be made to the spirits who guard the doors. Doors inside houses are referred to here. What is not quite clear is why the spleen should be sacrificed. The sacrifice of the viscera of an animal is a way of establishing an 'agreement' with the 'spirit of Spring', as it is in the five viscera of an animal (or of man) that the 'vital principles' that animate all living creatures are materialized and differentiated.

What happens in the animal world in the first month of Spring? Among land animals, those that hibernate are mentioned, since Winter is coming to an end. The east wind, which is the wind of Spring, brings with it the thaw: animals re-emerge from their hiding places. There is undoubtedly a correspondence between the atmospheric movement which frees the waters and the physical movement of the animals shaking off their Winter torpor: the stream of life begins to flow again. Water animals, fish, leave the ice and return to free waters. The otter, living by rivers 'sacrifices' fish to the spirits. Migratory birds, the wild geese, return.

The world of men is governed by the Emperor. His rest and activity must be in harmony with the direction of Time, the quality of the Season. When at rest the Son of Heaven inhabits the Hall of Resplendency (of the Virtue) residing in him, which be must reflect in the right direction. In the first month of Spring, the Son of Heaven occupies the apartment in the north-east corner of the complex of buildings forming the Hall of Distinction. When in motion, he rides in a carriage embellished with bells, drawn by six horses called azure dragons. His clothes, his jewels and his ornaments, like the standard on his carriage, are all blue-green, the colour of the season.

The Virtue of the Son of Heaven is sustained by food whose taste is in harmony with the season: wheat and mutton. Mutton has a strong flavour, corresponding well to the acidity of Spring.

The inauguration of Spring is an impressive ceremony. The Grand Astrologer (or recorder), Guardian of the Calendar, formally announces the arrival of Spring three days before the event, informing the emperor that 'the energies of the season are fully seen in wood'. To ensure that no harmful influence affects the Virtue which must invest the Prince on this occasion he devotes himself to self-purification.

NOTES

1. The figures in brackets refer to the numbered ideograms on pages 38 and 39.
2. 'I need not again insist on the untranslatability of this word, which has connotations similar to the *pneuma* of the Greeks and to our own conceptions of a vapour or a gas, but which also has something of radiant energy about it, like a radioactive emanation.' (Note by Joseph Needham in *Science and Civilization in China*, Volume II, Chapter 13 (e)).
3. Marcel Granet, *La Pensée Chinoise*. Éditions Albin Michel, Paris, Passim. cf. Index: 'temps' (time).
4. For example: *China Illustrata* by Athanasius Kircher, 1667, or *Description Géographique, etc . . . de la Chine et de la Tartarie Chinoise* by J.-B. de la Halde, 1735.
5. Better known at present as the *Shu Ching*, a title which is sometimes translated into English as the *Historical Classic* or the *Book of History*, but which should, strictly speaking be called the 'Canon of Documents'. It is a mixed collection, of which one of its best translators, Séraphin Couvreur, has written: 'The *Shu Ching* acquaints us with ideas which were current if not 2,000 years at least 1,000 years B.C. and gives us reliable information about the times which followed the rise of the Chou dynasty.'
6. Whether or not the Shang were in fact Chinese is open to question but the dynasty is known to have existed and the traditional chronology of fourteen ancestors and thirty kings was confirmed by the archaeological discoveries made at Anyang at the beginning of this century.
7. *Les Mémoires Historiques de Se-Ma Ts'ien*, translated and annotated by Édouard Chavannes, Paris, Adrien Maisonneuve, 1967, III, p. 1.

8. *China*, Berkeley and Los Angeles, 1946.
9. Four elements each correlated with a point of the compass, revolving around an element correlated with the centre.
10. The translation reproduced in this English version is an extract from that by James Legge in *The Sacred Books of the East*, Vol. XXVII, first published by the Clarendon Press, Oxford, in 1885, and reprinted by Motilal Banarsidass, Delhi, in 1966 as part of the 'Unesco Collection of Representative Works'. The system of transcription used by Legge has, for purposes of convenience, been followed in both Appendix 1 and Appendix 2.

BIBLIOGRAPHY

CHAVANNES, E. *Les mémoires historiques* (a translation of the *Shih Chi*). Paris, A. Maisonneuve, 1967. (A two-volume selection from this work has been translated into English as *Records of the grand historian of China* by Burton Watson. Columbia University Press, 1961.)

COUVREUR, S. (the translator of the Classics). *Les annales de la Chine*. Paris, Cathasia (reprint). (An English translation by James Legge entitled the 'Shu Ching' was published in *The Chinese classics*, Hong Kong, 1861–72.)

——*Mémoires sur les bienséances et les cérémonies*. Paris, Cathasia. (An English translation by John Steele entitled the *Book of etiquette and ceremonial* was published in 1917.)

——*La chronique des printemps et des automnes* (The spring and autumns annals or the Ch'un Ch'iu).

——*La chronique de la Principauté de Lou* (The annals of the principality of Lu).

EBERHARD, W. *Histoire de la Chine*. Paris, Payot, 1952. (Translated into English as *A history of China*. London, 1950.)

FONG YEOU-LAN. *Précis d'histoire de la philosophie chinoise* (A short history of Chinese philosophy). Paris, Payot, 1952.

GRANET, M. *La civilisation chinoise*. Paris, Éditions Albin Michel, 1929 (since published in paperback). (An English translation was published under the title *Chinese Civilization*, New York, Meridian Books, 1958.)

——*La pensée chinoise*. Paris, Éditions Albin Michel, 1934 (since published in paperback, 1968).

It would be difficult to find among existing works a better account of what time and history mean to the Chinese than that given by M. Granet.

HOUANG KIA-TCHENG. *La voie et sa vertu* (The way and its virtue). Paris, Éditions du Seuil, 1949.

KALTENMARK, M. *Lao Tseu et le taoïsme* (Lao Tzu and taoism). Paris, Éditions du Seuil, 1965.

MASPERO, H. *La Chine antique*. Paris, Imprimerie Nationale, 1955.

NEEDHAM, J. *Science and civilization in China*. Cambridge, Cambridge University Press, 1954.

WILHEM, R. *The I Ching*. New York, 1950, 1967.

TIME AND HISTORY IN THE TRADITION OF INDIA:[1] *KĀLA* AND KARMA

Raimundo Panikkar

Appendix: Empirical apperception of time

Dr Bettina Bäumer

'Above time has been placed a vessel full to overflowing.'[2]

The existence of the universe—and hence the history of man and of the cosmos—comes under the sway of two superior forces: *kāla* (time) and karma (the act).

The first part of this study will accordingly be devoted to time, and the second, which is shorter, to history. We shall approach the problem of time by following the various paths of the tradition which is summed up in a passage of Bhartṛhari:

The vision of time varies according to whether time is regarded as power, the Self or a divinity. In a state of ignorance [time] is the first thing to manifest itself, but in the state of wisdom it disappears.[3]

Time

TIME AS THE FRUIT OF RITUAL ACTION

In the earliest experience of Vedic India, time was perceived as the actual existence of the beings we describe as temporal. There is no such thing as empty time. Time is an abstraction which does not exist. What does exist is the (chronological) flux of beings: and it is this process which makes sacrifice possible.

Time is born with sacrifice, and it is by sacrifice that it is once again destroyed. This concept is at the root of the intimate relationship between worship and time, and provides us with a key to the understanding of the central place of sacrifice and man's participation in the unfolding of time. In this sense time is something which man makes, in close collaboration with the gods: time, i.e. the continuing existence of beings, is a theandric product.[4]

In the Vedas, in the Saṃhitā period, we find several words to designate time, for example *āyus*, life-time, life span,[5] or *ṛtu*, the right time for sacrifice, the season.[6] Abstract time is of no interest to the *ṛṣis*, the poet-sages of the Vedas, for whom there is no continuity of time apart from ritual activity or the act of a god (for instance Indra).

This time . . . has no reality, that is to say efficiency, except in the moments in which divine or sacred acts are concerted. . . . In this succession of acts linking moments it would be vain to look for a given continuity: continuity is no more than the fruit of the constructive activity which recommences day after day.[7]

In the Vedas the unit of time is the day, which is the centre of all experience of time.[8] Dawn and twilight are 'junctions', the most 'critical' moments in the whole day. It is 'from day to day' (*dive dive*)[9] and by dint of the daily sacrifice, the *agnihotra*, that time endures and existence continues. Hence the well-known saying:

If the priest did not offer up the sacrifice of fire every morning, the sun would not rise.[10]

Later, as the sacrifice became increasingly elaborate, and the building of the fire altar in the Brāhmaṇas stretched out over a year, it was the year which became the larger unit of time. The sacrifice remained the foundation of the temporal structure, each brick of the altar corresponding to one day in the year.

It was the *puruṣa*, the cosmic man of the Ṛg Veda[11] and Prajāpati in the Brāhmaṇas, who was originally immolated in order that the world might exist: the world exists only by virtue of this primordial sacrificial act.[12] In a second act—which is, however, performed in the reverse order—it is the sacrifice which reconstitutes the Lord of living beings. Since Prajāpati is identified with time, symbolized by the year,[13] this reconstitution corresponds to the consolidation of time, the structuring of the year. In the Vedas this activity is frequently compared to that of weaving,[14] the weft being made up of the day and the night[15] and ritual moments.[16]

Another very ancient image which represents the rhythm of time is that of the wheel (*cakra*), the symbol of the solar cycle. This image plays a vital part, even today, both in speculations on time and as a folk symbol of the 'cycle' of existence.

To sum up, in this intuitive Vedic view of time there is, first, the idea of a relationship between time and the act of worship ('karma' in the intrinsic sense of the word) which is so close that the one does not exist without the other; and secondly, Vedic man—unlike man in subsequent periods—aspires either to long life, or to a certain kind of continuity which does not seem to be guaranteed by the cosmological events.[17]

TIME AS A COSMIC POWER

A second fundamental intuitive notion of time, which is moreover akin to the first, goes so far as to consider time as a cosmic power which is the *fons et origo* of reality. Not only is this a very ancient concept, for which there are analogies in other civilizations, but above all it is a widely held popular view, belonging probably to the less Brahmanic stratum of Indian tradition. This would explain why nearly all orthodox schools reacted vigorously against what they called *kālavāda*, i.e. the doctrine which places time at the centre of reality and ascribes to it a universal causality. Any vehement negation presupposes precisely the existence, even the predominance, of that which is denied: thus the markedly a-temporal and trans-temporal tendency of a certain kind of Hinduism might be accounted for precisely by the important role played by absolute time in the outlook of the period.

Time as an absolute principle: fate

We shall leave aside the question whether the concept of absolute time was imported into India from Babylon or Greece,[18] and to what extent this concept is traceable to Iranian influences.[19] Our primary concern is with the importance of this doctrine from the period of the Atharva Veda onwards. The exaltation of Great Time in two hymns of this Veda is the earliest expression of this vision of Time as 'the creator of the creator', Prajāpati, who is *brahman* (the ultimate principle of the universe) itself:

1. Time draws (the chariot like) a horse with seven reins,
   a thousand-eyed, fruitful-loined, immune to age.
   Astride it are poets who understand inspired songs.
   Its wheels are everything that exists.
2. Thus time draws seven wheels,
   it has seven hubs, its axle is (called) non-death.
   On the hither side of all these existences
   it advances, first among the gods.
3. A full vessel has been placed above Time.
   We see (Time) even though it is
   in many places (at once).
   Opposite all these existences
   Time (is also seated), they say, in the highest firmament.
4. In oneness Time bore these existences,
   in oneness it encompassed them around.
   Time the father became time their son.
   No glory higher than his.
5. Time engendered Heaven above,
   Time also (engendered) the Earths we see.
   Set in motion by Time, things which were
   and shall be are assigned their place.

6. Time created the Earth;
in Time burns the Sun;
in Time (yes), Time, the eye sees far off
all existences.
7. In Time is consciousness; in Time,
breath; in Time is concentrated the name.
As Time unfolds
all creatures rejoice in it.
8. In Time is (sacred) Fervour, in Time (yes), in Time
is concentrated the all-powerful *brahman.*
Time is the lord of all things,
Time was the father of Prajāpati.[20]

All reality depends on Time, and even sacrifice, which elsewhere in the Vedas is considered as the supreme force, is likewise subordinated to Time. It is important to note the relationship, spoken of in practically all texts on time, between absolute time and empirical time, the creator and the creature, father and son[21] cause and effect. Here space is supported by, and extended in, time.[22] Even inner realities—consciousness and breath—are under the sway of time.[23] A universal dynamism sets everything in motion. To put it succinctly, *kāla* is here the supreme divinity which is subject neither to the personified creator (Prajāpati) nor to the impersonal universal powers of the sacrifice or of the *brahman:*

After conquering all worlds by the Word, time advances, the supreme god.[24]

The Maitrī Upaniṣad, which reflects several concepts of time, quotes a sentence from the doctrine of absolute time (*kālavāda*):

From time flow beings, through time they grow old, in time they are destroyed: Time that is amorphous assumes a shape.[25]

There are, accordingly, two aspects of time: transcendental time and time become incarnate in the sun, the planets and the empirical divisions of time.

It is difficult for us to establish all the connexions between this ancient *kālavāda* doctrine and the much later texts on time the Mahābhārata, for whatever we know about this doctrine comes mainly from quotations occurring in texts which seek to refute it.[26]

Besides, what is reflected in the Mahābhārata is more of a popular concept, which probably had a profound influence on the attitude of less 'Vedic' circles, namely the concept of time as fate.[27] A certain Hindu passivity, which is almost fatalistic, too readily ascribed to a Moslem influence in India, has its roots in this vision of time.

The most frequent quotation, which is attributed to the *kālavādin*, is the following:

Time ripens beings, time enfolds creatures. Time keeps watch when all are asleep. Time is hard to overcome.[28]

While it is obvious from the Mahābhārata that many different views have been held about time, the predominating one certainly seems to be that of an insurmountable fate.

(Time is) the Lord who works change in beings—that which cannot be understood and that from which there is no return. Time is the destiny (flux: *gati*) of everything; if one does not follow it, where can one go? Whether you try to flee from it or remain motionless, you cannot escape from time. The five senses cannot grasp it. Some say that (*kāla*) is Fire, and others that it is the Lord of the creatures (Prajāpati). Some conceive of time as a season, others as a month, a day or even an instant. . . . There are those who say that it is the hour (*muhūrta*): but that which is uniquely One has many forms. Time must be acknowledged as that which controls everything that exists.[29]

Here as in many other texts, time is perceived as indivisible and omnipotent, beyond divisible and measurable time.

Time is the cause of all, it is time that creates and destroys,[30] that binds men by its links[31] and causes the joys and sufferings of men, regardless of their actions.[32] According to this conception man is purely and simply delivered up to fate, and his actions and efforts are powerless to alter his lot. In the end, the destructive aspect dominates: it is Time which hastens the progress of all beings towards dissolution.[33] Time is compared to an ocean where one can see neither the other shore nor any island of refuge.[34] Time becomes the great destructive power, sometimes synonymous with death.[35]

The frequently expressed idea that time 'matures' or ripens beings means simply that it leads to old age and ultimately to death. The Buddhist view of the impermanence of existence, in the context of an ever-fluctuating and fleeting dynamic motion, seems to have influenced this vision of time.[36]

The Purāṇas still retain echoes of the conception of time as a divinity, but they often attempt to integrate it in their respective theologies. The statement that *kāla* is without beginning and without end, ageless, omnipresent and supremely free, that it is the great Lord,[37] is a continuation of the ancient *kālavāda:* 'Time, being infinite, caused the end; being without a beginning, creates the beginning, the immutable'.[38] However, the Purāṇas tend rather to regard time as a divine power.

Time as a power of God

The Atharva Veda already spoke of 'a full vessel placed above time',[39] and time can be visualized as being for ever replenished from that source. This fullness beyond time can be understood in the light of the Maitrī Upaniṣad, according to which '*brahman* has two forms: time and timelessness'.[40] Thus there is no longer absolute time or relative time, but time on the one hand and, on the other, pure timeless transcendence. This is evidence of a radical transformation which springs from the Vedic concept of sacrifice but which did not produce its full impact until the Upaniṣadic and Vedāntic period: the eternal is no longer thought of as limitless time or absolute time, but as something which transcends any kind of temporality. The vessel full of time, from which time flows out, is not itself temporal: it contains time, while being itself timeless: 'time ripens (matures) all beings in the great Self—in which time itself is matured: he who knows this knows the Veda'.[41]

But this transition does not take place smoothly or without controversy: theism, of which one of the earliest documentary testimonies is the Svetāśvatara Upaniṣad, attacks the *kālavāda* as being materialistic and atheistic:

> Some sages say that (the cause of the world) is nature, others say time. They are mistaken, it is the power of God which cause the *brahman*'s wheel to turn in this world.[42]

Time is not an independent reality; it is the Lord who is the 'knower and creator of time',[43] and time is his instrument.[44] The Upaniṣad emphasizes the transcendence of the Lord vis-à-vis time:

> He is the origin . . . he is beyond threefold time . . . He is higher, he is other than the tree (of the world), other than time and forms . . .[45]

He, Rudra, repossesses the worlds at the end of time.[46]

In both the Śaivïte and Vaiṣṇavïte theologies any reality which is not identical with God—though very frequently identified with him—becomes his power or *śakti*. Because of its cosmological importance, time is one of the god's earliest powers: *kālaśakti*, his instrument in the creation, preservation and destruction of the universe. However in the Purāṇas there are many doctrines regarding time. For instance, the Śiva Purāṇa recognizes three levels of time, from which one can trace the process by which absolute time was absorbed by Śaivïsm. In its first stage, time is not different from Śiva, it is eternal. In its second stage, it becomes the power of Śiva, Śiva being the innermost essence (*ātman*) of time. Śiva rules the universe by means of time. In the third stage, time is considered as a limiting principle, being the product of *māyā*, cosmic illusion. Only in this last stage is time divided up, and causes succession, duration and limitation. What has happened is that the transcendent absolute aspect of time has been transferred into the sphere of the god, and its empirical aspect into the sphere of the *māyā*, that which veils reality. However, the concept of *kālaśakti* strikes a certain balance between these two extremes.

Vaiṣṇavïsm accepts the same theory. In the Mahābhārata the pre-eminent place of time is expressed thus:

Beyond the spirit is intelligence, beyond intelligence Great Time: (but) beyond time is Lord Viṣṇu, from whom proceeds all the universe.[47]

In the Bhagavad Gītā it is Kṛṣṇa who is identified with time, in its indestructible[48] but destroying aspect.[49]

On the subject of the divine immanence the Bhāgavata Purāṇa says:

The Lord penetrates all existences by his own power (*ātmamāyā*): within he takes the form or the spirit (*puruṣa*); on the outside (he takes) the form of time (*kāla-rūpa*).[50]

The cosmological role of *kāla* is frequently described in the Purāṇas, which say that time exists in a latent state during the dissolution of the world, and is awakened by the god at the moment of the re-creation.[51]

Yet *kāla* is, and remains, more closely linked to Śiva than to Viṣṇu, and it is its destructive aspect which dominates all other cosmological aspects. Śiva himself is called *mahākāla*, Great Time, meaning death.[52] The destructive goddess Kālī is perhaps the female counterpart of the god Rudra-Śiva, who is identified with time.[53]

The conception of *kālaśakti* profoundly influenced Hindu thought. Even a philosopher like Bhartṛhari makes it the first power of the One:

Because they depend on its time-power, which is held to be responsible for differentiation, the six transformations (*pariṇāmas*) like birth, etc. become the cause of the variety of existence.[54]

And the first commentary explains that this power is independent (*svātantrya śakti*) and the cause of everything.[55]

The two concepts dealt with so far encompass a great variety of views, and have in common the fact that they belong to a religious universe: whether they deal with cultic time or with time as an absolute or divine power, these concepts represent two aspects of time as a sacred value, though many others have been traditionally entertained.

Time devoid of real power

For some civilizations the 'overflowing vessel' of time has shattered into countless pieces, and all that remains are the different temporal parameters of the different spheres of reality. For others, the vessel is, as observed above, the symbol of the author of time.[56] But there is still another view, which has found illustrious adherents in India: the view of time as the supreme form of cosmic illusion.[57]

It is relatively easy to trace the development of this thought. When the anthropomorphic features of the 'vessel above time' recede, the vessel ceases to be the lord of temporal reality, becomes its impersonal cause and takes over the full import of its reality, so that everything which overflows from it is no longer fully real.[58]

Time thus becomes devoid of reality, or at least of any power of reality. It even becomes the symbol of illusion. The vessel above time always remains full to overflowing, for the reason that it never really empties; there is no time which runs out, nothing falls from the timeless vessel.[59] The eternal here devours time.[60] Time here belongs to *māyā*, interpreted as illusion; it is based on *avidyā*, or cosmic ignorance. It is merely something superimposed on the Absolute, the *Brahman*.[61]

Philosophical speculation subsequently sought to modify this vision, and we shall now see that much of Indian philosophy might be characterized by the degree of reality that different systems ascribe to time.

LINGUISTIC HERMENEUTICS

Indian philosophy took an interest in time, starting primarily from a consideration of grammar and language, but also (this is striking in Yoga) on the basis of a spiritual desire to transcend time. The other philosophical systems gave little thought to time; at the most they included it in their systematization of the factors of existence, without however basing their conception of the universe on the phenomenon of time.[62]

We shall confine ourselves here to referring by way of example to the analyses of time carried out by the philosopher of language, Bhartṛhari, in his Vākyapadīya. In his chapter on time[63] Bhartṛhari studies the concepts of time which existed in his day[64] and expounds his own views.

It is obvious that time is closely linked to action, for as stated in a tantric text, space is a limitation of form and time of action.[65] Bhartṛhari maintains that time, as an absolute, is only differentiated and divided up because of actions (*kriyābhedas*),[66] for there is no perceptible time without some action which suggests a before and an after, speed or slowness.[67] An action consists of a succession of instants (*sakramas*). On the strength of the analysis of its two functions the role of time is described in detail: the permissive force (*abhyanujña*) and the preventing or retaining force (*pratibandha*). These are the two functions of time which maintain the order of the universe: without them everything would be produced or destroyed simultaneously.[68] The first function enables the virtual to become real, to blossom forth in time, the second prevents things from materializing before their time and ensures that they do not continue beyond their allotted time. Thus time is called the secondary[69] or efficient[70] cause, which alone can regulate and activate the other causes.

Some schools of philosophy have denied the existence of time independent from action.[71] Bartṛhari, on the contrary, recognizes only the existence of time as such, utterly independent of any division between time past, future and present.[72] He considers that it is the sequence of actions which causes us to speak of past, future and present, time itself being always the same. In other words, we speak of the past because an action is completed, and we think of the future when we imagine coming events. The proof of the existence of time in the present is more difficult to establish, and implies a detailed analysis of grammatical usage, which we shall not go into in this study.

Time is called the pure mirror that reflects the real form of beings.[73] It is time which, so to speak, strips bare the reality of things.

Lastly, the grammarian philosopher Bhartṛhari recognizes that all action would be impossible without time; whether or not one tries to make it relative, a purely mental concept, one cannot get away from a fact.[74]

Already in the Mahābhāṣya and Kaiyaṭa's commentary thereon we find the asseveration that it is change (*pariṇāma*) in beings that forces us to accept the reality of time.[75]

These examples are sufficient to show that empirical and phenomenological analyses are indeed to be found in the Indian tradition. Yet the fact remains, significantly, that language is the starting point of these reflections. Other analyses, to be found in Yoga and Buddhism, which are just as detailed, show a purely spiritual concern, and lead not to an empirical affirmation but rather to the negation of any objective reality of time.

THE INTERIORIZATION AND TRANSCENDING OF TIME

The Vedas sought the continuity of time through the sacrificial act, but the Upaniṣads began to question the permanence of this act and this continuity.[76] Immortality, the sole concern of the Upaniṣadic sages,[77] was no longer ensured by the performance of the rite. Continuity was no longer to be found externally, in the ritual or the cosmos, but internally, within man, or more exactly within the Self, the *ātman*. And yet cosmic connotations are not lacking in this new vision.

One of the first factors to be descried in the search for this continuity is the breath of life, *prāṇa*.[78] *Prāṇa* is, in the first place, the life principle and the individual aspect (*adhyātma*) of the unabating, omnipresent cosmic wind (*vāyu*);[79] secondly, *prāṇa* is not merely physiological breath, but the rhythm of respiration which also becomes a spiritual exercise (*vrata*) to overcome death.[80] This is the beginning of yoga exercises to control breathing (*prāṇāyama*). If even the sun is said to rise and fall in the *prāṇa*, one begins to realize the cosmological importance of the breath. Later on, *prāṇa* is identified with immortality (*amṛta*)[81] and *brahman* itself. The important point is that respiration corresponds to an internal time, and it is the mastering of this internal rhythm, especially in Yoga, that leads to the transcending of time—both externally and internally.

The transition from the cultic time of the Vedas to the interiorized time of the Upaniṣads occurs evidently at the point where respiration, interpreted as a sacrifice, takes the place of the sacrifice of fire (*agnihotra*).[82]

In addition, the Upaniṣads look for what is beyond the past and the future;[83] they seek infinitude (*bhūman*)[84] and plenitude (*pūrṇam*), which they find symbolized more in space than in time: the atmosphere, infinite space (*ākāśa*) is present also in the innermost chambers of the heart (*hṛdākāśa*).

The Kālacakratantra contains a distant echo of this interiorization of time as a spiritual exercise designed to transcend time.

(The yogi) relates inhalation and exhalation with day and night, and then with fortnights, months and years, gradually working up to the major cosmic cycles.[85]

The purpose of this and other similar practices is patently to succeed in discovering the unreality of time,[86] and eventually to transcend time.

From the Upaniṣadic period onwards both time—succession and duration—and the universe of the act (karma)[87] are divested of their value, and at the end of this process it is the doctrine of the cycle of existences (*saṃsāra*) which gives rise to a negative conception of time. The metaphysical schools which have liberation (*mokṣa*) as their goal tend in theory to deny time any real value, and seek to achieve a state of existence which is beyond time—to use a Yoga term 'the cessation of mental states',[88] one of which is time.

In order to affirm the relativity of time, these schools then envisage time as an intellectual conceit having no counterpart in any 'real thing'. This almost psychological reduction of time is expressed, for instance, in the Yoga Vāsiṣṭha, which attempts to demonstrate the unreality of instants and cosmic ages.[89] It says that, depending on the mental state of the subject, an instant may appear as a *kalpa* (aeon) or, contrariwise, an aeon may be experienced as a single instant.[90] In short, time *per se* does not exist. He who is absorbed in meditation knows neither day nor night[91] and in the end, Self-knowledge, illumination, encompasses all the future in an instant.[92]

The philosophical schools following the Upaniṣads and Buddhism take the instant, *kṣaṇa*, as their fulcrum for the 'leap into timelessness'. Here it should be noted that the doctrine of instantaneousness and the 'propitious instant of liberation'[93] profoundly influenced Hindu spiritual teachings.

The interiorization of time, the first step towards transcending it, thus leads towards the discovery of 'subtle time', the infinitely small unit of time, in which time and eternity, movement and stability meet, since: 'it is on the stasis (*sthiti*) of time that all quietude depends.'[94]

In his *Yoga Sūtra* Patañjali recommends 'meditation on the instant and the succession of instants in order to attain knowledge born of discernment'.[95]

The commentary defines the instant—the sole 'real' facet of time—in terms of atoms (*aṇus*) and their movement.[96] The succession of instants, and units of time—here the influence of Buddhism is visible—are not real (*na asti vastu-samāhāraḥ*), but exist solely in the mind (*buddhi*) as an intellectual or verbal concept. Time is empty of reality (*vastuśūnya:* without substance), and the yogis admit only the present instant, without past or future. Hence the purpose of meditation (*saṃyama*) is to attain the perception of the instant which is pure and—paradoxically—unflawed by temporality, for it is this subtle time (*sūkṣma*) which is the springboard for the timeless and the eternal. Transformations (*pariṇāmas*) are not denied, but they are reduced to the sole instantaneous dimension of time.

Not only in Buddhism, but also in other philosophical schools, the instant acquires a kairological connotation—in other words, salvation, the awakening, the release from the yoke of time, may be achieved at any instant, or else at the propitious instant (and here, a certain notion of grace is implied).

The Śaïvism of Kaśmīr (the Trika school) goes still further:

> Since no time unites instants in one substance, the yogi will be able to separate and penetrate the liberating interstitial vacuum (*madhya*) in between two succesive instants.[97]

According to this system the instant is described as the vibration of consciousness; it is the eternal present which alone confers plenitude and felicity,[98] a state governed by neither space nor time.[99] It is through the instant that one penetrates into timeless reality.

Can we try to define more closely the concept of time in traditional India? We have quoted the richly evocative symbol of the overflowing vessel. We may perhaps hazard a guess as to some aspects of this vessel overflowing with time.

The first aspect is the co-extensiveness of time and beings. There is time so long as beings exist, and beings exist so long as they have time (to exist).

The second aspect is that there exists the same degree of reality between beings and time. If beings are regarded as real, unreal or half-way between (*sadasadanirvacanīya*),[100] time partakes of the same degree of reality.

Although language is inadequate to express the third aspect, most of the systems of India hold that time, and with it beings, does not exhaust the whole of reality. The vessel which contains time makes time possible, but is not itself temporal.

History

The very notion of history raises some preliminary problems of terminology. Are we talking about the concept of history, or about the way in which history is experienced, or about the historical dimension of man?

Should we start from a Western conception of history and look for corresponding elements in other cultures? Manifestly, we do not seek to express Indian categories in Western terms, nor vice versa; our object is rather to discover the intuitive views of India and to situate them in the Indian world of thought, where they may possibly occupy a place homologous to that occupied by history in Western thought.[101]

A further comment in regard to history is appropriate here: it seems that the 'idea' of history and of historicity (as distinct from the 'experience' of history) makes its appearance precisely at the time of a break with, or deep crisis in, tradition. It is when tradition is challenged that one most fully realizes the historical character of existence: reflection needs a certain perspective. The West is going through a crisis with respect to its own tradition, and is keenly aware of its historicity. India, on the contrary, is still, despite its manifold crises, living in tradition, without the perspective of historical self-reflection, i.e. without being fully convinced of 'living through' history. There are admittedly some very diverse historical levels within the modern culture of India, but history in India is the living of tradition rather than any subsequent reflection on this culture.[102]

As regards the tradition itself, the concept which has played, and still plays, a role comparable to that of the historicity of man in Western philosophy, might be said to be the concept of karma.[103]

KARMA AND THE HISTORICAL DIMENSION OF MAN

In dealing with time we saw that action is intimately linked with time. Both in the world of the Vedas and in the analysis of factual experience it is often the deed, the human or divine action, which determines time. Apart from certain doctrines of absolute time, the law which governs time and history taken together as a whole is the law of karma.

Karma is in the first place action,[104] then the residuum of the action which produces good or bad results[105] and which lives on after the person,[106] and lastly, the law that governs the retribution of actions and the network of interconnexions between the karmas of beings. This 'universal causality', as the law of karma is commonly known, explains virtually all the relations in the universe, and goes far beyond any individual conception of transmigration. Karma combines personal elements (the repercussion of each action unto the outermost limits of the cosmos) with impersonal ones (the element of 'creatureliness' that all beings have in common) in such a way that karma may be said to be inexhaustible, i.e. without end, as the aggregate of the residues of human acts. The being who attains *mokṣa* may be released from his karma, but the karma as such is not ended.

Who then is the subject of karma? While the Western world of today tends to regard the individual, or particular individuals, as the subject or subjects of history, India tends to deny that the illusory Ego can form the subject of karma. Sankara's saying has become classic: 'There is no transmigrant (subject) other than the Lord.'[107]

Karma as a universal law, does not reflect the externals of history, an explanation of events (though such an explanation may be inferred from it) but rather the inner historicity, subtle and hence invisible. Reflection on karma is more of a reflection on the causes of events.

Furthermore, the very term 'event' should be understood not as connoting something which happens externally, or even as an external change in a constellation of space and time, i.e. a change in the position of beings, but as meaning a karmic modification, i.e. a modification in a being's karma. This is a question rather of anthropological incidences than of sociological accidents, achievements rather than occurrences.

The question of man's freedom with respect to his own or the universal karma has also preoccupied the Indian mind. Philosophical and religious schools have proposed different paths for escaping from what appears to be determined and have defended the free human act (*puruṣakāra*), i.e. man's power to break the actual chain of the causality of actions and reactions. Some of the more determinist views come very close to the interpretation of *kāla* as fate;[108] and it was to get away from these views that there were developed on the one hand the idea of *puruaṣakāra* (which is, for example, basic to Yoga: man's own effort to transcend his karma) and, on the other, the doctrines of divine grace.

This being said, there is no school or religion in India, perhaps even in all Asia, which would deny the law of karma, however diversely interpreted.

The relationship between karma and time, the counterpart of that which exists between historicity and time in Western thought, is twofold. In the first place, time's *raison d'être* is precisely the existence of karma. So long as karma exists in the world, time will be necessary. Karma is, as it were, the intrinsic quality of time, that which gives time substance and density. Secondly, without time karma would be unrealizable, but would remain in a latent state; and without the collaboration of time, so to speak, beings would not be able to attain either their goal, through the performance of their duty in this world, or the liberation for which the consummation of all karmas is a prerequisite.[109] The example of those 'liberated during their lifetime' (*jīvanmuktas*) demonstrates this relationship: for the individual who has 'raced through' all his karmas time has, as it were, ceased; he lives outside time, and his body is said to continue to exist only until the consumption of all the subtle vestiges of the karma, of which his body is but the condensation.

Karma is thus linked less to history, in the sense of historiography, than to the intrinsic historical character of beings, whereby their past determines the present and the future, and not a single one of their actions is wasted or is without repercussions. The structure of reality is based on this historicity, which makes possible reciprocal interactions throughout the world, in a pattern of universal solidarity.

MYTH AND HISTORY: *ITIHĀSA* AND *PURĀṆA*

A people's vision of history indicates how it understands its own past and absorbs it into the present. But it is not so much the written interpretation as the way in which the past is experienced, and continues to be experienced, that bears witness to a people's attitude to history. India has experienced its past much more through its myths than by interpreting its history as a recollection of past events. This is not to say that there is no such recollection—in certain regions there is even an acute consciousness of history in this sense[110]—but there are no criteria for differentiating between myth and history, a disconcerting fact for the Western mind, which does not realize that history is its own myth. Commenting on that great epic, the Mahābhārata, G. Dumézil has said that it 'is not what we think of as history, but takes the place of history, and renders the same services both to dynasties in search of great ancestors and to a host of listeners longing to hear of a glorious past.'[111] In other words, it is myth as the counterpart of history.

The recognized expressions for 'mythical history' or 'historical myth'—the two are inseparable from each other—are respectively *itihāsa*, 'it happened thus', used to designate epic literature, and *purāṇa*, 'ancient narrative', used to designate more specifically mythical literature, in which historical elements are obviously intermingled.[112]

Myth and history should not be correlated to legend and truth, but should be regarded as two different horizons of reality. Within a historical view only the myth appears as legend, i.e. as being less real than historical facts. Within a mythical view, on the other hand, history is interpreted as inferior to myth. What the Westerner considers as history in the West, he would regard as mythin India. In other words, what he calls history in his own world is experienced by Indians as myth. But conversely, what in India has the degree of reality of history is what in the West an Indian would call a myth. Put differently, what an Indian in India would call history is experienced by Occidentals as myth. From the Western point of view, it is not history which carries weight in the Indian mind: whatever is of importance in a people's historical consciousness is precisely mythical.

The personalities and events which profoundly mark and inspire Indian life (in Western terms, which carry historical weight) inevitably give rise to myths, since any event which has what we may call existential 'consistency' enters into the realm of myth. 'Myth' has a greater degree of reality than 'history'. This statement might be illustrated by a reference to the popular reaction at the time of the birth of Bangladesh.

The process of the creation of myths has not come to an end, and it has been amply proved by M. Eliade that 'archaic man' is more interested in archetypes than in the uniqueness of an historical situation.[113]

If it is conceded that this 'mythical consciousness' corresponds to the Western 'historical consciousness', at least in respect of its function of preserving and integrating the past, it should be said that, while India has not thought profoundly about 'history', it has organically assimilated historical facts into 'myths'. This assimilation might be compared to sacred trees like the pipal, the secondary roots of which reach down from the air to the soil, take root again and sometimes survive even when the trunk has gone.

REINTEGRATION OF HISTORY

Nearly all Indian traditions have regarded the ultimate meaning of life as a-temporal and in a certain sense non-historical. They have placed greater emphasis on detachment and the surrender of historical values than on temporal commitment, since true history always transcends the temporal. Yet such commitment has not been lacking, and its justification is to be found precisely in a religious conception of secular duty. The teaching of the Bhagavad Gītā was, and still is, an outstanding example of this attitude.

It has been said that it was no accident that the Bhagavad Gītā was rediscovered in our time, and that it has provided a spiritual basis for many political movements. The reason is that it teaches that the path of action (*karmamārga*) is as valid as the traditional paths of knowledge (*jñānamārga*) and of loving devotion to a god (*bhaktimārga*). The advice given by Kṛṣṇa to Arjuna on the battlefield (the plain of *Kurukṣetra*) was precisely not to relinquish his duty (*svadharma*),[114] but to fulfil his role in a given historical (i.e. mythical) situation. Action must be purified (*karmaphalatyāga*),[115] and it is this unattached action which alone is capable of maintaining the universe and the order of the world (*loksaṃgraha*).[116]

The great leaders of modern India, like Mahātma Gandhi, Vinoba Bhave and others, found their source of inspiration in this spirituality of action in the Bhagavad Gītā. They purged political action of personal aspirations and gave a divine significance to history. They approached history not as an end in itself—as if a more perfect future society might form the aim of mankind's expectations—but as a duty assigned by God, which must be carried out with total commitment, yet at the same time with the greatest possible detachment.

Gandhi's interpretation of history may be summed up as follows:[117]

1. The meaning of earthly life and the meaning of history are identical.
2. The ultimate meaning of life is a-historical or trans-historical, but at the same time it is conceived as being dependent on the social order.
3. Since this ultimate meaning of life is transcendent in relation both to history and to the social structure, man's hope does not lie in a future utopia.
4. Since the ultimate meaning of life is a-historical, there is no absolute concept of history.

One might conclude this study with a reference to the familiar metaphor of the circularity of time and history as an expression of the quintessence of Indian experience, while giving it its proper interpretation.

The circularity of time, hence the repetition of history, does not imply that time is infinite or history unlimited—quite the contrary. Circularity is the symbol of the contingency, ontological limitation and closure of time, as also of the enclosure of history and the contingency of events. The circumference is limitless, and the circle indefinite, only in a unidimensional or two-dimensional world. This metaphor from geometry signifies precisely that reality has other dimensions, and that one must break through encircling time if one is to save oneself and achieve being. One must escape from the domination of time, not by running towards a future which is always ahead, but by leaping out of the circle.

It there were nothing else but time, the 'successive' points of passage through the same point would be absolutely identical, in other words, there would be only one single point. This is the cycle of *saṃsāra*, or, perhaps, hell: this is what history would be, were one not able to escape from it. . . .

APPENDIX

Dr Bettina Bäumer

Empirical apperception of time

WORDS DESIGNATING TIME

Āyu, āyus: vital force, life span, duration of life (especially important in the Veda); cognate of the adjective *āyu*, lively, mobile, changing. (cf. *Aiōn* αἰών), (Greek concept analysed by G. Pàttaro on p. 173).

Abhīka: critical instant, decisive moment (Veda), literally: meeting, collision.

Kāla: fixed time, space of time, time; occasion, fate, death.

Ṛtu: regular time, season, propitious or effective time. In the Vedas designates the specific time for sacrifice, and subsequently the season of the year. From the same root as *ṛta*, cosmic order.

Samaya: literally, meeting, agreement, arrangement; subsequently occasion, suitable time, fixed time, rule, coincidence; final moment.

Velā: literally, limit, river bank or shore; time limit, period, season, hour, opportunity, moment of death, last hour.

Kṣaṇa: instant, moment, the smallest unit of time (twinkling of an eye); propitious moment (particularly for salvation, liberation), also free time. Frequently (in the modern languages of India as well) signifies feast day, rest time, leisure; interval of time.

Muhūrta: propitious moment (fixed by astrology for occasions such as marriage), instant, moment, a unit of time (one-thirtieth of a day).

Kalpa: literally, that which is constructed or imagined; fixed time (fixed by the imagination), a period of the world, aeon (see ages of the world).

Yuga: human generation; astronomical cycle; age of the world, period of time which elapses between generations.

Diṣṭa: literally, that which is determined; fate, death, time.
Qati: course or flux (of time), movement, destiny.
Krama: duration as a succession of elements ('*krama* is the unbroken succession of instants').[118]

Most of the words mentioned above have a meaning strongly associated with fate and death. *Kāla*, the divine power or the power of the godhead, becomes the supreme destructive power, death personified (*mahākālā*), and is thus associated with Śiva, the great destroyer, or Kāli, the goddess of destruction. Since time itself is the force which 'matures' and 'digests', i.e. ripens beings (*pacatis*),[119] which causes them to revolve and envelops them (the root *vṛt*, with different prefixes) and carries them off (*saṃharati*),[120] the only way of overcoming time will be to 'destroy' it in an act of intuition (*jñāna*), or else by yoga.

From *kāla* comes the adverb *kālya*, which in most of the modern languages of India (derived from Sanskrit) has taken the form *kal*, and means tomorrow, or yesterday, or both. Thus the adverbs of time, yesterday and tomorrow, the day before yesterday and the day after tomorrow, are expressed by the same word, the important characteristic being the distance from the centre (today, which is in itself non-temporal), without favouring one direction over the other.

TIME AS REFLECTED IN SANSKRIT GRAMMAR

In classical Sanskrit, the present tense predominates, and the future often takes the meaning of the present. The verb tends to be eclipsed by substantive and adjectival expressions. The temporal relationship of anteriority is expressed primarily by the unattached participle or the past participle. The well-known 'substantive character' of classical Sanskrit, with its juxtapositions, combinations, repetitions, etc., and the predominance given to passive rather than active verbs shows a preference for static over dynamic relationships, a certain primacy of being over becoming; it reflects a tendency to eliminate action as such. It is noteworthy that most nouns expressing static qualities have an intrinsic positive value, whereas nouns which express movement and change possess a pejorative value.

MEASUREMENT OF TIME

Since ancient times, India has been acquainted with subtle divisions of time.[121] The Viṣṇudharmottara Purāṇa gives the following illustration of the extreme subtlety of time (I, 72, 4): if one pierces 1,000 lotus petals with a needle, the foolish man thinks that they are all pierced simultaneously (I, 72, 5), but in reality they were pierced one after the other (*kālakrameṇa*, 'in order of time'), and the subtle difference between the instants in which the successive petals have been pierced represents the subtlety of time (I, 72, 6).

There are considerable divergences between texts, particularly as regards the smallest divisions of time. It will be enough to give two examples. The most minute division of time, which is for that very reason compared to the atom (*aṇu* or *paramāṇu*), lasts for the twinkling of the eye, or the time required to utter a short vowel;[122] it is called *nimeṣa* or *kṣaṇa*. According to the counting system used in the above-mentioned Purāṇa,[123] two *nimeṣas* equal one *truṭi*, ten *truṭis* equal one *prāṇa* (= breath), six *prāṇas* equal one *vināḍikā*, and sixty *vināḍikās* equal one *nāḍikā* or *ghaṭī* (= twenty-four minutes). A unit comprising day and night (*ahorātra*) is made up of sixty *nāḍikās* (or *ghaṭīs*) or else of thirty *muhūrtas* (two *nāḍikās* = one *muhūrta*). From the *ahorātra* onwards, the divisions are the same in all systems, namely: half-month (*ardhmāsa*), month (*māsa*), season (*ṛtu*), which normally consists of two months, half-year (*ayana*, consisting of three *ṛtus*) and year (*varṣa*, *saṃvatsara*). Divisions longer than a year are aeons, the ages of the world, which we shall deal with separately.[124]

A rare example of an extremely subtle division of time is to be found in the Bhāgavata Purāṇa (III, 11, 3–10). A more common measurement is found (among others) in the Manu Smṛti (I, 64), using the *nimeṣa* as a base: eighteen *nimeṣas* equal one *kāṣṭhā*, thirty *kāṣṭhās* equal one *kalā*, thirty *kalās* equal one *muhūrta* and thirty *muhūrtas* equal the day-and-night unit (*ahorātra*).

THE CALENDAR, ASTROLOGY, FEAST DAYS

As the Hindu calendar contains at one and the same time astronomical, astrological and religious elements, it would be artificial to separate them. In fact, the calendar is useful not so much for fixing the date, since the quantitative and chronological aspect of time is entirely secondary; it is consulted in order to determine the times of worship and feast days, and the propitious time for a particular undertaking. The whole of life is regulated by the laws of 'theo-cosmic' time.

Owing to the combination of solar and lunar time the Hindu calendar is not easy to establish. Without going into complicated astronomical discussions, it is important to note that in general the solar month (*sauramāsa* or *sāvanamāsa*) is almost exclusively the 'quantitative' time for measuring the year; and that in all matters concerning cultic time, times of fasts, observances (*vratas*) and feasts (*utsavas*), as well as individual events and activities, the lunar month (*cāndramāsa*) is the more relevant unit of measurement. Very often, however, it is precisely the relative positions of the moon and the sun which are decisive.

Most texts affirm that time (*kāla*), which is in essence indivisible and eternal, is divided up solely because of the movement of the sun (and other heavenly bodies). The sun is even said to be the source of time.[125] The classic definition of time is given by Patañjali in his Mahābhāsya:[126]

People say that kāla is that by which one observes the waxing and waning of solid bodies, and it is also called 'day and night' when it is associated with a certain activity. What activity? The movement of the sun. It is by the repetition (of the same movement) that we have the month and the year.

The lunar month (*cāndramāsa*) is divided into two fortnights (*pakṣas*) of lunar days or *tithis*. The 'black' fortnight (*kṛṣṇapakṣa*) begins with the full moon (*pūrṇimā*, and the 'light fortnight' (*śuklapakṣa*) with the new moon (*amāvāsyā*). Religious activities are regulated by lunar days.[127]

There is no unified calendar for India as a whole, and as a consequence of divergent calculations it can happen that the same feast days are celebrated on different dates in the north and in the south. Generally, the Hindu calendar (called *pāncāṅga*) contains the following elements: at the beginning, the name and the divinity of the year, with the year's horoscope; then the name of the month, the length of the solar day, the lunar day (i.e. the name of the *tithi* and the *pakṣa*), the days of the week, the beginning and end of the *tithi*, and the *nakṣatra* or constellation; the *yoga*, or propitious or unfavourable times for various activities (determined by the relation of the sun and the moon), with the *karaṇas* (since each *tithi* has two *karaṇas*, there are sixty *karaṇas* in the lunar month); then the *rāśis* or signs of the zodiac. The times of sunrise and sunset (important for the rites of *sandhyā*, dawn and dusk) and of the rising and setting of the moon are recorded, as well as the mid-point of the year (the southern or northern course of the sun—*dakṣiṇāy* or *uttarāyana*—which is important, for example, in ancestor worship). At the end are indicated all the prescribed ritual actions, feast days, etc.

It is interesting to note that at the beginning of each ritual act (*pūjā*), at the moment of 'resolution' (*saṃkalpa*), the definition of the present instant is recited first, beginning with the aeon (*kalpa*), the *yuga* (current cosmic age), then the year, the month, the fortnight, the *tithi* and the *muhūrta*. Worship is a cosmic activity which assumes time and space in a special way. Thus even the science of astronomy (*jyotiṣa*, subsequently astrology) is justified as follows:

The Veda exists for the purpose of accomplishing sacrifice; sacrifices are prescribed according to the order of the times; thus he who knows astronomy (*jyotiṣa*), which is the science that regulates time, knows the times of sacrifices.[128]

The year in India is generally divided into six seasons: spring, (*vasanta*), summer (*grīṣma*, hot season), the rainy season (*varṣa*, monsoon), autumn (*śarad*), winter (*hemanta*) and the cold season (*śiśira*), which comes between winter and spring. In several regions the Hindu year begins half way through the month of *caitra* (March-April), but many regions have their own new year.

Dates are fixed according to different eras, the most common of which are the Vikrama era (from the victory of Vikramāditya in 58 B.C.) and above all the Śaka era (beginning in A.D. 78), both of them fairly close to the Christian era. Sometimes the date is given by reference to the beginning of the current *kaliyuga* (which is supposed to have begun about 3102 B.C.).

While a certain a-temporal interpretation of Hinduism (influenced by neo-Vedānta) has always denied the value of time, the importance in Hindu life of propitious or inauspicious times (*muhūrta* has become the commun noun for a favourable moment) can hardly be overstated. Cosmic, individual and religious times are inseparably bound up. The notion of an individual human destiny separate from the rest of the cosmos is unthinkable, and this is reflected in man's relationship with time. No important religious or secular activity is undertaken without consulting the astrologer. It is the qualitative aspect of time, its ontological 'density' which predominates. There is no 'neutral' time —such as implied by technology.

Festivals are condensations of cosmic and mythological time. Some festivals are purely cosmic in origin, such as the solstices (*saṃkrānti*), full moons (*pūrṇimā*), etc., although they are often linked with original or subsequently added myths. Other festivals are mythological or historical (for example, the night of Śiva or Śivarātrī, or the birth of Rāma or Rāmanavamī). The quality of the feast-time is basically different from that of ordinary time; the festival represents so great a concentration and condensation of time that time is forgotten. In other words, participating in a festival means entering into truly full, condensed time, it means transcending time and entering into eternity.

There is yet another difference between this eternity, based on the time condensed in the festival, and the eternity of the timelessness of contemplation. Contemplation cannot even be approached from the temporal aspect, nor can it be visualized as contrasting with action, since practically all Hindu philosophical schools affirm that contemplation (properly speaking: *samādhi*) is by definition outside time. The only temporal definition of contemplation to be found in both Yoga and Buddhism is the instant (*kṣaṇa*).[129]

MYTHICAL TIME, AND AGES OF THE WORLD

While the well-known 'in the beginning' (*agre*) of the Veda can be interpreted as a time of origin, revealing an original state of things, in post-Vedic periods it was held that this origin continually reproduces itself (cf. *punaḥ punaḥ*, *yuge yuge*, etc.), since each creation is preceded by the destruction of the previous creation, and so on. Time (*kāla*) has neither beginning nor end (*anādi*, *ananta*). The complete systematization of this concept is to be found in the doctrine of the *yuga*, the *kalpa* and the *manvantara*.[130] The catalogue of the divisions of time (particularly in the Manu Smṛti and the Purāṇas) passes without a break from the instant, the twinkling of the eye, to cosmic ages: there is no qualitative difference, because whatever is under the sway of the temporal is relative.

The smallest of the ages is the *yuga*, the unit of human history, and four *yugas* of varying length make up a great age (*mahāyuga* or *caturyuga*). The *yugas* reflect a conception of history which places the golden age at the beginning of creation, with a progressive decline up to the fourth *yuga*. Thus we have the *kṛtayuga*, also known as the *satyayuga*, the age of truth or golden age, which is supposed to last 4,000 (divine) years,[131] the *tretayuga* lasting 3,000 years, the *dvāparayuga* lasting 2,000 years and the *kaliyuga* lasting 1,000 years. Each *yuga* is separated from the next by the time of the dawn which precedes it and the twilight which follows it. Thus the duration of a *mahāyuga* is 12,000 years. The destruction of the cosmos (*pralaya*) occurs at the end of a cycle. We are at present in the *kaliyuga*, the degenerate age. A thousand *caturyugas* make up a *kalpa*, which is one day (or one night) of Brahma, the creator. According to another fairly ancient conception, a unit of seventy-one *mahāyugas* is governed by a Manu (progenitor of the human race), and is known as a *manvantara*. Thus a *kalpa* consists of fourteen *manvantaras*.

Whereas within a *mahāyuga* there is a certain (in fact negative) development, and each *mahāyuga* has a certain historical character, the major cycles are formed of unceasing changeless repetitions. The repetition and circularity of time by no means signify limitlessness, and even the expressions for infinite time (*anādi*, *ananta*) are more suggestive of the slavery of time, its contingent and limited nature. The circle tends rather to be a symbol of the finite, and the determinate complete system of the ages of the world reprensents time closing in on itself. Here we have complete relativity, which includes the gods, who are also under the sway of time, while having their own specific times. Beyond time there is only the undifferentiated *brahman*. Thus the object is not to go back to an origin in time, the golden age, etc., but precisely to break the temporal limits, without relapsing into a more subtle or more elevated form of time (a time of salvation, etc.). The vista of the cosmic circles demonstrates the evanescent and illusory nature of existence.[132] No one is afraid of wasting or 'losing' time, precisely because 'lost time' is Being regained.

NOTES

Following is a list of abbreviations used in the notes below:

AV	Atharva Veda
BG	Bhagavad Gītā
Bhāg Pur	Bhāgavata Purāṇa
BS	Brahma Sūtra
BU	Bṛhadāraṇyaka Upaniṣad
CU	Chāndogya Upaniṣad
Kaṭh U	Kaṭha Upaniṣad
Mah Nār U	Mahānārāyaṇa Upaniṣad
Mait U	Maitrī Upaniṣad
Māṇḍ U	Māṇḍūkya Upaniṣad
Māṇḍ Kār	Māṇḍūkya Kārikā
MBh	Mahābhārata
RV	Ṛg Veda
SB	Śatapatha Brāhmaṇa
SU	Śvetāśvatara Upaniṣad
Vākyap	Vākyapadîya (Bhartṛhari)
Viṣṇu Pur	Viṣṇu Purāṇa
YS	Yoga-Sūtra (Patadjali)
Y Vās	Yoga Vāsiṣṭha

1. Despite India's close connexion with Buddhism, the fact that Buddhism developed outside India and that Indian Buddhism alone would require a separate study will be our excuse for this limitation of the field to India. We are the first to deplore this limitation of the field.
2. AV XIX, 53, 3. *Pūrṇaḥ kumbho'dhi kāla āhitaḥ. . . .*
3. Bhartṛhari, Vākyap, II, 233.
4. cf. R. Panikkar, *Le Mystère du Culte dans l'Hindouisme et le Christianisme*, in particular the chapter on 'Le Culte et le Temps', p. 43–52, Paris, Éditions du Cerf, 1970.
5. cf. RV X, 17, 4.
6. cf. RV I, 49, 3; 1, 84, 18.
7. L. Silburn, *Instant et Cause*, p. 43, Paris, Vrin, 1955. The quotation is a Unesco Secretariat translation, from French.
8. cf. RV X, 37, 9 etc., and SB IX, 4, 4, 15 for the continuation of the tradition, for example.
9. cf. e.g.: RV I, 1, 3; X, 37, 7.
10. SB II, 3, 1, 5.
11. cf. RV X, 90.
12. cf. R. Panikkar, 'La Faute Originante ou l'Immolation Créatrice, Le Mythe de Prajāpati'. In: E. Castelli, *Le Mythe de la Peine*, p. 65–100, especially p. 70–9, Paris, Aubier, 1967.
13. cf. SB V, 2, 1, 2; VII, 1, 2, 11; X, 4, 3, 3, and also BU I, 5, 14; Praśna U I. 9; etc.
14. cf. RV IV, 13, 4; V, 5, 6; AV X, 8, 37 et seq.; etc.
15. cf. AV X, 7, 42–3, etc.
16. cf. RV II, 3, 6; X, 130, 1–2; etc.
17. cf. RV II, 33; etc.
18. cf. O. von Wesendonck, '*Kālavāda* and the Zervanite System', *JRAS*, Jan. 1931, p. 108–9,
19. cf. J. Scheftelowitz, *Die Zeit als Schicksalsgöttin in der Indischen und Iranischen Religion.* Stuttgart, Kohlhammer, 1929.
20. AV XXI, 53, 1–8. by Trans. by L. Renou, in: *Hymnes Spéculatifs du Veda* (Verses 9 and 10 have been deleted), Paris, 1956. The quotation is a Unesco Secretariat translation, from French.
21. *Hymnes Spéculatifs du Veda*, op. cit., 54, 3.
22. *Hymnes Spéculatifs du Veda*, op. cit., 54, 2.
23. *Hymnes Spéculatifs du Veda*, op. cit., 53, 7.
24. *Hymnes Spéculatifs du Veda*, op. cit., 54, 6.
25. Mait U VI, 14.
26. cf. Gauḍapāda's reference in Māṇḍ Kār 8 to the *Kālacintakāḥs*, 'those who reflect on time' and regard it as the origin of everything.
27. *Kāla* is very close to *niyati* and *daiva.*
28. MBh XII, 231, 25; XII, 227, 79; etc. cf. however: 'But no one here on earth knows him in whom Time is ripened', XII, 244, 2.
29. MBh XII, 224, 5–54.
30. Mbh XII, 227, 73.
31. Mbh XII, 227, 81–2.
32. Mbh XII, 227, 85.
33. Mbh XII, 227, 103.
34. Mbh XII, 231, 23 and 27.
35. cf. MBh XII, 27, 44 which speaks of 'the ocean of time infested by the great crocodiles of decrepitude and death'.
36. Even the gods are subject to this impermanence; cf. the discourse between Bali and Indra, MBh XII, 224.
37. cf. Viṣṇu Pur I, 2, 26, etc.
38. Bhāg Pur IV, 11, 19.
39. AV XIX, 53, 3.
40. Akāla, Mait U VI, 15.

41. ibid.
42. SU VI, 1.
43. SU VI, 2.
44. SU VI, 3.
45. SU VI, 5–6.
46. cf. SU III, 2.
47. Sāntiparva (crit. ed.) 199, 11.
48. BG X, 33.
49. BG X, XI, 32.
50. Bhāg Pur III, 26, 18. cf. also Viṣṇu Pur I, 2, 14.
51. cf. op. cit., III, 8, 11, etc.
52. This intuition is of fairly ancient date; it occurs already in the Brāhmaṇas, where Prajāpati is identified with time and death. cf. L. Silburn, *Instant et Cause*, op. cit., p. 53 et seq.
53. Despite the other etymology 'the black (goddess)'.
54. Vākyap I, 3.
55. Vrtti on Vākyap I, 3.
56. cf. *kālakāra* in the SU VI, 2 (and VI, 16), already quoted above or the 'lord of the past and the future' in the Kaṭh U IV, 13 (II, 1, 13).
57. cf. the notion of *nitya-anitya-vastu-viveka*, 'discerning between the temporal and the eternal' in Sankara, BS Bhāsya I, 1, 1. cf. also Vivekachudamani, 20.
58. cf. Māṇḍ U I, 1, 1 with the reduction of the past, present and the future to the *Om*.
59. cf. *The Doctrine of Sattvaśūnya* in the *Tattvatraya* of the Rāmānuja school (Chowkhamba Sanskrit Series, No. 22), p. 62: *sattvaśūnyam kālaḥ/ayaṃ ca prakṛti-prākṛtānām pariṇāmahetuh* 'Time is empty of being. It is (merely) the cause of the modification of nature and of its evolution'.
60. cf. BG XI, 32.
61. cf., for example, T. M. P. Mahadevan, *Time and the Timeless*, Madras, 1954.
62. cf. E. Frauwallner, *Geschichte der Indischen Philosophie*, II, p. 111, Salzburg, 1956.
63. Kālasamuddeśa, Vākyap III, 9.
64. Fifth century and early sixth century, according to Frauwallner.
65. cf. Tripurā Rahasya XI, 46.
66. cf. Vākyap III 9, 32; cf. also *Nyāyamañjarī* (Kashi Sanskrit Series, 1936), p. 123–7.
67. cf. Satyavrat Śastri, *Essays on Indology*, p. 174 et seq., Delhi, 1963.
68. cf. Vākyap I, 3 with Vṛtti, and III, 9, 3–8.
69. *Sahakārikāraṇa*, Vṛtti on Vākyap I, 3, etc.
70. *Nimittakāraṇa.*
71. cf. for example Yuktidīpikā, quoted by Satyavrat Śastri, *Essays on Indology*, op. cit., p. 192.
72. There is a certain correspondence between *trikāla*, triple time, and *triloka*, the three worlds.
73. cf. Vākyap III, 9, p. 56. K. A. Subramania Iyer (ed.).
74. cf. Vākyap III, op. cit., 9, 58.
75. Mahābhāsya II, 2, 5, and Kaiyaṭa's Pradīpa.
76. cf. Kath U II, 10–11, etc.
77. cf., for example, BU IV, 5, 3.
78. cf. the competition of the vital organs, which is won by *prāna* since the other organs depend on it; BU I, 5, 21–3.
79. cf. BU I, 5, 22: 'As *prāna* is the central breath, so Vāyu (the air) is the central divinity. Other divinities interrupt their activity, but not Vāyu, Vāyu is the divinity which knows no rest.'
80. cf. BU I, 5, 23: 'This is why one must . . . observe one single practice. One must breathe out and in, in order to avoid succumbing to Mṛtyu the evil [one] . . .'
81. cf. BU I, 6, 3.

82. cf. the entire Prāṇāgnihotra Upaniṣad, which is based on this substitution. Annotated translation by J. Varenne (ed.), *La Mahāṇārāyana Upaniṣad et la Prāṇāgnihotra Upaniṣad*, Paris, De Boccard, 1960.
83. cf. Kath U II, 14 (1, 2, 14).
84. cf. CU VII, 24, 1, etc.
85. Quoted by M. Eliade in *Images et Symboles*, p. 113, Paris, Gallimard, 1952.
86. *Images et symboles*, op. cit., p. 112: 'By working in this way on his breathing, the yogi works directly on experienced time.'
87. See 'Kārma and the historical dimension of man', page 79 in this chapter.
88. *Cittavṛtti-nirodha*, YS I, 1.
89. cf. Y Vās III, 20, 29.
90. cf. Y Vās III, 60, 21; III, 103, 14, etc.
91. cf. Y Vās III, 60, 25–6.
92. cf. Y Vās III, 60, 171.
93. cf. L. Silburn, *Instant et Cause*, op. cit., p. 408 et seq.
94. cf. ibid.
95. YS III, 52: *kṣaṇa-tatkramayoḥ saṃyamād-vivekajaṃ jñānam.*
96. Vyāsa Bhāṣya on YS III, 52.
97. L. Silburn, *Le Vijnāna Bhairava*, p. 60, Paris, De Boccard, 1961. The quotation is a Unesco Secretariat translation from French.
98. cf. Abhinavagupta, *Parātriṃśikâ*, quoted by L. Silburn, op. cit., p. 62.
99. *Digdeśakālaśūnya*, Vijñāna Bhairava, op. cit., Vol. 22, p. 76, where the experience of plenitude beyond time is still linked to the practice of respiration ; also Vol. 24.
100. cf. BG IX, 19 and later Vedantic speculations. cf., for example, BS Bhāṣya I, 3, 19; I, 4, 3; II, 1, 27; etc.
101. cf. R. Panikkar, 'La Loi du *Karma* et la Dimension Historique de l'Homme', in: E. Castelli (ed.), *Herméneutique et Eschatologie*, p. 205-30, Introduction, Paris, Aubier, 1971.
102. Clearly, therefore, the sources which we shall cite as regards modern Indian culture are not so much modern books on history (which are in any case quite rare) as a certain, contemporary school of phenomenology.
103. cf. article quoted above, by R. Panikkar, for a detailed description.
104. See 'Time as the fruit of ritual action', page 63 in this chapter, the act of worship in the Veda.
105. cf. BU IV, 4, 6.
106. cf. BU III, 2, 13, etc.
107. BS Bhāsya I, 1, 5: *satyam neśvarād anyaḥ saṁsārī.* (Literally: 'in truth no other than the Lord (trans)migrates'.)
108. The diffrence being that *kāla*, in this case, is an external though encompassing power, whereas karma is the result of the specific history of each being.
109. cf. the two functions of time described by Bhartṛhari, Vākyap I, 3.
110. It is enough to quote Śivajī's role in the Maharashtra, the king who repelled the Moslem invasions (1627–80).
111. G. Dumézil, *Mythe et Épopée*, p. 239, Paris, Gallimard, 1968. The quotation is a Unesco Secretariat translation from French.
112. All the *Purāṇas* give, for instance, the genealogies and dynasties of the kings (*vaṃśas*).
113. cf. M. Eliade, *Le Mythe de l'Éternel Retour: Archétypes et Répétition*, *passim*, Paris, Gallimard, 1949.
114. cf. BG II, 31 and 33, etc.
115. cf. BG V, 12, etc.
116. cf. BG III, 20 and 25.
117. Dr Minoru Kasai, who is writing a study on Gandhi's idea of history, has communicated to me the results of his research, from which I have taken these four points.
118. YS Bhāṣya III, 51.
119. cf. e.g. MBh Strīparva II, 24, etc.

120. cf. e.g. MBh Ādiparva I, 248, etc.
121. cf. Vājasanayi Saṃhitā, 32, 2; BU III, 8, 9; Mah Nār U I, 8, etc.
122. cf. Viṣṇudharmottara I, 73, 1, etc.
123. Viṣṇudharmottara I, 73.
124. We are disregarding the divisions of the years from Jupiter onwards (Bṛhaspati). cf. L. Renou and J. Filliozat, *L'Inde Classique*, II, p. 725 et seq. Paris, Imprimerie Nationale 1951.
125. cf. Mait U VI, 14: *sūryo yoniḥ kālasya.*
126. Mahābhāṣya on Vārtika 2, Pāṇini II, 2, 5.
127. cf., for example, the traditional fast on the eleventh day of the moon (ekādaśī).
128. *Vedānga-Jyotiṣa*, 41.
129. cf. YS Bhāṣya III, 51.
130. cf. MBh Vanaparva 149; 188; Śāntiparva 69; 231–2; Manu Smṛti I, 61–74; Viṣṇu Pur I, 3; VI, 3; etc.
131. The unit of measurement used is the divine year (*divya*), one human year being one day of the gods; thus a *mahāyuga*, or age of the gods, consists of 4,320,000 human years (cf. Kane, *History of Dharmaśāstra*, Vol. V, Part I, p. 688 et seq. Poona, 1958).
132. cf. M. Eliade, 'Le Temps et l'Éternité dans la Pensée Indienne', in: *Mensch und Zeit—Eranos Jahrbuch, 1951*, p. 219–52, Zurich, Rhein, 1952.

BIBLIOGRAPHY

BEDEKAR, V. M. The doctrine of *svabhāva* and *kāla* in the Mahābhārata and other old Sanskrit works. *Journal of the University of Poona* (Humanities), no. 13, 1961, p. 17–28.

BENVENISTE, E. Expression indo-européenne de l'éternité. *Bulletin de la Société Linguistique de Paris*, vol. 38, no. 112, fasc. 1, 1937, p. 103–12.

BHATTACHARYA, U. C. Problems of time in Indian thought. *Calcutta review*, no. 52, 1934, p. 302–9.

COOMARASWAMY, A. K. *Time and eternity*. Ascona, Artibus Asiae Publishers, 1947.

CORNELIS, H. Le discontinu dans la pensée indienne. *Revue des sciences philosophiques et théologiques*, no. 41, 1957, p. 233–44.

DAS, S. R. Notion of time in Indian philosophy. *Indian Historical Quarterly*, no. 9, 1933, p. 149–53.

ELIADE, M. *Le mythe de l'éternel retour: archétypes et répétition*. Paris, Gallimard, 1949.

——. Symbolismes indiens du temps et de l'éternité. *Images et symboles*. p. 73–119. Paris, Gallimard, 1952.

——. Time and eternity in Indian thought. *Man and time, Eranos Year Book 1958*, p. 173-200. London, Routledge & Kegan Paul.

HIRIYANNA, M. An Indian view of present time. *Quarterly journal of the Mythic Society* (Bangalore), no. 14, 1924.

HOGG, A. G. The challenge of the temporal process (Principal Miller lectures, 1933). *Journal of the Madras University*, vol. VI, no. 1, January 1934, p. 233–7.

HUBERT, H.; MAUSS, M. La représentation du temps dans la religion et la magie. *Mélanges d'histoire des religions*. p. 190–229. Paris, Alcan, 1909.

MADHAVATIRTHA. *The concept of time in Indian philosophy*. Ahmedabad, Vedant Ashram, 1951.

MAHADEVAN, T. M. P. *Time and the timeless*. Madras, Upanishad Vihar, 1953.

MALKANI, G. R. The temporal and the eternal. *The philosophical quarterly*, Amalner, vol. XXX, no. 1, April 1957, p. 11–18.

——. Time and the absolute. *Journal of the Philosophical Association* (Nagpur), no. 5, 1958, p. 1–7.

MANDAL, K. K. *A comparative study of the concepts of space and time in Indian thought.* Varanasi, Chowkhamba Sanskrit Studies, vol. LXV, 1968.

MONCHANIN, J. Le temps selon l'hindouisme et le christianisme. *Dieu vivant*, no. 14, p. 111–20.

NAKAMURA, H. Étude comparative de la notion d'histoire en Chine, Inde et Japon. *Diogenes*, no. 42, 1963, p. 44–59.

——. Time in Indian and Japanese thought. In: J. T. Fraser (ed.), *The voices of time*. p. 77–85. New York, G. Braziller, 1966.

PANIKKAR, R. *Le mystère du culte dans l'hindouisme et le christianisme*. Paris, Éditions du Cerf, 1970.

——. The law of *karma* and the historical dimension of man. *Philosophy East and West*, vol. XXII, no. 1, January 1972, p. 25–43.

Toward a typology of time and temporality in the ancient Indian tradition. In: *Philosophy East and West*, no. XXIV, no. 2, April 1974, p. 161–4.

PRZYLUSKI, J. From the Great Goddess to Kāla. *Indian historical quarterly*, 1938, p. 267–74.

SAMARTHA, S. J. *The Hindu view of history*. Bangalore, CISRS, 1959.

SĀSTRI, P. S. Time and the philosophy of history. *Prabuddha Bharata*, no. 60, 1955, p. 211–34.

SĀSTRI, S. Conception of time in Post-Vedic Sanskrit literature. *Essays on indology*. p. 149–204. Delhi, Meharchand Lachhmandasa, 1963.

SCHAYER, S. *Contributions to the problem of time in Indian philosophy*. Cracow, Polska Akademia Umiejetności Prace komisji orientalistycznej, 1938.

SCHEFTELOWITZ, J. *Die Zeit als Schicksalsgöttin in der indischen und iranischen Religion*. Stuttgart, Kohlhammer, 1929.

SENART, E. *Bṛhad-Āranyaka- Upaniṣad.* 2nd ed. (trans. and annotated). Paris, Les Belles Lettres, 1967.

SILBURN, A. *Svetāśvatara Upaniṣad* (trans.). Paris, A. Maisonneuve, 1948.

SILBURN, L. *Instant et cause. Le discontinu dans la pensée philosophique de l'Inde*. Paris, Vrin, 1955.

——. *Le Vijñāna Bhairava*. Paris, De Boccard, 1961.

WESENDONCK, O. von. Kālavāda and the Zervanite system. *Journal of the Royal Asiatic Society*, January 1931, p. 108–9.

THE EMPIRICAL APPERCEPTION OF TIME AND THE CONCEPTION OF HISTORY IN BANTU THOUGHT

Alexis Kagame

This study is concerned specifically with the Bantu zone and, in practice, is also relevant to the Sudanic zone. Although the language system of Sudanic civilization differs from that in the Bantu zone, it has been possible, from evidence gathered by sampling, to identify many affinities between the fundamental thought processes in the two zones. Consequently, although this study concentrates on Bantu Africa, I am convinced that its conclusions are also valid, at least to a large extent, with regard to Sudanic culture.

The conception of time in Bantu culture

In 1851, W. H. I. Bleek submitted a doctoral thesis at the University of Bonn on the 'class languages' spoken in southern Africa. This phenomenon had been known since the seventeenth century from publications by missionaries mainly in Angola and Mozambique. In 1852, K. A. Barth applied the term '*Ba*-Sprachen' to the entire group of these class languages owing to the fact that all such languages which were known at that time used the form *Ba-ntu* as the plural of *mu-ntu* (man). As the root *NTU* denoted MAN in all these languages, Sir G. Grey later referred to them as *BAntu languages*.[1] The term was therefore originally applied only to languages but was later extended by cultural anthropologists to peoples and cultures using these class languages.

THE METAPHYSICAL CONCEPTION OF TIME

Ontologically speaking, Bantu culture regards everything which can be conceived or formulated as falling within the following categories:
1. Being endowed with intelligence (man).
2. Being without intelligence (things).

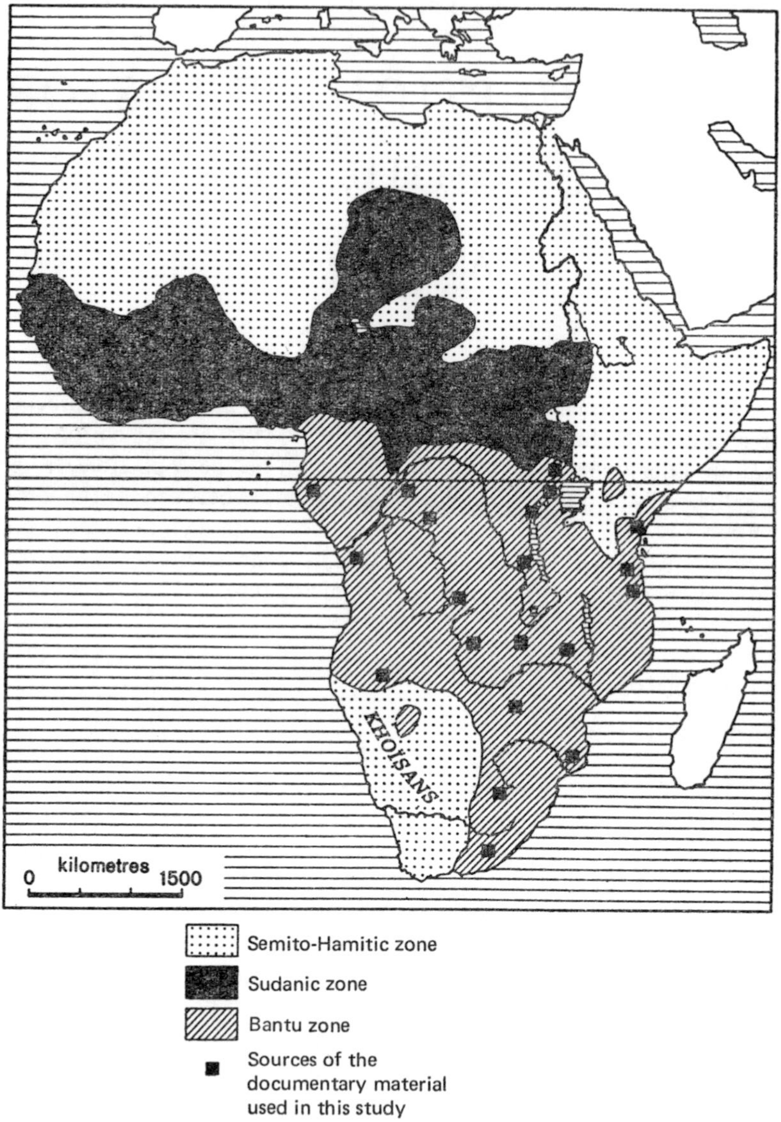

Map taken from C. G. Seligman, *Les Races de l'Afrique*, Paris, 1935.

3. Localizing being (place-time).
4. Modal being (accidentality, or modification of being).

The fourth category takes in all entities which, by their nature, are incapable of independent existence but, like quantity and quality, have to be attached to a substance-being; or which consist essentially in a relationship between two beings (relation, possession, position, etc.).

The third category, which is the subject of this paper, is expressed in Bantu languages by '*there where*', the true significance of which can be rendered by the term 'localizer'. The Bantu 'there where' is expressed by an element which grammarians have rightly classified among the locatives. This basic locative element is *HA* in the eastern zone, with its variant forms *PA* and *KA*. In the western zone, its equivalent is *VA*, whereas in the south-eastern zone it is rendered by *GO*. Thus, in the *HA* zone, *HAntu* (and *PAntu*) signify place or situation. This word includes the root *ntu*, which has already been noted in *MUntu* (man) and *BAntu* (men). The root *ntu* signifies being, the nature of which is indicated by the element prefixed to the root. Thus, in *HAntu* the localization is expressed solely by the element *HA*.

It should be added that this basic element often appears in conjunction with other complementary elements, for example: *aHA* = here (variant form: *aPA*), or with the demonstrative suffix *o* = *aHao* = *aho* (variant form: *aPao* = *apo*), etc.

I have therefore translated *Hantu* as 'localizing being' and have stated that it expresses the place-time entity. Far from being mere pedantry, this conclusion is based on a detailed analysis of the actual structure of the terms, of which I have already given an account.[2] The cultural data compiled at the time in our Interlacustrine zone were collated, between 1956 and 1971, with those from the Bantu zone as a whole, with a view to establishing correspondences and divergences. I consulted 231 works on the various Bantu languages and sent out a questionnaire to areas on which I had no information. Replies were received from scores of correspondents.

The authors of the works consulted, of course, had no intention of philosophizing when they composed their grammars and dictionaries.

A number of them, however, noticed and specifically drew attention to the phenomenon, although the majority merely listed the elements concerned without dwelling on them; Roland, for example, in his *Grammaire de la Langue Kisanga* notes on page 112: '*ponka* = *là*', adverb of place, and next to it: '*ponka* = *là*', adverb of time.

Among the works in which the place-time entity is explicitly mentioned are the following: (a) E. Jacottet, *A Practical Method to Learn Sesuto:* on the subject of *KA* (a variant of *HA*), the author specifies that *KA* also indicates the moment at which an action is performed (p. 88); (b) MacLaren, *A Xhosa Grammar:* after a detailed account of the locative *E-NI* which is peculiar to this language, the author adds that it also indicates a point in time (he further specifies that the locative *PHAKADE* signifies infinite space or time) (p. 31–4); (c) *Luba-*

Sanga Grammar: on the subject of *PA* (a variant of *HA*), the author states that this locative is used in forming prepositional words which are widely used to indicate place, time and circumstances in general (p. 12); (d) M. Guthrie, *Grammaire et Dictionnaire Lingala*: 'In European languages there is one range of words to specify the time when an action takes place and another to specify the place in which it occurs. In Lingala, the same expressions are used for time and for place' (translation from the French, p. 77).

The examples cited were, quite naturally, noted by these authors because they were analysing the languages in question, but in everyday conversation the Bantu themselves were unaware of the phenomenon. It must be added that the Bantu make a clear distinction between space and time, the former serving locate existents and the latter to measure duration. This is quite normal in everyday life, for in such a context people are often satisfied with analogical notions. But at the underlying levels of thought which can be inferred from the structure of locative terms, the two entities merge into a single notion which is that of localization. As Bantu culture was in the past, and still is, unwritten, this is a purely empirical conception.

THE METAPHYSICAL JUSTIFICATION FOR MERGING PLACE AND TIME INTO A SINGLE CATEGORY

We must now go further and try to account for the fact that the Bantu have merged the concepts of place and time. The explanation undoubtedly lies in an effort to localize and situate something, that something necessarily belonging to one of the four categories of 'being'. The latter term is used here in order to draw the reader's attention to the fact that, in Bantu philosophy, being = *Ntu* expresses the essence or the entity which is conceived of by the mind independently of its existence. If entities are universalized to such a degree, it is superfluous and, indeed, impossible to localize them in space or time. Furthermore, it cannot be claimed that what is known is localized in the mind, because the mind is not a place. It follows that the Bantu have merged the concepts in this way with a view to localizing not beings, but existents assigned to one of the other three categories.

The category of attached entities (the modifications of being) does not, of course, postulate the direct localization which belongs to the existent-substance. Once the latter has been localized, its internal modifications (for example, its quantity and its qualities) are also concomitantly localized. Was there any necessity, however, to merge place and time in order to localize existents? Surely space alone would have been sufficient. And why should the space which localizes the existent form a single entity with time? Does this mean that the existent is linked equally with space and with time? Undoubtedly. And this provides us with the makings of a satisfactory solution.

First, any existent, as soon as it appears, necessarily has a 'before' and an 'after'. Hence, the existent—whether animate or inanimate, whether or not endowed with immanent movement, motionless, at rest or fixed—is fraught with existential movement and proceeds upon its trajectory towards its connatural consummation. This existential movement is metaphysical and defies direct observation; we are aware only of its effects: for instance, we increase imperceptibly in age with each passing second.

This transition, not subject to observation, from 'non-such' to 'such' has been more than implicitly perceived at least once in our culture. Indeed, there is a story in which the protagonists are Death and a certain Sacyega. The latter had incurred a debt towards Death and owed him a calf. One day, Death came and stipulated that the animal should be neither male nor female. Sacyega was at a loss what to do in this impossible situation. But his son Ngoma, with whose name all tales concerning the solving of riddles are associated, suggested a way out: 'Tell him that you have found a suitable calf but that, in order to take possession of it, he will have to come between night and day. By day the stars are invisible and by night they are visible. Let him come between the two.' [3]

The story-teller took the tale no further, his purpose being merely to set one impossibility against another: a sexless calf, and the complete absence of any precise moment of transition between the non-visibility and the visibility of the stars. This is exactly parallel to the famous axiom of classical philosophy: between being and non-being there is no middle term. Between the non-visibility and the visibility of the stars, there is no moment of transition.

A clarification is, however, called for at this point. In discussing the question of existents, it must be remembered that the originators of Bantu culture, in accordance with the principle of causality, postulated a pre-existent, by virtue of which the *Ntu* essences pass to the higher stage of existents. This pre-existent has no place in the four categories of beings (essences): it is neither man (*Muntu*), nor thing (*Kintu* or *Kiuma* or *Kiloko* or *Ciro*, etc., depending on the regional term for being without intelligence); it is neither a localizer (*Hantu*, *Vuma* or *Golo*, etc.), nor the mode of existence of a being. By thus excluding it from the categories of beings (essences), the originators of Bantu culture indicated that that which causes the appearance of existents is not an essence, that is to say that we cannot, even theoretically, conceive of it as not existing. It is thus the necessarily existent, the existence of which has had no beginning. This provides the ultimate explanation for the emergence of existents. Accordingly, as far as Bantu culture is concerned, it is incorrect to refer to it—as ethnologists do—as the supreme being: it should be called the supreme existent or simply the pre-existent.

Thus, when we attribute existential movement to existents, this does not apply, of course, to the pre-existent, because the latter can have no 'before' or 'after'.

In addition to this existential movement which is its fundamental attribute, the existent itself executes other movements which may be either immanent or a combination of translation and rotation, or again internal and invisible to the naked eye in existents which are apparently motionless; each existent, in short, acts or is acted upon in accordance with the dynamic disposition of its nature.

The movements made by existents—whether actions or passions—are entities falling into the fourth category. Entity implies individuality: each entity must be itself and is distinct from previous and subsequent entities. How, then, are the movement-entities of each existent to be individualized? By the point in space in which the movement was made? This is out of the question, for a given point in space can accommodate an infinity of movements. Furthermore, if a particular point in space could individualize a movement and serve to distinguish it from any other movement, it would mean that this movement would occupy the given point in space without beginning to occupy it. It would consequently no longer be a movement but an eternally fixed entity occupying the same point in space, since the fact of being separated from it would mean that the entity would cease to be itself. Furthermore, this entity defined by a particular point in space would by the same token serve to define the space, so that, as soon as the entity was separated from its point in space, the latter would cease to be itself. This would lead to a series of inextricable corollaries: since the two would be united without beginning to be united, they would be of infinite duration, and this infinitude would necessarily imply their being of infinite extent so as to occupy all space, which would become a single point in a single entity. It is, therefore, impossible for any movement to be individualized by virtue of the point in space in which it is performed.

Could the movement at least be individualized and distinguished from previous and subsequent movements by virtue of the instant or point of time in which it was performed? This is impossible, for a given instant is the receptacle of an infinite number of movements made simultaneously by all existents.

How, therefore, do we individualize the movement of each existent? We can do so by combining the point in time and the point in space. The movement performed at-a-given-point-at-a-given-instant thus becomes a single entity; not only did it not take place in the past, but also it will never take place in the future. It is unique among the totality of possible and imaginable movements. If the same existent repeats an analogous movement at the same point in space, it will necessarily be a different existent for, just as the earlier instant had never previously occurred, so it will never recur.

That is the ultimate justification, at the underlying level of thought processes, for the merging of place and time in Bantu culture.

It should be noted that this metaphysical unification of place and time is deeply embedded in Bantu philosophy and that it is as old as Bantu language. Not only have the Bantu incorporated it in their language without becoming explicitly aware of it, but their culture, having no written form, cannot aspire to scientific self-analysis. A distinction must therefore be drawn between this place-time unity and the four dimensional space-time unity postulated by Minkowski and Einstein. [4,5] For the purposes of their scientific discoveries, these scientists applied the term 'chronotopical co-ordinate' to the place-time combination; for our present purposes we prefer to call it the 'individualizing co-ordinate' of all movements (i.e. actions and passions) of existents.

EXISTENCE AND 'LIFE'

Before proceeding further, we must explain how Bantu culture approaches the concept of existence.

Throughout the Bantu zone, the verb 'to be' can never express the idea of existence nor, therefore, can the word 'being' express the notion of existing. The celebrated axiom 'I think, therefore I am' is unintelligible, as the verb 'to be' is always followed by an attribute or by an adjunct of place: I am good, big, etc., I am in such and such a place, etc. Thus the utterance '. . . therefore I am' would prompt the question: 'You are . . . what? . . . where?'

The verb 'to be' may be expressed by two roots: *LI* and *BA*. The former does not appear in any perfect tense form (expressing a completed state) nor in any future tense. It refers exclusively to the present. The latter, on the other hand, *BA*, is used in all tenses of the past, present and future.

The verb 'to exist' may be formed from either of the two roots *LI* and *BA* with the addition of the adverb of place *HO* = *LIHO*, *BAHO*. This adverb *HO* is composed of two contracted linguistic elements:

HA = localizer (cf. above section).

O = demonstrative element: the *A* of *HA* is elided: *HA-O* = *HO* which can be rendered in English by the word 'there' or, more literally: 'place-there'. Thus the verb 'to exist' is rendered in Bantu by:

liho = is there (without the infinitive particle *KU*);

baho = to be there (with the infinitive particle, *KUBAHO*).

The adverb *HO* has a number of regional variant forms: thus, *liho* becomes *lipo*, *liko*, etc.; and *baho* becomes *bapo*, *bako*, *wapo*, *wako*, etc.

Lastly, there are other zones which express the notion of existence by using the verb *kuikala*, with its variant forms *kukala*, *kujala*, etc., which means: to be seated, to take up one's position there, to settle there.

The use of the form *liho* amounts, therefore, to a statement that the existent concerned is there, with the further implication that it will cease to exist; and, in general, it refers to a living being. It cannot be applied to the deceased because its use would be tantamount to a statement that they are not yet dead.

In order to express existence, both actual (the field of reference of *liho*) and habitual, past and future, the form *baho* must be used. This is also the form which must be used when one wishes to exclude the idea of living, for example in the case of the deceased, or if one mentally rules out the idea of ceasing to exist (through death or otherwise) in speaking of the Pre-Existent.

Finally, people and animals form a special category among existents in that, in Bantu culture, they have the attribute of 'life'. The vegetable kingdom is different in this respect. The only existents which have life are those which are born, are endowed with immanent movement and with feeling and which, by dying, reach an end of their living existence.

Existence and life are separate concepts; as long as men and animals both exist and live, the word *liho* = 'existing-not-yet-dead' is applied to them.

During their 'living existence', the word *baho* will of course be used in referring to what is habitual, past and future; but once this 'existence linked with life' has ended, *baho* will be applied to people alone, for Man's vital principle of intelligence continues to exist, whereas the vital principle of animals vanishes at the moment of death.

In conclusion, it may be noted that the term 'to live' is expressed by the same forms as the verb 'to exist'; the idea of 'life' and of 'living being' is rendered by a special term in each cultural zone: *ubuzima* in Interlacustrine Africa; *Bomoi* in Lingala; *oruhupo* in Kiherero; *mweo* in Kiluba; *ubumi* in Kibemba, etc.

It is evident, at all events, that Bantu culture in its language structure makes a clear distinction between 'existence' and 'living'. The latter is, so to speak, only an accessory stage on the existential trajectory of two categories of existents.

EXISTENTIAL MOVEMENT, TIME AND DURATION

As we have said, existential movement is a fundamental attribute, a connatural condition, of any existent which has made its appearance at a given moment—because it necessarily implies a before and an after. But the notion of this movement which we apply to the existent is not confined solely to each existing entity taken individually; it is similarly applied to all of them considered collectively in their totality or cosmos, in other words to the existents and the environment in which they evolve, space itself being an entity which has sprung into existence. The initial explosion which brought the cosmos into being imbued it with existential movement, the active principle of its expansion. The cosmic expansion is matched, for each individual existent, by what we have called the 'existential trajectory'.

The existential movement governs the phenomena of generation, corruption, augmentation, and diminution, decline, action and passion.

1. The *existential movement*, considered in itself as an entity, is the transition 'from non-being to being' (from 'non-being' X to 'being' X) or, in Bantu cultural thinking, the transition from 'non-being-there as' X to 'being-there as' X: the transition from 'non-starlight' to 'being-there as starlight', to take the example mentioned in the tale featuring Ngoma, son of Sacyega.

2. Existential movement is contrasted with *eternity*, the fundamental attribute of the pre-existent, which may be defined as real existence which has not emerged and which represents, in the present moment, the sum total of all duration.

Thus eternity is not subsumed in the genus 'movement'. By defining it as 'real existence', we wish to make it plain that this existence is not so termed merely by analogy but that it is an authentic 'being-there' and not a logical existence created by our minds, like the existence which we attribute to 'impossibility', 'contradiction', the notions of 'genus' and 'species', etc.

3. *Existence* seems to be susceptible of definition as the 'progressive sum of individualizing co-ordinates of the movements of the existent' launched on its existential trajectory, from its emergence up to its 'connatural', consummation.

The term 'connatural consummation', in this context, is used to indicate accidents such as death, corruption, decay, the limit beyond which the existent ceases to be what it was and its component elements give rise to another existent: *corruptio unius, generatio alterius.*

4. *Eviternity* is real existence which has come into being but which will have no limit, its connatural consummation being perpetuity.

Eviternity is therefore subsumed in the genus 'movement', for it is an existent which implies a before and an after.

5. *Becoming* is synonymous with 'the transition from non-being to being' ('non-being there as' such and such to 'being there as' such and such). It may thus be defined as 'existential movement considered in the existent as the latter proceeds upon its trajectory'. It follows that the essence of becoming is the relationship established between existential movement and a particular existent as it progresses towards its connatural consummation.

In this sense, becoming is also synonymous with existence, the difference being that the latter represents the 'progressive sum of individualizing co-ordinates', whereas the former refers to the existent in the effectuation of these same individualizing co-ordinates.

6. *Lasting* and *duration:* the meaning of these two terms does not appear to be identical: (a) duration seems to be the sum regarded as an over-all whole, of the individualizing co-ordinates already realized by the existent in a particular stretch of time; (b) the idea expressed by the verb 'to last', on the other hand, seems to correspond with the idea of 'continuing to exist'. Since it is synonymous with existing, it also expresses existential movement; (c) in the same sense, *duration* is synonymous with *existence*, both ideas expressing the static aspect of reality, the dynamic aspect of which is rendered by the verbs to exist and to last.

7. *Living* is the mode of *existence* peculiar to two categories of existents, man and animal in Bantu culture, and also plant life in non-Bantu culture.

Similarly, life is synonymous with *existence* and *duration*, all three notions being applied in the same way to this category of existents as long as they are passing through the stage of 'beings endowed with life'.

8. *Time*, from whatever angle it is considered, is the metrical entity of existential movement.

In order to determine its essence, it may be considered in its three phases: the past, the present and the future. The 'past' is an imprecise idea from the metaphysical point of view. It is measured by 'time' as duration already actuated by existents. Consequently, we should not seek the essence of 'time' in the 'past' for 'being-there' (existence as such) precedes 'lasting'. It follows that the being-there of 'time' precedes the past. Nor is the essence of time to be found in the future, in the 'time to come', for this is a mere projection of the mind. The essence of 'time' is, consequently, to be found in the present. But where is the true present? There is one principle which will provide us with a means of approaching the problem: admitting that time is the 'metrical' entity of movement, which is beyond dispute, it should already be applicable to the initial atom of existence (of duration, etc.). That is to say, it should already be applicable to movement at the initial stage of its effectuation and individualization. It is in this way that the individualizing co-ordinates are instantaneously marked during their imperceptible transition from 'non-being-there' to 'being-there'. It would be impossible for 'time' thereafter to measure them *a posteriori;* for that would imply that they had already been measured and enumerated at the precise moment of their individualization.

The essence of time therefore coincides with existential movement at the level of the emergence of the individualizing co-ordinate entity—existential movement being the realizer, and time as the measurer.

Concomitantly with both these, of course, existence continues at the same pace, adding the individualizing co-ordinate to those previously effectuated, as does duration considered as the total and static sum of these co-ordinates.

To sum up: (a) in their everyday speech, the Bantu make a clear distinction between the entities of place and time; (b) their linguistic structure suggests that, at a particular level, these two entities merge into a single category; (c) if one ponders the underlying reason for this unification, one discovers that the two entities are species of the genus 'localization'; (d) if one probes still more deeply in order to discover the 'localizable' element which postulates this unification, one ultimately discovers that it is a matter of the individualization of the movement of the existent (movement = action and passion); (e) it follows that an analysis of the conception of 'time' in Bantu culture would be incomplete if time were considered without reference to the conception of place. It is, no doubt, possible to set aside this unification if we confine ourselves to everyday speech, as has been done, for example, by research workers who were not concerned with philosophical reflection. But, once the topic has been approached from the philosophical angle, this problem of place-time unification cannot be evaded.

Empirical apperceptions of time in Bantu culture

THE FUNDAMENTALS OF TIME SERIATION

The first section of this essay was concerned with metaphysics; the topic to which we now turn comes under the head of cultural anthropology. We shall, however, have occasion to note that the metaphysical approach is also relevant to the experimental estimation of time. There is nothing surprising about this, for everyday language cannot be separated from its underlying basis, which is the structure of the linguistic system.

It has already been mentioned that, in everyday life, the Bantu clearly distinguish between the entities of place and time. There are three factors underlying the apperception and seriation of time:

1. The rotation of the earth, which is the cause of night and day.
2. The movement of the earth around the sun, which determines the seasons.
3. The movement of the moon around the earth, which is the basis of the months, together forming the year.

TIME 'STAMPED' BY THE EVENT

In Euro-American and other similar cultures, time is considered almost as an entity which runs parallel to existents and which, in a sense, travels along simultaneously with them. Indeed, time is used, or, in other words, advantage is taken of it in order to accomplish specific acts. Time is lost or wasted when one relaxes one's endeavours and remains inactive for a moment; in which case, it can be made up through increased exertion. It even has a commercial value: time, as the saying goes, is money. Such expressions indicate a precise, obsessive and feverish conception of time.

In traditional Bantu culture, however, time is a colourless, neutral, entity as long as it is not marked or stamped by some specific event: an action performed by the pre-existent, by man or animal, a natural phenomenon (earthquake, appearance of a comet, eclipse of the sun, an accident caused by lightning, flood, drought, etc.). As soon as the action or the event impinges on time, the latter is marked, stamped, individualized, drawn out of its anonymity, and becomes the time of that event.

It should be noted in this connexion that the Bantu have no substantive such as those which exist in the languages of Euro-American culture to denote 'time' in the abstract sense. For the Bantu, the only time is the time of this or that, the time propitious for this or that. The time thus marked and individualized by the event may be very short or very long, depending on the duration of the event which individualizes it. In speaking of the monarch, of a particular armed expedition or invasion, the terms reign, expedition and invasion are synonymous with time, for they are included in such formulations as: during the reign of so-and-so, when so-and-so launched such-and-such an expedition, etc. Once the event which stamped time has come to an end, the empty moments are devoid of any reference point, and their passing is marked only by the countless activities of everyday life. The latter are undoubtedly important for each existent, and each individual knows them to be marked by his own daily business, but the principle remains true: these personal activities are also interspersed with empty, insignificant moments.

It is evident that time thus marked by the event is, on the plane of everyday experience, a prolongation or transposition of the individualizing co-ordinate analysed on the metaphysical plane, with the additional distinction that the place is implied by the 'marking' event in question. The latter, indeed, cannot take place in a void: it occurs in a particular place. A particular monarch reigned over a country known to the speakers; a particular expedition was launched against a particular country; a particular comet made its appearance in the sky and a particular drought in a particular country caused a particular kind of famine (each such disaster having its own special name).

THE THREE PHASES OF TIME: PRESENT, PAST AND FUTURE

As stated above, the event, throughout the period during which it continues to unfold, individualizes the time necessary for its accomplishment. It is obvious that, on the metaphysical plane, this continuing event never ceases to recede into the past. But it will be regarded as a 'present' event until it has been accomplished. This can easily be explained, even on the metaphysical plane, by the fact that each event is considered as a special, individualized entity, distinct from those which preceded it and those which are contemporaneous with it. A reign, for example, however long, will remain in the present and will be referred to as the 'present' reign; it will become part of the past only on the death of the monarch. Clearly this is not peculiar to the Bantu: it is a universal form of expression. Thus, present time is time which is currently being 'marked' by existents which continue to proceed on their existential trajectory.

The 'past', on the other hand, is so called by reason of the 'stamp' which has previously been put upon it. In other words, the 'marking' entity (the event) has completed its connatural course. It is therefore of little consequence whether the existent which causes the event has itself completed its connatural course or not, for in this context 'past' time will be qualified in relation to the event and not in relation to its author, the cause of the event. Thus, the existent, while remaining in the 'present' (following the course of its existential trajectory) will have accumulated a considerable volume of 'past', representing those of its activities which had previously marked time.

The dead, not only distant ancestors but also those recently deceased, have completed their existential trajectory as living beings. In this respect, they belong to the 'past', which means in reality that their activities have marked earlier time as succeeding generations have completed their term as living beings. They still continue their existential trajectory as existents, however, for their connatural end is eviternity, or perpetual existence, by reason of their vital principle of intelligence which is immortal. But as there are innumerable ancestors and it is impossible to know them all by name, an attempt will be made to classify them chronologically as contemporaries of the chiefs who left the most noteworthy stamp on their own age. In certain regions, such chiefs are themselves classified under their respective kings and it is said that they were 'living' (that they were putting their stamp on time) in the reign of a particular monarch.

For a number of reasons, the past is of paramount importance in Bantu culture.

First, because, were it not for the past, the 'present', the time of the present generation, would not exist. Although this may seem to be a self-evident truth, it is, nevertheless, of fundamental significance. It implies not only the obvious fact that the men of today would not exist, but also that the language of the region concerned would not have been formed, that its territory would not have been created, that its social customs would not exist, that its political institutions would not have been established, that its Customary Law would not have been formulated, that its economic system and its range of crafts, trades, etc. would not exist. In short, it means that the culture peculiar to this region would not have been formed and that, consequently, its inhabitants would have vanished from the face of the earth. This is the first aspect of the 'past' (that is to say, the sum total of the activities by means of which the ancestors stamped their own time and which they have transmitted to their descendants). For all this, the men of the 'present' are indebted to generations of ancestors and are proud of their achievements.

Furthermore, there is in Bantu culture a close relationship between ancestors and their descendants, who are convinced that they would cease to exist in the 'present' and would be unable to perpetuate their line without the protection of their ancestors, to whom they must therefore look for the required patronage. This does not mean, however, that they are unconcerned with future times, for the ultimate goal of man, in the Bantu philosophical system, is the perpetuation of one's lineage. They thus look to the 'past' to secure their individual future and the future of their descendants (cf. below, p. 111).

On the metaphysical plane, 'future time', as we have said, is merely a projection of our minds. In order to appreciate the extreme limit of such anticipation, a distinction must be made between the individual and the social or political group.

John S. Mbiti, in *African Religions and Philosophy* (p. 17) writes:

> The future is virtually absent because events which lie in it have not taken place, they have not been realized and cannot, therefore, constitute time. If, however, future events are certain to occur, or if they fall within the inevitable rhythm of nature, they at best constitute only *potential time*, not *actual time*.

I therefore agree with this excellent writer's opinion, although our starting-points are different. The 'future' cannot be marked by actual events and therefore cannot be regarded as knowable time. A man who projects his mind into the future is not even certain of being there on the morrow. As a Rwandese proverb has it: *iby'ejo bibara ab'ejo:* 'the things of tomorrow occupy the conversation of the people of tomorrow'. In other words, 'If I am there tomorrow, I shall see about it'. In practice, however, everyone makes plans for the future, for he is certain that, if he should disappear prematurely, his heirs will carry on his work. According to Rwandese customary law, all debts contracted must be paid at the end of a year, in the lunar month of Nyakanga (July), the season of the millet harvest: 'to show someone the ear of millet' is a legal expression meaning 'to ask a debtor to pay his debt'.

As the time cycle in Bantu culture is limited to the year, as will be shown below, it might be expected that an individual would be unable to make plans extending beyond this twelve-month period.

A social or political group (a large family, a tribal nation, etc.), on the other hand, is on a different level. The territory occupied by the members of the group, and their common heritage, were bequeathed to them by their ancestors who formed a similar group. They defend them and even struggle to enlarge them in order to bequeath them in their turn to their own heirs, who will pass them on from generation to generation. It is evident that, for them, 'future' time is infinite.

It is also in the context of such groups that certain cyclical initiation or dynastic ceremonies are performed at periods ritually fixed by the ancestors. Although some of these ceremonies, such as the ceremony of initiation, are obviously performed in the present, they duplicate actions of the past in order to guarantee the indefinite continuance of the group. Some dynasties in regions which have a monarchical system give their monarchs reign names every four generations; once all four names have been used, the cycle begins again, the same names being used from one cycle to another throughout the future. It is therefore clear that, in every such case, 'future' time is anticipated as certain to be marked by the activities of the group, which will perpetuate itself indefinitely in its descendants.

THE CULTURAL SERIATION OF TIME

The day

One important remark should be made at the outset: it has already been stated that the Bantu languages all have the same structure; but what has not so far been stated is that all these languages, throughout the region where they are spoken, from north to south and from the Atlantic to the Indian Ocean, use the same word, the same root, to express a range of fundamental ideas which must certainly have been current before the dispersal of the tribes and the differentiation of the regional cultures. Let us take, for example, the term meaning 'moon': in the languages of Interlacustrine Africa, the term is *kwezi;* in Kinyanja (a Malawian language): *mwezi;* in Kiluba (the language of the Baluba, in Central Zaire): *kwezi;* in Kitabwa, on the western shore of Lake Tanganyika, in Zaire: *kwezi;* in Kibemba (northern Zambia): *mweshi;* in Kishona (in Rhodesia): *mwedzi;* in Kisukuma (south of Lake Victoria in Tanzania): *ngweji;* in Kiswahili (on the east coast in Tanzania and Kenya): *mwezi.*

The day, as might be expected, is closely associated with the sun. A number of roots, which it would take too long to enumerate here, are used to express both these notions. In certain languages, both are even designated by a single word; thus in Kishona (in Rhodesia), both are called *zuva* (cf. Biehler, *Shona Dictionary*). The name Kishona is applied to an extensive region in which thirty-seven dialects are spoken.[6] Similarly, in Kitabwa, both the sun and the day are called *koba*.[7] In the Kisanga language, also in Zaire (in the province of Shaba, formerly Katanga), the sun and the day are called *dyuba*.[8] The same applies in the zone of the Pahouin (South Cameroon and Gabon) in which the same two meanings are attached to the word *dzo*.[9]

An important distinction is made between what may be termed 'daylight' and 'daytime'; the former begins as soon as the first light of dawn heralds the sunrise and ends in the evening twilight shortly after sunset. 'Daytime', on the other hand, means the time during the day when one can feel the warmth of the sun.

Lastly, it should be noted that the day is quite distinct from the night: the Bantu traditionally had no concept of a revolution of the earth taking twenty-four hours. The role of the day and that of the night were separate.

The notion of 'instant' is expressed by a special term in each language. For example, in the languages of Rwanda, Burundi and Buha, which is part of Tanzania, the instant is *akanya*, a diminutive of *unwanya*, moment. (It should be noted that these three languages are, for all practical purposes, dialect variants of a single language.) The instant is termed *felé* in Lomongo, a language of west central Zaire; *mwila* (little moment) in Kitabwa; *kimye* in Kisanga; *akafimbo* in Kwanyama, in southern Angola, etc.

Obviously the idea of 'hour' could have no part in traditional culture, but all Bantu regions expressed its equivalent by referring either to the apparent movement of the sun or to the sequence of daily activities, which ultimately depended on the movement of the sun. By comparing the names denoting these traditional 'hours' with the hours shown by our watches, we can calculate approximately their actual duration.

John S. Mbiti, in the book already quoted, gives an example referring to the Nkole Bahima in Uganda. These Bahima were a pastoral people and their hours, consequently, were determined by the tasks connected with herds of cattle. Thus 6 a.m. for Europeans, in other words the first hour of the day, is milking time, and so on until the first hour of the night (7 p.m.) which is the time of the evening milking.

In Rwanda, on the other hand, where the Batutsi (Hamitic herdsmen, cousins of the Bahima) were a completely settled population, time was indicated by combining agricultural and pastoral occupations, with additional references to the effects produced by the sun on the landscape. It should be added that the day began with the first light of dawn, *umuseke* (literally, the laughing) and was followed by *mu bunyoni* (literally, song of the little birds). Around 8 and 9 a.m. occurred *agasusuruko*, the heat of the sun. Around 10 a.m., *ku kareka-macu*, 'the moment when' (in certain seasons) 'the clouds are driven' (from the sky). Around 11 a.m. to 12 noon, *amahingura*, the return from the fields (the workers being overwhelmed by the heat). Around 12 noon or 1 p.m., *amashoka*, the time to water the cattle. This sequence continued, each portion of the day having its own name, until sunset when the hours of night began.

The situation was similar everywhere else. Thus, Van Acker says that 'the Batabwa indicate the time by pointing to the place where the sun is'.[10]

Among the Bakongo (around the Zaire estuary), the sun is termed *ntangu*, which also means: time, present time, hour, occasion, propitious time, precise moment, etc. Thus, in order to ask, 'What time is it?', one asks, 'What sun is it?'

For the Basukuma, south of Lake Nyanja (Victoria), the times of day are reckoned in terms of the position of the sun, indicated by the position of the arm. There are also a number of precise terms: *Makingo*, early dawn; *Wela*, bright dawn; *Lyafuma*, the first appearance of the sun; *Dilu*, morning (until noon); *Lyaseba*, 10-11 a.m; *Ntwe gati*, noon; *Lyabinza nkono*, 1 to 2 p.m.; *Lyasalika*, 4 to 5 p.m.; *Lyaloka*, 5 to 6 p.m.; *Lyagwa*, sunset.[11]

In his reply to the questionnaire on the Bahaya, living to the west of Lake Nyanja (Victoria), W. Matthijssen gives a complete list of the times of day and night, the names for which combine references to the movement of the sun, pastoral life and agricultural activities.

Farther south in the Bantu region and also in Chinyanja (in Malawi), we find exactly the same approach. Among the Thonga (southern Mozambique), the 'hours' are also indicated in accordance with the movement of the sun.[12]

To conclude this section on the 'day', let us consider it with respect to its present centre which is 'today'. In the language of Rwanda-Burundi-Buha, we express 'today' by *none*. In this respect we are an insignificant minority, for in the eastern region, between central Zaire and the Indian Ocean, including Zambia and Malawi, the term *lelo* is used. By aphaeresis, the coastal variety of Kiswahili drops the second *l* and says *leo*. The other regions employ their own terms, none of which is used over anything like so wide an area as the word *lelo*.

Two different attitudes may be observed with regard to the two days before and the two days after 'today'. Six of the eleven languages on which we have collected full information use the same term for yesterday and tomorrow and another for the day before yesterday and the day after tomorrow, whereas the other languages have specific terms to express these different ideas. The table below will make this clearer.

It may be noted that the language of Rwanda (Kinyarwanda) goes even further and has a name for a third day: *ejobundi-buriya* (literally: 'after-tomorrow-over-there' and 'before-yesterday-over-there').

In conclusion, it is clear from the position, as shown on the map, of the sources of the information used in this study that: (a) the Bantu all have the same approach to the classification of the hours which make up the day and that the clock which they have in common is the sun (we have given no des-

Language	Day before yesterday	Yesterday	Tomorrow	Day after tomorrow
Kiluba	*maipi*	*dikelela*	*dikelela*	*maipi*
Kisanga	*masosi*	*kenshya*	*kenshya*	*masosi*
Kibemba	*bulya-bushiku*	*mailo*	*mailo*	*bulya-bushiku*
Kiganda	*lwa bbiri*	*jjo*	*jjo*	*lwa bbiri*
Kinyarwanda (Kirundi-Giha)	*ejobundi*	*ejo*	*ejo*	*ejobundi*
Kitabwa	*bolya-busiku*	*lukere*	*lukere*	*bolya-busiku*
Kinyanja	*dzana*	*dzulo*	*mawa*	*mkuca*
Kishona	*marimwezuro*	*nezuro*	*wedza*	*kuskwera wedza*
Kikongo	*ezuji*	*ezono*	*ombaji*	(?)
Pahouin	*ozan*	*anghoghi*	*kerie*	*ozan*
Kiswahili	*dyuzi*	*dyana*	*kesho*	*kesho-kutwa*

cription of the hours of the night because we have received too little explicit data on the subject); (b) these hours are designated by reference to a fact, thus an event, which normally occurs each day. This exemplifies the principle of the 'stamping' of time by the event.

The week

In certain areas of Bantu Africa, the days were grouped together to form a week of five days; the people worked on the land for the first four days, the fifth being a day of rest. In Rwanda, the fifth day was called *icyumweru*, a term which has since been used to designate Sunday. In the Bushi, an area in Zaire bordering on Rwanda, it was called *umugobe*. The same institution existed among the Baluba in central Zaire[13] and among the Bakongo, in the region situated around the Zaire estuary, where the fifth day is called *nkandu*, each of the days having its own name.[14]

Certain cultural zones do not have this institution of the week: for instance, in the tradition of the Buhaya and the Busukuma, living respectively to the west and south of Lake Nyanja (Victoria), it was unknown. In most areas, in fact, it is for the present impossible to draw conclusions because we have not enough information. But it may, at all events, be said that the week is a cultural element which apparently stems from north-eastern Africa. It remains an open question whether it exists among the Bakonga and the Baluba, whose areas seem not to have been settled by Hamitic populations. As for the fact that the Burundi had no concept of week whereas the Rwanda did recognize such a concept, this proves that there were successive waves of migrants and that one group which was familiar with this institution settled in Rwanda without spreading farther south.

The month

Mention has already been made of the linguistic components of the terms used to express the month. The same terms denote the moon except in certain languages which we have mentioned. Among the Baluba (central Zaire), it was believed that each new moon was really a different moon, in fact a new creation.[15]

In Rwanda, the new moon is called *umataho*, return (of the moon which had disappeared), and the full moon *inzora*, complete unfolding. These are the two great events of the lunar month. The new moon was the occasion for ceremonies in many zones throughout the Bantu region, where it was believed that the earth's satellite was auspicious for those who honoured it and ominous for those who paid it no attention. The full moon, on the other hand, indicates the middle of the month or, in other words, the end of moonlit nights and the onset of dark nights. The majority of the Bantu never counted the days of the month; those who have done so, for example in the Swahili zone on the East Coast, have adopted this practice as a result of contact with non-African cultures.[16]

In general, the months bear proper names to most of which is attached a phrase indicating the state of the food crops, etc. Thus, among the Babemba, the month of February is *Kabengele kakalamba:* the month in which cucumbers and pumpkins are plentiful.[17] The same occurs in the Kishona zone.[18] Here the months are indicated by reference to the seasons of rain, wind and heat. The same applies among the Bakongo, around the Zaire estuary: January: *ntasu*, hunger; February: *kyuni*, scarcity of rain; March: *nkazi andolo*, feminine rain (light rain); April: *nuni ndolo*, masculine rain (heavy rain); May: *mawalala*, distant rain; June: *mumu tsi*, parched landscape; etc.[19] The list of examples could be extended, particularly with regard to the names of the months in the present writer's own region.

It may be noted, however, that the names of the months are specified by reference to the seasons, for the moon does not itself create the circumstances which enter into the designation of the successive moons. This is a further instance of the 'stamping' and marking of time by the event, without which it would be anonymous, impossible to determine, observe or remember.

The seasons and the year

The movement of the earth around the sun determines the cyclical return of the seasons. This cyclical return is at the basis of the number of months: people observed the recurrence of the same climatic phenomena and ultimately counted the number of 'moons' in the full cycle which included two dry seasons and two rainy seasons. Having established that this cycle consisted of twelve 'moons', the Bantu grouped them into a whole which they called a 'year':

from then on it was an easy step to classify the months according to the heavy and light rains and the seasons of intense and moderate heat.

Of the authors whom we have consulted, only Biehler (*Shona Dictionary*) has recorded the existence of a term denoting the season, *mugino* (with the plural form *migino*), which signifies division. It is very likely that this is a word of his own invention, for the Bantu considered it sufficient to attach proper names to each season and did not feel the need for a generic term.

In the eastern zone (from central Zaire, including the southern part of the territory, as far as the coast), the year is denoted by the root *ak-a: mu-aka* (the 'u' of the classifier becoming 'w' because it is followed by a vowel, hence *mwaka*); in the Kishona region, in Rhodesia, this term is replaced by *ligore* (in the plural: *magore*). In the western sector, on the other hand, the root *ak-a* seems to be unknown; indeed, the year is called *mvu* by the Bakongo and *mbu* by the Pahouin. In both cases, however, the term used for 'year' does not indicate solely a period of twelve months; the same term also means season, period, epoch, year.

In the Interlacustrine zone (including Rwanda), in Malawi[20] and also in the region in which Kikongo is spoken, around the Zaire estuary[21], the idea of harvest is rendered by the term which signifies year.

Among the Babemba (in Zambia), there seems to have been an attempt at greater precision through the use of two different terms: *c(h)aka* (as in Malawi) means a year of twelve months, whereas *mwaka* is used variously to indicate year, season and period.[22]

To sum up, the year seems to be the longest unit of time; although it generally corresponds to a period of twelve months, it may be further extended. Indeed, in its connotation 'period' it may refer to times stretching fairly far into the future, as among the Babemba.

As for expressing the concepts of season and harvest by the term meaning year, these are metonymic transfers of meaning, in so far as these 'events' are intimately bound up with the cyclical passage of time measured by the unit of the year.

Bantu culture has never conceived any longer unit of time such as the century or, *a fortiori*, the millennium.

The remote past

Each language has its own term to convey the idea of the remote past: *kale*, formerly, in Kinyanja; *kule* in Kitabwa, *kera* in Kinyarwanda-Kirundi-Giha, etc. Kiswahili and similar languages of the East Coast also use the term *kale*, which means in ancient times, formerly, of old, antiquity.[23] Kiswahili also uses the term *zamani*, of which John S. Mbiti has made much, although wrongly, it seems, because it does not unambiguously and exclusively indicate the 'past'. Its exact connotation may conveniently be indicated by quoting what is said by C. Sacleux, who is fully qualified to pronounce on the subject:

Zamani, time, epoch, moment; used in both the plural (*zamani za*) and in the singular (*zamani ya*), in the time of, in the days of, in the epoch of, in the centuries of, in the age of (when speaking of a period of time). *Zamani za kale*, in former times, in ancient times, in antiquity, of old, long ago. *Zamani za sasa*, nowadays, in the present times.[24]

This last acceptation shows that the term fluctuates between the 'past' and the 'present' except when supplemented by *kale*. The idea of 'centuries' may be explained by the fact that the East Coast has been strongly influenced by Arab and Indian cultures.

These analyses by C. Sacleux are all the more significant evidence on the 'stamping' of time in that the author did not approach the matter from our own standpoint. Furthermore, it will be noticed that, in spite of several centuries of acculturation, the Bantu of the East Coast have not modified the traditional conception.

The idea of eternity, however, in the sense of the totality of duration (and consequently comprising pre-time, all past and all future times, as eviternal existents will eternally be linked with time), could not have presented itself to the Bantu. The adverb of time 'always', in the documentary material which we have before us, may be broken down into 'all the days', that is to say each day, which amounts to a continuous, or undefined time.

The idea of eternity was probably introduced by missionaries. However this notion remains unintelligible—which is not wholly unexpected, in view of the fact that a finite intelligence cannot grasp the infinite. This explains why all expressions introduced by missionaries remain ambiguous. In our zone, for example, we say: *iteka lyose*, eternally, but this expression means the each-time-total, the always-total. In Kikongo, one says: *mvu ka mvu*, year after year (always, eternally). Lastly, among the Pahouin, one says: *ngan-tul*, the days-all. Eternity is thus expressed by conventional terms which are far from corresponding exactly to the notion of eternity.

The conception of 'spiral' time: a corollary

To conclude the discussion on the subject of time, we still have to analyse a corollary not explicitly considered by the Bantu, namely the overall direction taken by time.

In the language of Rwanda there is a saying which has been attributed to a woman living in the time of the Mibambwe III Sentabyo, a king who reigned around 1741–46. This woman is reported to have exclaimed: 'As it is day and then night, what will the end be?'[25] This saying would have vanished into oblivion if it had not become a proverbial expression applied to events which resume their uninterrupted course at the moment when the final point of the series seemed to have been reached.

The succession of day and night is similarly reflected each year by the seasons. Consequently, it might be said that Bantu time is cyclical. This assertion would seem to be supported by the cyclical initiation ceremonies and the repetition of dynastic names which have already been mentioned.

These socio-political phenomena co-exist, however, with the universal conviction that time which has been stamped does not return: what belongs to 'past' time—the entities which have completed their existential trajectory—can never recur.

Thus the irreversibility of time serves in a sense as the central point pivot around which the cycles revolve, like a 'spiral', giving the impression of an open cycle. Each season, each new generation to be initiated, each fourth dynastic name returns on the same vertical but at a higher level. In other words, they do not return either to the same point in space or to the same instant—which is the logical counterpart of our individualization of the entity 'movement'.

It is immediately obvious that there is no return to the same instant. It is even easier to grasp that time does not return to the same point in space. Indeed, as the sun itself both rotates and travels round in unison with the galaxy, the days and nights, the seasons and years which succeed each other on earth do not recur regularly at the same point in space. Hence the path taken by the earth, which is elliptical in relation to the sun, is spiral in relation to the galactic movement.

The view of history in Bantu culture

THE EFFICIENT CAUSES OF HISTORY

A civilization, if it is to be recognizable as such, embodies a number of constituent elements. First, a linguistic system; second, a corpus of fundamental political laws or customs which underlie the organization of the public and private life of all types of communities, whether based on the clan or on the nation. It also has a system of social customs which forms the basis of the various rites governing relations between persons, households and families and, above all, the rite represented by the education of children. It also has an economic system underlying the production of commodities and providing a structure for their circulation and distribution for consumption within the groups concerned. It also has a corpus of technical know-how which is related to the real needs of such groups, and on which are based the various crafts and trades indispensable to those groups. Again, it has some system of scientific knowledge even if, as in certain essentially speculative branches, such 'knowledge' is merely an invention of the mind, unrelated to reality. It also has a philosophical system or an underlying theory of the nature of being, which is at least implicitly affirmed in the conception of the world and in everyday speech. Lastly, it has a religious system which governs the relations between the living and the dead, with real or imagined hypersensual forces, and with the eternal existent, and which provides a comforting solution to the highly important problem of the origin of man, of his earthly existence and of his ultimate end.[26]

Before becoming the background and cause of historical events, all these and other elements were themselves facts of history. They did not descend out of the blue in a perfectly structured form: they must have been tentatively created by innovators whose efforts were gradually improved by their successors from generation to generation until each element reached a point of stability.

But it remains to be considered what prompted the earliest innovators to initiate the first activities which gave rise to such cultural elements. It is certain that in each case, the first initiatives must have been taken by an individual, a household or, at most, a patriarchal family. The two latter cases would, in any event, suggest the existence of 'collaborators' who assisted the initiator. Whatever the case, these cultural elements came into being, were realized, in order to ensure survival through: (a) the production of commodities which effectively met the real needs of the group concerned; (b) effective protection against danger from outside; (c) adaptation to the climatic condition of the area and mastery over nature.

Within the context of a particular civilization, we consider such elements only in their evolved and highly complex stage, as concerning vast groups of human beings. But it nevertheless remains true that each 'invention' is due, at its inception, to an individual. Consequently, in view of the fact that a vast group of human beings—a body corporate—is a mass of individuals, it reflects on a large scale the basic trend which inspired the initiators of its civilization.

We must keep in mind the principle referred to above of the 'stamping' of time. The initiators left a deep mark on time during their existence on earth; in other words, they launched a series of entities (their 'inventions') on their existential trajectory, and their descendants, from generation to generation, repeat the stamping of time on a large scale, for the production of commodities, protection against outside danger, and adaptation to climatic conditions, ever-increasing emphasis being placed on the mastery of nature.

In particular zones, of course, a significant contribution to these fundamental cultural elements may have been made by immigrants having a more highly developed technology. But in addition to peaceful immigration, which, in a sense, passes unobserved, there may be armed invasion which makes a stronger mark on time; the purpose of the assailants may be merely to make a raid and then withdraw, or they may wish to conquer and annex the territory. A raid tends to enhance the economic strength of the group making it, whereas conquest strengthens its defensive capacity, since the conquered people become an additional source of mobilizable manpower. The same objectives motivate the representatives of more advanced cultures to embark on the enterprise of colonization. They come in search of raw materials for their industries and of consumers to provide a market for their surplus manufactured goods.

In short, the three fundamental concerns which we have just indicated as conditions of survival, both for the individual and for society, seem to form three headings under which the other cultural elements enumerated at the beginning of this section may respectively be classified, except for the linguistic system which pre-exists them.

THE REAL PURPOSE OF HISTORY

Some people imagine that a society is formed of the members of the present living generation. In fact, those who are at present alive are only one component of their society; the territory they occupy is another component, and so is their language, not to speak of all the cultural elements which distinguish them from other similar groups. But the most important and most decisive element is that of the ancestors of each generation, who have progressively created and bequeathed to posterity the territory, the language and all the cultural elements by virtue of which, taken as a whole, those who are now living are what they are, and without which they would be entirely different. Thus all generations together form a living whole.

Successive generations all follow the same basic policy; they defend and develop the national heritage without which the community as such would cease to exist and would be swallowed up by its neighbours. Each generation brings up its children in the moral climate of this over-all policy, inculcating in them the ideal which determines the inner behaviour of each citizen. And the aim of each generation is to bequeath to the next what it has inherited and holds in trust from the one before it.

The heritage which engenders the national mentality in this way has been formed by the sum total of the successive events of the 'past'; that is to say that the instigating agency—whether an individual or a body corporate—has produced a particular event—an entity launched on its existential trajectory to continue placing its mark on time. Certain events of lesser intensity may end their course as a result of another and more significant event; thus the outbreak of the French Revolution theoretically put an end to the monarchy in France. To sum up, such events have sprung into existence in the 'past' and, having stamped time by their emergence, have been launched on their existential trajectory, continuing to stamp the time of subsequent generations, in some cases right down to the present generation.

THE PRESENCE OF ANCESTORS IN THE EVERYDAY LIFE OF NEGRO-AFRICANS

The purpose of this section is to show that the views analysed in the preceding section are not the personal ideas of the present writer. In many cultures, particularly Euro-American culture, the influence of the biblical tradition has led to an over-stylization of the link between the living and preceding generations. In other cultures, however, particularly among the Negro-Africans, the dead are the constant companions of the living. It will suffice to instance the following statements:

Belief in the continued influence of the departed fathers of the family and tribe is exceedingly strong in all West Africa . . . The ancestors . . . are felt to be still present, watching over the household, directly concerned in all the affairs of the family and property, giving abundant harvests and fertility . . . It is difficult for the modern European to realize, and always to remember, the extent to which the ancestors are considered in West African life.[27]

The same attitude is found among the Bakongo around the Zaire estuary:

The dead have their own village just like the living . . . In their village, the ancestors have their houses and their fields . . . The ancestors are masters and owners of the earth and the water, the forests and the bush, with all the animals which inhabit them and the wine-palms which grow there. They also possess arable land and they grant abundant harvests if they deign to permit them. Should a native wish to fell and burn an ancient forest in order to turn it into a cassava or maize field, he will previously ascertain the opinion of the ancestors by means of a little test called *kifudikila.* He goes in broad daylight into the forest and clears a very small space; . . . if, during the night, he has strange dreams and feels tired in the morning, it is because the ancestors do not wish this part of their forest to be touched.[28]

The same thing applies among the Baluba in central Zaire:

The dead protect those who honour them, preserve them from misfortune, defend them against their enemies, and wreak vengeance upon the latter. They are the natural tutelary spirits of the household.[29]

The situation is the same in Interlacustrine Africa and in Zambia.[30]

Again, Radcliffe-Brown and Daryll Forde state that:

In South-east Africa, a man's own ancestors of his own lineage are believed to watch his conduct and punish him for any breach of duty.[31]

In confirmation of the foregoing, here is a passage concerning the Thonga in southern Mozambique. These people believe that the spirit of every deceased person becomes a god, *shikwembu,* the ancestor-god. The plural of the term *shikwembu* is *psikwembu;* this will make clear the meaning of the following passage:

The natives believe that the *psikwembu* are the masters of everything: earth, fields, trees, rain, men, children and even of *baloyi,* wizards! They have full control over all these objects or persons. The gods can *bless:* if the trees bear plenty of fruit, it is because they made it grow; if the crops are plentiful, it is because they sent good wizards to increase them, or hindered bad ones who tried to spoil them; if you come across a pot of palm wine, it is your god who has sent you that windfall . . . Often when a man has narrowly escaped drowning, or having his ankle sprained by a stump which has caught his foot, he will say 'The gods have saved me' . . . but they can also *curse*, and bring any amount of misfortune on their descendants. If the rain fails, it is owing to their anger; if a tree falls on you, they have directed its fall; if a crocodile bites you, the gods residing in the pool have sent it; if your child has fever and is delirious, they are in him, tormenting his soul; if your wife is sterile, they have prevented her from childbearing.[32]

In short, for Negro-Africans, the life beyond is not merely hypothetical: it is a conviction of a very practical kind which has repercussions on the daily life of the living. The dead are considered the masters and are involved in the life of their descendants, granting them success in their undertakings, protecting them and preserving them from all danger and, above all, ensuring the continuation of their lineage. If, however, the living neglect to pay due honour to the dead, the latter have it in their power to show their displeasure by causing various misfortunes (loss of property, sickness, etc.).

It is generally believed that nobody can succeed merely through a rational use of his natural endowments: success will be attributed to the tutelary spirit of his ancestors. Similarly, if someone's property is in a bad way or if he suffers physically (sickness, infirmity, death), everything will be attributed to a malevolent ancestral spirit which may act directly or strike at him through the medium of another living being, for example an animal or a poisoner, or through natural phenomena such as lightning, drowning, the fall of a tree, etc.

In this context, the importance of the soothsayer will readily be appreciated; he is credited with the power of identifying the deceased person who is making the attack, the precise reason for the attack, and the form of worship which should be offered in order to appease his rage. If it is impossible to identify the assailant, the soothsayer will endeavour to find another departed person to serve as protector, who will see to it that the assailant relinquishes his hostility. Thus the relations between the living and the dead are an obsessive and all-embracing problem, for whatever happens to the living, for good or evil, the ancestors are believed to have had some hand in it.

THE INTERVENTION OF THE DEAD AND OF THE SOOTHSAYER IN HISTORY

Thus, no occurrence is regarded as purely secular, or fortuitous, or dependent solely on human agency however skilfully exercised. The influence of the supernatural is discerned in every event. If the country is invaded, it is inconceivable that the attack could have been launched by the invader without the propitious divinatory oracle provided by the soothsayer. If the group under attack is organizing itself to resist the assailant and wishes to ensure its success, a soothsayer is first consulted and indicates the ceremonies which are to be performed in honour of a particular ancestor, who is thus promoted unseen 'commander in chief' of the armed forces. Success and failure, on either side, are attributed not to the prowess or incompetence of the 'visible' commander but to a higher concentration of supernatural forces on the side of the victor and a lesser concentration on the side of the vanquished.

Thus, all historical events occur in reality but are assessed in terms of this magical logic.

We do not wish to imply that the expression 'magical logic' refers to the prelogical mentality which a certain school of thinking has wrongly attributed to 'primitives'. What we have termed 'magical logic' is not a stage of thinking which is advancing towards Cartesian logic; it is a system of thought which is complete in itself but of a different kind. It coexists with a conception of the world which is in keeping with it; it cannot evolve, and is abandoned entirely if a different conception of the world is acquired.

In conclusion, it may be said that the Negro-African view of the 'ancestral past', once it has been separated from its magico-religious excrescences, provides a basis on which the true meaning of history may be grasped; it is not concerned with the 'past' as such, but describes present events as they occurred and sprang into being in the past.

NOTES

1. cf. G. Van Bulck, *Manuel de Linguistique Bantoue*, p. 25–9, Brussels, G. van Kampenhout, Académie Royale des Sciences d'Outre-mer, 1949 (Mémoires).
2. cf. A. Kagame, *La Philosophie Bantu-Rwandaise de l'Être*, p. 246–78, Brussels, Académie Royale des Sciences d'Outre-mer, 1956 (Mémoires, coll. in 8º, Louv. sér., 7, 12, fasc. I).
3. cf. Kagame, op. cit., p. 264–6.
4. cf. A. Aliotta, 'Tempo', *Enciclopedia Filosofica*, col. 1124–31, Venice and Rome, Istituto per la Collaborazione Culturale, 1957.
5. cf. Henri Bergson, *Durée et Simultanéité*, p. 140-76, Paris, Presses Universitaires de France, 1968.
6. cf. C. M. Doke, *A Comparative Study in Shona Phonetics*, p. 247, Johannesburg, Witwatersrand University Press and Routledge, 1931.
7. cf. Van Acker, *Dictionnaire Kitabwa-Français*, Tervuren, G. van Kampenhout, 1907.
8. cf. Dom Hadelin Roland, *Vocabulaire Français-Kisanga*, Saint-André-Lez-Bruges, Abbaye Bénédictine, 1938.
9. cf. V. Largeau, *Encyclopédie Pahouine*, Paris, E. Leroux, 1901.
10. Van Acker, op. cit., p. 130.
11. Reply by S. Moravcik to the questionnaire entitled 'Enquête Linguistique sur la Pensée Profonde des Bantu', sent by the author to all parts of the Bantu zone.
12. cf. Henri A. Junod, *The Life of a South African Tribe*, Vol. II, London, 1912.
13. cf. E. Van Avermaet and B. Mbuya, *Dictionnaire Kiluba-Français*, p. 162, Tervuren, 1954 (Annales du Musée Royal des Sciences d'Outre-mer).
14. cf. A. Seidel and I. Struyf, *La Langue Congolaise*, p. 155, Paris, Jules Groos, 1910.

15. cf. Van Avermaet and Mbuya, op. cit.
16. See under the word '*mwezi*', in: C. Sacleux, *Dictionnaire Swahili-Français*, 2nd ed., rev. and enl., Vol. II, Paris, Institut d'Ethnologie, 1949.
17. cf. The White Fathers, *Bemba-English Dictionary*, p. 514, London, Cape Town and New York; Longmans, Green & Co., 1954, in which all the months are listed with the corresponding months in the Gregorian calendar.
18. cf. E. Biehler, *A Shona Dictionary*, 2nd ed., p. 149, Boston and Cape Town, Longmans, Green & Co., 1950.
19. See under the word '*ngondi*', in: K. E. Laman, *Dictionnaire Kikongo-Français*, p. 691, Brussels, Académie Royale des Sciences d'Outre-mer, 1936 Mémoires).
20. cf. under the word '*chaka*', in: D. C. Scott, *Dictionary of the Kinyanja Language*, 2nd ed., London, United Society for Christian Literature, Lutterworth Press, 1951.
21. Laman, op. cit., p. 1021.
22. See under the words '*caka*' and '*mwaka*', in: The White Fathers, op. cit.
23. cf. Sacleux, op. cit., Vol. I, p. 320.
24. Sacleux, op. cit., Vol. II, p. 1036–7.
25. Kagame, op. cit., p. 264.
26. A. Kagame, 'Un Aperçu Panoramique de la Culture Rwandaise', lecture delivered at Kigali on 4 January 1971 (mimeo.).
27. cf. G. E. Parrinder, *West African Religion*, p. 124.
28. cf. J. Van Wing, *Études Bakongo*. Vol. II: *Religion et Magie*, p. 37–8, Brussels, G. van Kampenhout, 1938.
29. See under the word '*mufu*', in: Van Avermaet and Mbuya, op. cit., p. 154.
30. See under the word '*mupashi*', in: The White Fathers, op. cit., p. 481.
31. cf. A. R. Radcliffe-Brown and D. Forde, *African Systems of Kinship and Marriage*, p. 36, Oxford University Press, 1950.
32. Junod, op. cit., p. 360.

BIBLIOGRAPHY

ALIOTTA, A. Tempo. *Enciclopedia filosofica*. Venice and Rome, Instituto per la Collaborazione Culturale, 1957.

ANON. *Luba-Sanga grammar*. Koni Hill Kalonga (Zaire), no date.

BERGSON, H. *Durée et simultanéité*. Paris, Presses Universitaires de France, 1968.

BIEHLER, E. *A Shona dictionary*, 2nd ed. Boston and Cape Town, Longmans, Green & Co., 1950.

DOKE, C. M. *A comparative study in Shona phonetics*. Johannesburg, Witwatersrand University Press and Routledge, 1931.

GUTHRIE, M. *Grammaire et dictionnaire lingala*. Cambridge, 1939.

HULSTAERT, G. *Dictionnaire français-lomongo*. Antwerp, De Sikkel, 1953.

JACOTTET, E. *A practical method to learn Sesuto*. Mo ja (Lesotho), Sesuto Book Depot, 1914.

JUNOD, H. A. *The life of a South African tribe*. London, 1912.

KAGAME, A. *La philosophie bantu-rwandaise de l'être*. Brussels, Académie Royale des Sciences d'Outre-mer, 1956. (Mémoires, coll. in-8°, Louv. sér., 7, 12, fasc. I.)

——. L'ethno-philosophie des Bantu. In: *Philosophie contemporaine*, vol. IV, p. 589–612. Florence, La Nuova Italia Editrice, 1971.

——. Un aperçu panoramique de la culture rwandaise. (Lecture delivered at Kigali on 4 January 1971) (Miméo.)

——. La mentalité religieuse préchrétienne des Bantu. (Butare, 1968, 42 p. (Miméo.)

LAMAN, K. E. *Dictionnaire kikongo-français*. Brussels, Académie Royale des Sciences d'Outre-mer, 1936. (Mémoires).

LARGEAU, V. *Encyclopédie pahouine*. Paris, E. Leroux, 1901.
LE VEUX. *Manuel de langue luganda*. Algiers, Société des Pères Blancs, Maison-Carrée, 1914.
MACLAREN, J. M. A. *A Xhosa grammar*. London and New York, 1942.
MATTHIJSSEN, M. A. J. M. Reply to questionnaire,[1] 1972.
MBITI, J. S. *African religions and philosophy*. 2nd ed. London, Ibadan and Nairobi, Heinemann, 1969.
MORAVCIK, S. Reply to questionnaire,[1] 1972.
NOËL, E. *Éléments de grammaire kibemka*. Elizabethville, Préfecture du Luapula Supérieur (Zaire), 1935.
PARRINDER, G. E. *Religion in Africa*. London, Pall Mall Press, 1969.
PÈRES DE SCHEUT. *Vocabulaire luba-français*. Luluabourg, Vicariat Apostolique du Haut Kasaï (Zaire), 1940.
RADCLIFFE-BROWN, A. R.; FORDE, D. *African systems of kinship and marriage*. Oxford University Press, 1950.
ROLAND (DOM HADELIN). *Grammaire de la langue kisanga*. Saint-André-Lez-Bruges, Abbaye Bénédictine, 1937.
——. *Vocabulaire français-kisanga*. Saint-André-Lez-Bruges, Abbaye Bénédictine, 1938.
SACLEUX, C. *Dictionnaire swahili-français*. 2nd ed., revised and enlarged, vol. II. Paris, Institut d'Ethnologie, 1949.
SCOTT, D. C. *Dictionary of the Nyanja language*. 2nd ed. London, United Society for Christian Literature, Lutterworth Press, 1951.
SEIDEL, A.; STRUYF, I. *La langue congolaise*. Paris, Jules Groos, 1910.
THOMPSON, T. D. *A practical approach to Chinyanja*. Zomba (Malawi), The Government Printer, 1955.
TOBIAS, G. W. R.; TURVEY, B. H. C. *English-Kwanyama dictionary*. Bantu Lexicographical Archives. Johannesburg, Witwatersrand University Press, 1954.
VAN ACKER, A. *Dictionnaire kitabwa-français*. Tervuren, G. van Campenhout, 1907.
VAN AVERMAET, E.; MBUYA, B. *Dictionnaire kiluba-français*. Tervuren, 1954. (Annales du Musée Royal des Sciences d'Outre-mer.)
VAN BULCK, G. *Manuel de linguistique bantoue*. Brussels, G. van Campenhout, Académie Royale des Sciences d'Outre-mer, 1949. (Mémoires.)
VAN WING. J. *Etudes bakongo*. Vol. II: *Religion et magie*. Brussels, G. van Campenhout, 1938.
WHITE FATHERS (THE). *Bemba-English dictionary*. London, Cape Town and New York, Longmans, Green & Co., 1954.

1. This questionnaire, entitled 'Enquête Linguistique sur la Pensée Profonde des Bantu' was sent by the author to all parts of the Bantu zone.

VIEWS ON TIME IN GREEK THOUGHT

G. E. R. Lloyd

The study of Greek views on time, as of many other aspects of their speculative thought, is important for perhaps three principal reasons. First, and most obviously, it enables us to trace the origins of ideas that have had a profound influence on the subsequent history of European thought, an influence which, in many cases, is still very much alive today. Secondly, it throws light on the transition brought about by the development of philosophy itself, providing an interesting case-history of the continuities, and discontinuities, between pre-philosophical and philosophical views. And, thirdly, the Greek philosophers themselves were responsible for important and lasting insights into certain aspects of the philosophical problems connected with time.

Nevertheless the difficulties of the study are severe. Our source-material, rich as it is, is still extremely limited. Quite apart from thinkers of whom we know nothing, there are many for whom the evidence is insufficient for us to speak confidently concerning their ideas on time. Moreover most of our evidence is literary in character. We cannot afford to forget that the study of both pre- and non-philosophical views on time is both handicapped and biased by the fact that they are mediated through literary sources. Unlike the social anthropologist, the student of ancient Greece cannot question his informants, and he must remember that almost all his evidence comes from texts designed as literary productions, whether prose or verse, of one kind or another.

The picture that emerges is a complex one, and it must be emphasized at the outset that there is no such thing as *the* Greek view of time. In particular, the attempt to contrast *a* Greek with *a* Jewish view of time, and to see the former as essentially cyclical, the latter as essentially linear, is—at least so far as the Greek material is concerned—quite misconceived. The so-called 'cyclical' conception of time meant, as we shall see, quite different things to different Greek writers. More decisively, there is clear evidence of linear as well as cyclical conceptions in Greece. Certain generalizations concerning dominant tendencies in Greek thought can be advanced. But one of the most striking, and significant, features of Greek thought on this subject is the very divergence of views that different authors expressed, a divergence that can be seen not only in the philosophers' debates and disputes concerning time, but also outside philosophy, where, for example, there are marked historical developments in the meanings of certain terms used to express ideas on time.

Pre-and non-philosophical views of time

Homer and Hesiod, the lyric poets and the dramatists, not to mention a wide variety of prose writers of the classical period, provide rich mines of information concerning pre-philosophical and early non-philosophical views and experience of time, and their evidence can be supplemented by what we know, from other sources, of relevant Greek religious beliefs, myths, customs and practices. Beginning with Homer, we find an extensive vocabulary of terms referring to temporal phenomena. Not surprisingly, no single term, whether in Homer or in classical Greek, is an exact equivalent to the English 'time'—itself, of course, by no means synonymous with the French *temps* or the German *Zeit*, let alone other non-Indo-European terms. There are, too, important modifications and developments in Greek terminology from Homer onwards.

Thus one of the commonest general terms for time in classical Greek, *chronos*, is used of intervals of time, and then only in certain types of phrase, in Homer. *Aiōn*, a word that came to be used of life-span, age or generation, and in Plato and later writers of eternity, originally meant 'life'/'life-force', to judge from Homeric expressions that refer to a man's *aiōn* leaving him on death. A third important later Greek word, *kairos*, fit or right time or opportunity, does not occur in Homer at all, although the adjective *kairios* is used in a spatial (not a temporal) sense, that is of the place where a mortal blow lands. Two of the most important words in Homer are *ēmar*, day, used extensively in such phrases as *nostimon ēmar*, day of return, and *doulion ēmar*, day of enslavement, and *hōra*. The latter term is used both of the seasons and of the right time for some action or activity, as, for example, the time for story-telling, or the time for marriage.

Broad indicators are used, in Homer, to mark the major periods of time, years, seasons, months, days. Among the expressions used of the passing of the years (*etos*, *eniautos*) are some where the verb has the prefix *peri*, suggesting, perhaps, a conception of the coming 'round' of the years, although in other phrases the verb has the prefix *epi*, suggesting that the years come 'on'.[1] Three seasons, spring, summer and winter (the word for which, *cheimōn*, also means 'storm') are distinguished. The word *opōra*, later used of autumn, refers literally to the ripening of fruit and grain and has that sense in Homer. Within the year the risings and settings of prominent stars or constellations, especially Sirius and Orion, are used as markers, and so too are such natural phenomena as the migrations of birds. Homer has *meis*, 'month'/'moon', but does not use the names of individual months as these later came to be established in the various calendars of the Greek city-states. The Greek custom of counting the night as beginning the night-day period can, perhaps, already be detected in the common Homeric use of a stock formula referring to 'nights and days' in that order. Within the night-day period, dawn, sunrise, noon and so on are used to mark the passage of time, and so too are human activities as in such a text as *Odyssey* 12 439, 'at a time when a man rises from the assembly for his evening meal. . .'. Finally there are texts that suggest that the day and the night were each divided—roughly—into three main parts.[2]

To look for an abstract conception of time, or for a precise method of measuring it, in Homer would be anachronistic. Homer speaks of a seer knowing 'what is, what will be and what was before' (*Il.* 1 70); the older heroes typified by Nestor often reflect on the deeds of bygone years; and there are myths and stories that describe events in an indefinite past. Yet there is in general little sense of time as an extended continuum. Although first Plato half-jokingly and then Aristotle more solemnly saw the references to Ocean as the begetter of the gods or of all things in *Iliad* 14 (201 and 246) as having a general quasi-cosmological significance,[3] there is little or no systematic thought concerning the origins of the world, or of men, in Homer. Broadly speaking, time is viewed in the Homeric poems not as a quality-less abstract continuum, so much as an affectively charged phenomenon. This is suggested by the use of the expressions 'day of return', 'day of enslavement', and so on that we have already noted: for each man the day itself possesses the quality of the events it contains. When as first in the *Odyssey* and then more frequently in the lyric poets the words *ephēmerios* or *ephēmeros* are applied to man or to his thoughts, it is, as H. Fränkel has shown,[4] the idea of man's dependence on his 'days', rather than his ephemerality in our sense, that is the chief significance of the term.

While abstract notions of time remain undeveloped, the two ideas of the transitoriness, and the fatefulness, of human life are powerfully expressed. In a famous simile (*Il.* 6 146 ff) the generations of men are compared with the growth and decay of leaves. The contrast between men and gods, mortals and immortals, is a constant theme in Homer, and it is important to grasp what the contrast does, and what it does not, imply. The conception of the immortals in Homer is at certain points ambiguous. They are regularly conceived as having been born, and they have, of course, varied and eventful histories. The belief in immortal gods does not, then, lead to the development of any clear idea of eternity. Rather the fundamental contrast between men and gods is that the former are, while the latter are not, subject to hated old age and death. Although men have an existence of a sort after death, in that their souls (*psychai*) go down to Hades, there is no doubt of the inferiority of that existence, as Achilles' bitter cry, that he would prefer to be a bondsman on earth than king of all the dead, makes plain (*Od.* 11 488 ff).

There is, too, a deep-seated ambiguity in the relation between fate, the wills of the gods, and the efforts of man, in Homer. A profound sense of destiny coexists both with the notion that the gods can and do intervene directly in human affairs, and with the idea that the heroes are not entirely passive agents, but can and do act. Men think the thoughts that Zeus sends them day by day, Odysseus says in the *Odyssey* (18 136 ff). Yet cunning and forethought are highly prized qualities, as Odysseus' own reputation proves. Once again there is no question of any abstract theory concerning the problems of free will and determinism. Rather the ideas we find expressed on these topics represent different and complex reactions to, and reflections on, lived experience.

These points can be strengthened and elaborated, though they must also be modified and supplemented, by referring to Hesiod. The main purpose of the *Works and Days* is to offer advice concerning the regulation of the activities of the year. As in Homer, but now with a far greater wealth of examples, natural phenomena such as the migrations of birds, and the rising and setting of constellations, are used to mark the passage of time. The reference to Sirius 'parching the head and knees' (587) for example suggests that the stars are thought to bring about certain changes directly. But we should be wary of pressing the literal interpretation of such statements too far, if only because it would be anachronistic to attribute any clear distinction between cause and concomitant to Hesiod. The last part of the work (765 ff) is devoted to an account of the particular qualities of the days of the month. The month itself is of thirty days, and particular days are of good, or evil, omen, appropriate or inappropriate for particular activities. Thus 'beware of the thirteenth day from the beginning of the month for starting to sow; but it is best for planting' (780 f). As Homer had conceived days as characterized by the quality of the fortune they contained, so, much more systematically, Hesiod sets out a schema of lucky and unlucky days, although he acknowledges that some are indifferent, 'without fate' (*akērioi*), that there are disagreements among men about the fortunes of such days, and that 'sometimes a day is a step-mother, sometimes a mother' (823 ff).

The richness of the mythological data in Hesiod is well known. The *Theogony*, with its account of an original 'chaos', or yawning gap, and of the subsequent births of the gods, including some that are more or less transparent personifications of natural phenomena, is undoubtedly the most important pre-philosophical text from the point of view of the later development of cosmological thought. But pre-eminent among the myths that reveal the central part played by ideas of time in Hesiod is that of the five races or ages of man (*Works* 109–201).[5] These are the golden, silver and bronze races, the race of heroes and that of iron, although within the last age Hesiod suggests a distinction between the present and a future race. Each race is characterized by a different experience of time, that is of birth, maturity and, especially, death. Thus the golden race, who live under Kronos, experience no old age. They die 'as if overcome by sleep' and thereafter become the guardians of justice among men on earth. The silver race spends a hundred years as children: once they have finally passed adolescence, they live only a short while. They are 'hidden' by Zeus in anger at their *hybris* (insolent excess) in that they refuse to worship the gods—and they then exist as 'the blessed' under the earth. Both the bronze race and the race of heroes are closely associated with war. The former, who 'eat no bread', 'care only for the groan-causing works and excesses (*hybries*) of Ares': they die by their own hands and go down to Hades as the 'nameless ones'. The latter are 'juster and better': of these some die in war, while others live apart from men in the Islands of the Blessed. For the men of the present race of iron there is no end to toil by day or night. Yet there is still good mixed with evil. Zeus will, however, destroy this race too 'when men are born with white temples' (181), a brief, but gripping, allusion to a future race in which the men will be born already old.

Many aspects of the interpretation of this highly suggestive myth are obscure or disputed. Nor can we say with any confidence how much of it is Hesiod's own or how much he has taken over from tradition. Yet in the myth as we have it, at least, it is fairly clear that just as the silver race differs from the golden in the excess or insolence it shows, in this case in respect to the gods, so the bronze race differs from that of the heroes in excess in regard to war. There appears, too, to be a third, analogous, contrast between the present, and the future, race of iron: certainly the latter is described in terms which suggest uncontrolled excess—sons dishonour parents, no oath is trustworthy, justice and shame do not exist, the criminal and the 'man of excess' are honoured. One of the messages of the myth is, then—to express the point banally—a warning against disproportion of any kind, indeed against the excesses that might be associated with each period of a man's life. The silver age is an age of excessive youth: it does not respect the gods and is punished by Zeus. The bronze age is an age of excessive concern for war (the activity, *par excellence*, of the adult) and this too leads to dire results. Finally, the future race of iron is an age where there is no youth at all, where the men are born old, and this upsetting of the natural temporal order, accompanied by the overthrow of justice, leads to the worst consequences of all, a situation where 'there is no defence against evil' (201).

The temporal, and the moral, order are indissolubly linked. Any disruption of the temporal regulation of man's life is accompanied by disastrous results. It is certainly not fortuitous that the Greeks identified the three divine *Hōrai* (Hours, Seasons) as *Eunomia* (Good Order), *Dikē* (Justice) and *Eirēnē* (Peace): they, and the three fates, Clotho, Lachesis and Atropos, are represented as the daughters of Themis (Right) and Zeus in the *Theogony* (901 ff). One may conclude that at an early stage, and certainly long before philosophical speculation began, the notions of justice and the moral order were intimately bound up with the notion of the regular ordering of time, both of the seasons of the year, and of the seasons of man's life. In the myth of the races, the two ideas interact: as justice is conceived, in part, as a matter of the orderly temporal regulation of man's life, so conversely time is not simply a natural phenomenon, but an aspect of the moral ordering of the universe.

After Homer and Hesiod, the material on which we can base our discussion of early Greek attitudes to and experience of time becomes increasingly rich, and certain developments can be traced. Some of these such as the establishment of calendars can be connected with the political development of the city-state and its institutions, others with the development of new religious beliefs, while yet others relate to ideas and attitudes expressed by writers in the new genres of lyric poetry, tragedy and so on. We have, in this survey, to confine ourselves to a brief mention of some of the most important points.

First, the calendar.[6] Not only did different city-states have different calendars, but in some cases a single city made use of two calendars, one to regulate the religious festivals, the other for the purposes of political administration. At Athens, for instance, the year was one of twelve lunar months of twenty-nine or thirty days each, a thirteenth month being 'intercalated' in certain years to keep the calendar more or less in agreement with the seasons. The decision when to make an intercalation, and the regulation of the calendar as a whole, were the responsibility of a magistrate. Although the number of extra months needed in a cycle of nineteen years had been worked out by the late fifth century by the Athenian astronomer Meton, this knowledge had, apparently, little or no effect on the calendar, adjustments to which continued to be made on an *ad hoc* basis rather than according to predetermined calculations. This was the calendar used to regulate the religious festivals, but after Cleisthenes' reforms there was also a simpler 'prytany' calendar that governed the terms of office of the representatives of the ten tribes in the Council. These reforms had both a practical, and a symbolic, importance, for they modified not only the political structure of the Athenian state, but also the accepted articulation of space and time within it.[7] It should, however, be noted that long after official state calendars had been set up to regulate religious and political life, the Greeks continued to refer, for many purposes, to natural phenomena to identify the main periods within the year. Greece was, and remained, an agricultural society, and the farmer's year continued to be regulated in much the way that Hesiod describes. Eventually the astronomers needed both a more rational calendar (for this they used the Egyptian calendar of twelve months of thirty days with five additional days) and a method of keeping count of the years (here Ptolemy, for instance, took the first year of the reign of the Babylonian king Nabonassar, i.e. 747 B.C., as his deadline). But rationalized calendrical systems were confined, in the main, to the astronomers themselves.

Our next point concerns the religious festivals themselves, and here we tread on slippery ground. It is clear that by the fifth century B.C. the Athenians, for example, had a complex and elaborate cycle of festivals honouring different gods or celebrating different events through the year. Different festivals mark the difference between 'profane' or 'secular' time and 'sacred', 'festival' or 'holiday', time in different ways. But in the Kronia, for instance, the contrast was evidently striking and emphatic. Although our direct information is fragmentary, it is clear that during this festival, as in the Roman Saturnalia, the normal roles of master and slave were reversed. Although the festivals belong to, and are determined by, the civil calendar, they represent, in an important sense, a 'discontinuity' in the experience of time.

As the year was punctuated by occasions marking the contrast between sacred and profane time, so in an analogous way a man's life was also punctuated by moments that marked the passage from one age or status to another. Again the early Greek evidence is neither as clear nor as definite as we should wish. With the Athenian *ephēbeia,* however, we are evidently dealing with an institution similar to many that have been reported by anthropologists from other societies, in which the passage from childhood to adulthood is made by way of a transitional period during which the young man, though no longer a child, is still not yet fully accepted as an adult. The duties of the ephebes (such as that of guarding the frontier areas) and what we know of the way their lives were regulated, suggest, as P. Vidal-Naquet has shown,[8] their ambivalent status, of being and at the same time not being full members of the city. Although the *ephēbeia* fell into disuse, there can be little doubt that in origin the institution had not only certain practical functions, but also a profound symbolic one, both marking and indeed effecting the transition of the young man to full adult status.

Two contrasting time experiences both receive profound expression in Greek thought. On the one hand, the cycle of the seasons and the daily and yearly movements of the heavenly bodies are the most obvious examples of 'repetitive processes', and on a social level, the recurrence of the same religious festivals year after year endorses or reinforces this idea of time. Yet the process of growing old is irreversible, the approach of death is ineluctable, and from Homer onwards Greek literature provides many moving statements of the transience of youth and of the inevitability of the onward march of time. Viewed abstractly, there is, of course, a contradiction between the two conceptions: repetitiveness and irreversibility are, strictly speaking, incompatible. Yet in religion, especially in beliefs concerning the after-life, the contradiction is palliated, if not removed.

As we have noted, a belief in immortality of a sort is found already in Homer. But other and more positive conceptions of immortality come to be expressed by some of the lyric poets and by some philosophers. The doctrine of transmigration, that is the belief that the soul is reborn either in another human being or in some other kind of animal or plant, is associated especially with the philosopher Pythagoras, whom we shall be discussing again later. One of his near contemporaries, the poet-philosopher Xenophanes, pokes fun at the doctrine in a poem in which he makes Pythagoras recognize the soul of a friend in the barking of a dog, and the belief is also referred to by Pindar and Herodotus as well as by other philosophers, notably Empedocles and Plato.[9] What this doctrine suggests is that death, so far from being the end of an irreversible process, is one stage in what is an essentially repetitive one. Life is followed by death, and death again by life, just as in the living man, waking is followed by sleep and sleep again by waking, or as in nature the heavenly bodies rise and set and rise again. And we find these analogies actually used to support a belief in immortality in, for example, Plato's *Phaedo* (71 b ff) and in the pseudo-Aristotelian *Problemata* (916 a 24 ff, referring in particular to Alcmaeon). It should, however, be emphasized that immortality as such is not seen as a source of consolation. On the contrary, the soul's being subject to rebirth is conceived as a misfortune. The cycle of rebirth came to be called the *kyklos barypenthēs*, the circle of grievous affliction. What the sage seeks, and what he hopes he will attain as a reward for living not just one, but a series of holy lives, is escape from the cycle of rebirth—when, like the gods, he will possess not just immortality, but an immutable immortality.

It is impossible to do justice, here, to the extraordinary wealth of ideas and imagery associated with time that we find in the lyric poets and the tragedians. The very variety of conceptions expressed by different Greek poets is astonishing. There are, for example, as J. de Romilly has recently stressed,[10] important differences between the three great Athenian tragedians in this respect. Certain dominant themes may, however, be identified. One such is that of the power of time, the 'father of all' (Pindar, *Olympian* 2 17), described in such epithets as 'all-accomplishing' (Aeschylus, *Choephoroi* 965). It brings welcome forgetfulness of sorrow. In Sophocles' *Electra* (179) it is even described as a *eumarēs theos*, a god that brings ease. But more often its role is that of a waster and destroyer. Experience brings an increase of wisdom, to be sure (*pathei mathos*), but old age is none the less hated for that. Two passages in Sophocles, especially, express the destructive power of time. In the *Oedipus Coloneus* (607 ff) Oedipus says: 'to the gods alone neither old age nor death ever comes. But all the rest all-powerful time confounds. The strength of the earth decays, the strength of the body also. Trust dies, distrust grows . . .'. And in the *Ajax* (714) the chorus say that 'great time' 'quenches' or 'withers' (*marainei*) 'all things'. So far as men are concerned, it is reputation or excellence alone that can withstand time.

Time itself is intimately bound up with fortune and its fluctuations. Pindar, who in one ode calls time (here *aiōn*) treacherous (*Isthmian* 8 14), elsewhere speaks of it bringing manifold changes 'with its rolling days: but the children of the gods are invulnerable' (*Isthmian* 3 18). A famous chorus in Sophocles' *Trachiniae* (129 ff) speaks of sorrow and joy 'circling' for all 'like the revolving paths of the Great Bear. Neither the star-spangled night abides for men, nor diseases, nor wealth, but straightway it has gone, and another man has his turn of joy and of mourning'. Here the 'circle' of human affairs conveys the idea not of their repetitiveness, but of their fluctuations. Finally the association of time with the order of the universe, which we have remarked on before, underlies the notion of time as witness, revealer, judge. Pindar speaks of time revealing or testing the truth (*Olympian* 10 53–55), a theme repeated in many variations in the tragedians. In Solon, justice who 'silently sees what happens and what was before' will come 'in time', and he invokes earth as a witness on his behalf 'in the court of time' (*en dikēi chronou*).[11]

Many of the motifs we have just mentioned are at least foreshadowed in Homer or Hesiod, though in many cases they receive their most powerful or poignant expression in the lyric poets or the tragedians. At the same time certain new ideas relevant to the understanding of, and attitude towards, time come to be developed in the fifth century. Before we turn to the philosophers themselves, we must outline some of these developments. Three important such notions are : (a) a greater awareness of the past; (b) a growth of ideas and theories concerning the development of civilization; and (c) an increasing sense of the value of history. In each case our main, though not our only, texts come from the historians Herodotus and Thucydides.

A greater awareness of the past. Although there are plenty of references in Homer and Hesiod to the events of bygone years, the conception of the past is an indefinite one. Admittedly the heroes often boast of being able to trace their genealogies back through several generations—though they soon reach the gods. And in Hesiod's *Theogony* genealogy provides the means whereby an account of the origin of things in general is given. In the development of a sense of the past a text in Herodotus may be said to mark a turning-point. In II 142–3 he reports what he learnt from the priests of Egypt concerning the genealogies of their high priests and kings, namely that these could be traced through 341 generations, a matter of—as Herodotus calculates—some 11,340 years. He goes on to mention his predecessor, the first Greek historical writer, Hecataeus, who 'made himself a genealogy which connected him with a god in the 16th generation'. The contrast with the Egyptian priests is twofold, first in that they did not name a god (according to Herodotus) throughout the 341 generations and, secondly, in that their genealogy was, of course, far more extensive. The veracity of the priests' report is open to doubt: they told Herodotus that twice during the period the sun had risen in the west. Yet the significance of the episode, in suggesting to Herodotus the possibility of an unbroken record stretching back over 11,340 years, remains. Stimulated, no doubt, by their contacts with Near Eastern civilizations, and in particular with Egypt, the massive visible signs of whose past greatness, such as the pyramids, made an extraordinarily deep impression on them, the Greeks came, in the fifth century, to a new awareness of the extent and continuity of the past.

A growth of ideas and theories concerning the development of civilization. A contrast between a life conducted without laws or rights, and a society properly regulated by them, is already implied in, for example, the description of the Cyclopes in the *Odyssey* (9 105 ff). But both a consciousness of the development of 'civilization' from primitive communities, and a pride in its achievements, grow during the sixth and fifth centuries. Theories about the origin of human society were probably first expressed by the philosophers, and usually in connexion with general cosmological speculations (see below). Yet ideas on the subject are certainly not confined to philosophical writers. In mythology Prometheus was responsible for giving men fire. What is striking about Aeschylus' handling of the theme in the *Prometheus Vinctus* is first the recognition of the variety of the *technai* (arts and crafts) and of their usefulness to men, and secondly the temporal contrast between man's state before he possessed the arts and now. At first (*to prin*), Prometheus says (441 ff), they were all like children: they had no brick-built houses, no carpentry, but lived like ants in holes or caves. They had no means of marking off the seasons, no numbers, no writing, no use of horses, no ships, no medicine, no techniques of prophecy, no metals, before he, Prometheus, showed them. Pride in inventions and discoveries, and admiration for the individuals purportedly responsible for them, become common themes in Greek literature. But while a schematic or ideological contrast between primitive or 'barbarian' society and the more advanced or civilized Greek cities of the fifth century is present in many writers, what the historians, particularly Thucydides, add is a firmer grasp of how the latter developed out of the former. Thus in the opening chapters of book I, Thucydides contrasts the earlier weak state of Greece (which he compares in respect of certain of its customs with existing barbarian societies) with the present power of Athens and Sparta, and he suggests reasons for this development, the establishment of more settled communities, the accumulation of resources, the improvement of communications and so on. Irrespective of whether these reasons have any validity, the important thing to note is that he attempts an explanation of what he sees as a continuous historical development. Although, as has often been remarked, the idea of progress in the future, whether in social institutions or in technology, is quite undeveloped in Greco-Roman antiquity—and this despite the fact that there was no lack of theorizing about the 'best' or 'ideal' state—many fifth-century writers had a clear conception of their own society as the end-product of a long process of advance.

An increasing sense of the value of history. Finally, the development of ideas concerning the nature, aims and value of history—a genre effectively created by Herodotus—can be traced in him and in Thucydides. Although Herodotus' work appears diffuse, it has a complex articulation. His preliminaries are elaborate and long-drawn-out. But his account of the Persian Wars inaugurates continuous historical narrative as we know it. He is already aware of the need to evaluate evidence—a problem that was all the more acute since he had to rely almost exclusively on oral tradition. Yet his own statement of his aim in I : 1 is a simple one, to preserve the fame of past deeds, an aim with which Homer would not have disagreed, for all the differences in how he would have set about achieving it. With Thucydides, the gulfs between history and poetry, and between history and myth, widen. He insists, even more emphatically than Herodotus had done, on the need for deliberate research to get at the truth about what actually happened. He explicitly excludes poetic ornament (I 21) and 'story-telling', *to mythōdes*, and he states his aim as being to produce, in the famous phrase, a 'possession for always', *ktēma es aiei*, which will be found useful so long as human nature is constant (I 22, cf. III/82). While history and myth may both be said, in their different ways, to provide insight into experience, the contrast in their attitudes to the past is fundamental and the appreciation of that contrast must be recognized as one of the outstanding intellectual achievements of the Greek historians.[12]

The philosophers' analysis of time

The reflections of Greek philosophers on time are complex, subtle, varied and original: in the case of four of the greatest Greek philosophers, Parmenides, Plato, Aristotle and Plotinus, to understand their conceptions of time we must go deep into other aspects of their metaphysics. Yet in the earliest stages of philosophical reflection on time, the links with ideas we have already discussed are strong. We begin with the very first original statement of any Greek philosopher that has come down to us, the remark of Anaximander quoted by Simplicius that certain unnamed things 'pay the penalty and recompense to one another for their injustice, according to the assessment of time (*kata tēn tou chronou taxin*).'[13] The problem of what the things in question are is disputed, but they appear to be cosmological factors of some sort, and it has plausibly been suggested that the cycle of the seasons provides one of the best examples of the type of interaction Anaximander seems to describe. We have seen how time is associated with justice in Hesiod, and how Solon—approximately contemporary with Anaximander—speaks of 'the court of time'. Similarly in Anaximander's cosmology the stable relationships between things are conceived as a matter of justice, and time is not merely, it seems, the neutral medium in which natural changes take place, but rather imagined as itself in some way responsible for the regulation of cosmic justice.

Yet the setting of Anaximander's idea is quite different from that of Hesiod's.[14] Primitive though it is, Anaximander's cosmology is no longer mythological. No personal gods are invoked to explain the way the world comes to be or is, which is conceived rather in terms of the interplay of forces which while thought of, no doubt, as divine, are nevertheless essentially natural. A far more striking example is provided by what we hear of Anaximander's ideas about the origin of living creatures and of man. He is reported to have held that living creatures were first generated when 'the wet' is acted on by the sun, and that man, in particular, was originally born in a different species of animal, that is, apparently, some sort of fish.[15] The details of the theory are lost. But his ideas on man seem to have been stimulated by reflection on the problem presented by the fact that after birth the child takes a long time to become self-sufficient. The contrast between his suggestion and, for example, Hesiod's myth of Pandora is obvious but important. Hesiod represents Zeus as creating Pandora, the first woman, in revenge for the trick played on him by Prometheus, and Pandora herself is made from earth and water by the craftsman god

Hephaestus.[16] The action of the myth flows from the wills of the gods and part of the point of the story (at least) is to convey a moral about the female sex. Anaximander's ideas are not myths, but theories, the first attempt to provide naturalistic accounts of the origins of living creatures and of man.

By the end of the fifth century or shortly afterwards, Milesian cosmological speculation had provoked two sharply differing reactions from Heraclitus and Parmenides. Heraclitus explicitly denied what the Milesians had tacitly assumed, that the world came to be. In fragment 30 he states that 'neither a god nor a man made this world-order (*kosmos*): but it always was and is and will be an ever-living fire, kindling in measures and going out in measures'. In the protracted debate in Greek philosophy on the question of whether the world was, or was not, created, Heraclitus stands at the head of those who maintained the latter view.

Yet whether he had achieved anything like a coherent conception of time is not clear. His cardinal insight concerns the co-existence, interdependence or unity of opposites, and we find temporal phenomena cited to illustrate this, along with other examples from such fields as that of morality. God, he states in fragment 67, is 'day night, winter summer, war peace, satiety hunger', and in another fragment (57) Hesiod is criticized for not knowing that 'day and night are one'. Other examples refer to the life of man, his death and (it seems) rebirth. Fragment 88 says that 'the living and the dead, and waking and sleeping, and young and old, exist as the same thing (in us): these things having changed are those, and those having changed again are these', and other later and less reliable reports have been taken as suggesting that he held that the human soul is subject to a cycle of rebirth of 10,800 years.[17] The interpretation of all this evidence is difficult and disputed, and with many of the fragments we may believe that more than one sense is not only possible, but intended. But although his doctrine of the interdependence of opposites was evidently of quite general application, it was its physical implications that were important for subsequent thought on time—and in particular the lesson that Plato especially was to draw from his philosophy, namely that every physical object is subject to temporal change.

While Heraclitus provides us with the first explicit statement in Greek literature that the world is everlasting, his contemporary Parmenides is often thought to have been the first to express the notion of timeless eternity. Here too, however, some of the evidence is obscure and caution is necessary. Where Heraclitus emphasized that things are subject to change, Parmenides denied that change can occur at all. In the Way of Truth he sets out a philosophy based on the assertion that 'it is' and the rejection of the assertion 'it is not'—on the grounds that this latter cannot be known or declared (fragment 2) for, as he says in fragment 3, 'the same thing is for thinking and for being'. Fragment 8 begins by speaking of the 'signs' on the Way of Truth, that is the characteristics that are to be established, namely that it is ungenerated and indestructible, whole, homogeneous, unmoved and complete. Then at verses 5–6 Parmenides states: 'nor was it ever, nor will it be, since it is now all together, one, continuous'.

The denial of change is certain; what is not clear is the force of the 'now' (*nyn*) in the verses just quoted. Having denied being in past time ('it was not') and being in future time ('it will not be'), Parmenides does not, as might perhaps have been expected, deny being in time at all, but says 'it is now all together'. Some scholars have interpreted the use of the temporal adverb 'now' as indicating that Parmenides has not grasped the idea of timelessness and is not describing what is as timeless. But others have argued that just as he has to use spatial terms in denying certain spatial characteristics to being, so too he has to use temporal ones to deny temporal characteristics to it.[18] Now there can be no doubt that the notions of eternity and timelessness are conveyed both more definitely and more distinctly by later writers who had, of course, the advantage of being able to build on Parmenides' work. Yet although his 'now' is unclear, and indeed potentially misleading (for by itself it might even be taken—although it undoubtedly should not—to imply a momentary existence), the denial of 'it was' and 'it will be' is fairly evidently to be interpreted as a definite denial of temporal duration.

As with Heraclitus, the implications of Parmenides' philosophy were far-reaching. It raises, for the first time, certain fundamental ontological and epistemological issues. Sensation is rejected in favour of reason in fragment 7. More important still, he suggests a radical distinction between two modes of being, or rather between a mode of true being (the subject of the Way of Truth) and a mode of (mere) seeming, based, he holds, on a confusion of 'it is' and 'it is not'. He presents an account of the latter, after the Way of Truth, in the Way of *Doxa* (seeming or opinion), and this contains a cosmology of a type comparable in certain respects with those of the Milesians. Yet he makes it clear that he does not consider this account to be true. Turning to it, he says (fragment 8 52 ff) 'listen to the deceitful ordering of my words', even though he includes it 'so that no judgement of mortals shall outstrip you'. Again Parmenides' conception of the precise relationship between the two Ways is controversial. Certainly later philosophers were able to draw both clearer and more complex ontological distinctions between different modes of being. But what can and must be credited to Parmenides is to have been the first to draw a fundamental distinction between, on the one hand, a changeless being, to be understood through the use of reason, and, on the other, the world of appearances.

Parmenides' denial of change posed a problem that split subsequent Presocratic philosophers into two main camps. On the one hand there were those who reinstated change and presented cosmologies based on the postulate of an initial plurality of things. Of these the most important, for our purposes, is Empedocles. On the other, there were those such as, especially, Zeno of Elea, who upheld Parmenides' position and brought further arguments against plurality and movement.

To understand Empedocles' notion of time, we must first back-track a little to discuss Pythagoras and the Pythagoreans by whom he was, in this aspect of his thought, clearly much influenced. The evidence for Pythagoras and his school is particularly unsatisfactory. There are few authentic texts and the sources we depend on are often late and untrustworthy. Yet the fact that (as already noted) Pythagoras himself taught the doctrine of the transmigration of souls is one of the few reliable pieces of information we have about him. Two other doctrines associated with his school are more difficult to evaluate, namely a cosmogony involving time, and some doctrine of temporal recurrence.

Our best witness for Pythagoreanism, Aristotle, reports that they held that all things are numbers and that the principles or elements of numbers are the odd and even or the limited and the unlimited. Evidence for the cosmological ideas that they put forward on the basis of these principles comes especially from a text that has been preserved from a lost work of Aristotle devoted to the Pythagoreans. This tells us that they held that 'the universe is one, and from the unlimited it draws in time, breath and void, which goes on distinguishing the places of each thing'.[19] This looks like a highly suggestive cosmogony in which the coming-to-be of the world is associated with the introduction, into it, of spatial and temporal determinations—along with life itself, if that is the role that we can ascribe to breath. But we must confess not only that we do not know when exactly these ideas were put forward, but also that their precise significance is very much a matter of conjecture.

Similar problems face us with the doctrine, or rather doctrines, of temporal recurrence. Many different conceptions representing time as cyclical or repetitive are found in Greek thought. The notion of the years 'coming round' is already present in Homer. In Sophocles, the circle of time is an image rather of the fluctuations of fortune. In Heraclitus, the primary idea seems to be one of a cycle of rebirth, and before Heraclitus, Pythagoras' own doctrine of transmigration suggests the repeated passage from life to death and back to life again. But in addition to these ideas, two others must be mentioned, the doctrine of the Great Year and the view that individual events are repeated. The Great Year is the period at the end of which the sun, moon and planets return to their original positions in relation to each other. Various versions of the doctrine, with various values for the Great Year, appear in different ancient writers, including Plato, and it may well have been put forward by some of the later Pythagoreans. Whether it goes back to Pythagoras himself, however, seems very doubtful, if only because it depends on quite detailed knowledge concerning the periodicities of the planets, and this astronomical knowledge is unlikely to antedate the middle of the fifth century in Greece. Secondly the view that time repeats itself in detail, in the sense that individual events recur, is also described as Pythagorean in a text of Eudemus (fourth century B.C.) quoted by Simplicius: 'if one were to believe the Pythagoreans, that the same individual events recur, and I shall be talking to you, holding my stick, as you sit there, and everything else will be as it is now, then it is reasonable to say that time repeats itself.'[20] Once again the date of the doctrine is uncertain, but Eudemus provides good evidence that at some stage, at least, the Pythagoreans adopted the doctrine of temporal recurrence in an extreme form. The tendency to extreme generalization is a common feature of Greek cosmological thought. While originally, it seems, the idea of recurrence—supported by such examples as seasonal phenomena—occurs particularly in the context of the belief in the immortality of the soul, the Pythagoreans did not shrink from carrying the idea to its ultimate logical conclusion in the suggestion that every single event is, in time, repeated.

Several 'Pythagorean' doctrines are found also in Empedocles and here we have the great advantage that we can refer to the extant fragments of his two works, the cosmological poem *On Nature*, and the religious poem *The Purifications*. The main theme of the latter is the progress of the soul (*daimōn*), its fall, reincarnations in living creatures of different sorts, and eventual escape from the wheel of birth. Empedocles himself says (fragment 117) that he has been boy and girl and bush and bird and fish. He is an exile from the gods (fragment 115), though in fragment 112 he calmly claims to be 'an immortal god, no longer mortal'. The moral significance of the doctrine of rebirth can be seen. Incarnation is a penalty for sin, particularly the sin of bloodshed. Living creatures rise or fall in the scale of beings depending on how they have lived, and the *Purifications* contain a number of precepts for life, such as abstention from certain foods, similar to those we know the Pythagoreans adopted. At the end the highest human beings are prophets, bards, physicians and princes, who achieve the escape from the wheel of rebirth which is promised 'after 30,000 seasons' in fragment 115.

The relationship between the *Purifications* and *On Nature* is problematic. Yet the two poems are evidently linked by certain common doctrines, especially those relating to the four physical elements (earth, water, air and fire) and to the two cosmic forces (Love and Strife), all six of which figure, though in differing roles, in both poems. Thus in the *Purifications* Strife is the reason for the soul's downfall, while in the cosmological poem it is responsible for separating the elements, as Love is for joining them. As the *Purifications* suggests a cycle in the peregrinations of the soul, so in *On Nature* there are references to cycles or periods both in the cosmos as a whole and, it seems, in the generation of living creatures, even though the precise interpretation of these themes has been much debated. That there is some alternation between rest and movement, and between Love and Strife—a rule of Love being followed by increasing Strife and a rule of Strife by increasing Love—is clear from Empedocles own words. In fragment 17, for instance, he says: 'I shall tell a twofold tale. At one time it grew to be one only from many, and at another it grew apart to be many from one. There is a double coming-to-be and a double passing-away of mortal things. . . . And these things never cease to alternate continually, now all coming together into one through Love, and now each being borne apart again through Strife's hatred.'

In his account of the rule of Love—a theme occurring in both poems—Empedocles shows how far he has gone from the traditional view of the golden age of Kronos. In the *Purifications* (fragment 128) the rule of Kypris or Love, when there was no Ares (Strife) and, he adds, no Zeus, no Kronos, no Poseidon, is an age of perfect bliss and innocence, while in *On Nature* under the rule of Love all four physical elements are perfectly mixed and indistinguishable—the form the cosmos takes is then that of a perfect sphere (fragments 27 and 28). Moreover just as Anaximander had spoken of the regulation of certain interactions 'according to the assessment of time' (see above p. 127), so Empedocles evidently conceived the alternations of Love and Strife as being subject to temporal regulations, determined by a 'broad oath'. Fragment 17 says that Love and Strife prevail in turn 'as time comes round', and again in fragment 30 Strife is said to 'leap up' to claim his prerogatives 'as the time came round which was fixed for them alternately by a broad oath'. Aristotle's rather vague statement concerning the equality of the cosmic periods has been subject to widely differing interpretations,[21] but it is clear that there is an over-all balance between Love and Strife and between the times they are given to rule.

The cosmological and physical purposes of the cycle are clear. Where Parmenides had denied change and coming-to-be, Empedocles restores them, explaining them in terms of the mixture and separation of already existing things. Indeed his cosmic cycle provides for the processes of mixing and separating to be everlasting. At the same time the moral overtones of the cycle are unmistakable. Strife is 'hateful' (fragment 109, 3) and 'accursed' (fragment 17, 19) and Love is 'blameless' (fragment 35, 13). The cosmic forces are opposed not only in their physical effects, but also, it seems, in their moral quality. Yet they must be kept in balance, and the way this balance is achieved is through time: they are given equal periods to prevail over each other in turn. How far precise parallelisms are intended between the religious cycle of the *Purifications* and the cosmic alternations in *On Nature* it is hard to say: certainly there are important disanalogies between the two cycles. Yet this much is clear, that the notion of alternating periods is fundamental to both poems, and in each case time—as in Anaximander, and more clearly than in him—has not merely a physical, but also a moral, indeed religious, significance.

Ranged against the cosmologists in the late fifth century were the followers of Parmenides, Zeno of Elea and Melissus of Samos. The latter, while maintaining Parmenides' basic doctrines of the unity and changelessness of being, modified his teaching on a number of points, and on one in particular that directly concerns us. Where Parmenides had written 'nor was it ever, nor will it be, since it is now all together', Melissus' fragment 2 states: 'it is and always was and always will be'. Melissus does not deny temporal duration, but asserts it: his one being is not timeless but everlasting.

But even more important than Melissus for the development of Greek philosophical thought about time is Zeno of Elea.[22] The over-all purpose of his arguments is reported by Plato in the *Parmenides* (128 c, d) as being to support Parmenides' doctrine of the unity of being by showing that the opposite view, that there are many, leads to absurd conclusions. Zeno's arguments against motion in particular are recorded by Aristotle and later sources as a group of four, and since Tannery[23] one school of interpretation has taken these arguments as forming a closely co-ordinated set, a multiple dilemma, which Tannery himself saw as directed not so much against common sense views of motion, as against certain contemporary Pythagorean doctrines and in particular against the theory dubbed 'unit-point-atomism' according to which no distinction is drawn between arithmetical units, geometrical points and physical atoms. Two preliminary points should be made at once. First, the direct evidence for the complex of views that Zeno was believed to be attacking is, in many cases, thin: indeed there is simply no direct evidence that any Presocratic held an atomic theory of time, that is that time is composed of discrete indivisible quanta. And secondly, it is as a whole more likely, in view of the evidence in Plato, that Zeno's arguments were general rather than particular in intention, that is that they aimed to refute pluralism of any kind. But the question of whether the four arguments form a multiple dilemma takes us to the heart of the problem.

According to the view that stems from Tannery, the arguments form two pairs, the first attacking motion on the assumption that space and time are continuous and infinitely divisible, and the second attacking motion on the assumption that space and time are discontinuous and composed of indivisibles. Now it may readily be agreed that the first two arguments, known as the Dichotomy and the Achilles, do indeed attack motion on the assumption that space (at least) is continuous. The Dichotomy argues by means of an infinite regress that motion cannot begin. On the most likely view, the argument claimed that before you reach the end of the space to be traversed, you must first reach the half-way point; and before you reach the half-way point, you must reach the point half way to it; and since this process of division can be continued *ad infinitum*, a point can always be found between the point to be reached and the starting point, and so motion cannot begin. The more famous Achilles takes a similar form, though here Achilles and his opponent (it is the commentators that identify this as a tortoise) are both imagined as moving, and at different speeds. However much faster Achilles moves, he will never catch the tortoise. He must first reach the point from which the tortoise starts; when he has reached that point, the tortoise will have advanced a certain distance, and Achilles must then reach that point. Again this process can be continued *ad infinitum* and so, as Aristotle puts it in reporting the argument, 'the slower will always have a lead'.

Precisely how these two arguments should be answered is disputed: but their structure is clear enough. Aristotle, at least, considered the second argument guilty of *ignoratio elenchi*. Zeno has shown that Achilles is not level with the tortoise at any of the points arrived at by carrying out the division according to his—quite arbitrary—rules. But he has not shown that there is not some other point at which Achilles is level with the tortoise. But it should be noted that although in the chapter devoted to Zeno in *Physics* VI (Chap. 9) Aristotle dismisses these two arguments quite briefly, he returns to the Dichotomy later at *Physics* (263 a 4 ff). 'For if one leaves out of account the length and the question of whether it is possible to traverse an infinite number of lengths in a finite time, and asks the same question about the time itself (for time too is infinitely divisible) our former solution is no longer adequate.' Two points emerge from this: (a) it suggests that in the form stated by Zeno himself, the argument took account of the infinite divisibility of space only, not that of time; and (b) it shows that Aristotle recognized that once the infinite divisibility of time is assumed, the problem posed by the Dichotomy is more serious. Aristotle's own further solution, in terms of a distinction between actuality and potentiality, has found little favour among the many modern writers who have commented on the paradoxes, among whom a wide divergence of opinions can be detected. Some revert to the view that the Dichotomy and the Achilles fail through *ignoratio elenchi.* Many have claimed that the paradoxes have been cleared up by advances in the understanding of the mathematics of the continuum and the infinite. Yet the view that—despite those advances—difficulties still remain also has its advocates. Thus it has recently been argued (by Whitrow [24]) that the applicability to motion of the hypothesis of the infinite divisibility of time poses a problem. Cantor's theory of the infinite allows us to treat the infinite set of positions through which Achilles passes as a totality: but that does not guarantee that the successive acts of Achilles passing though them may be treated in the same way. To reconcile the notion of the infinite divisibility of time with the possibility of Achilles actually catching the tortoise we have, then, to introduce a further logical fiction, that in the limit he performs an infinite number of successive acts with infinite rapidity. Despite the vast quantity of literature devoted to the subject in the intervening period, we may still wish to agree with Ross' remark, in 1936, that 'Zeno's first paradox still awaits its final answer'.[25]

Zeno's third and fourth arguments, the Flying Arrow and the Moving Rows, are immediately controversial in that the correct interpretation of the underlying assumptions is disputed. It is obvious that in reporting the Arrow, Aristotle has abbreviated the argument, but the essential steps appear to be:

1. Everything is always at rest when it is 'at a place equal to itself'.
2. The moving object is always at a place equal to itself 'in the now' (*en tōi nyn*). Therefore :
3. The moving object is at rest.

The interpretation of the argument is complicated by the ambiguity of the expression 'the now', which can be used either (a) of the durationless instant (the analogue, in the continuum of time, of the geometrical point) or (b) of an indefinitely small interval. The argument can be read in two quite different ways depending on which sense of 'the now' we take. (A) If we take it to mean 'durationless instant', then proposition 2 is true, but the conclusion that follows is that the arrow is neither in motion nor at rest. It is meaningless to talk of either motion or rest taking place *in* an instant—though we can, of course, talk of motion, or rest, *at* an instant. (B) But if 'the now' refers to an interval, however small, then proposition 2 is false. The plausibility of proposition 2 depends on taking 'now' as instant: but for the conclusion in step 3 to follow, 'now' must be taken in the other sense, as a minimal interval.

It has often been assumed that Zeno's opponents adopted a view of time as composed of atomic quanta. Yet, as already noted, there is no direct evidence for this, and the first clear general distinction between *nyn* used of an instant and *nyn* used of a minimal interval comes in Aristotle. Whereas Aristotle was undoubtedly able to see his way through the problem, it is not at all obvious how clear a notion Zeno may have had on what motion 'in the now' might mean. The paradox rests, as we have seen, on a confusion of two senses of 'now': although it is possible that this confusion was one in Zeno's opponents, there is simply no evidence to confirm that hypothesis, and it is as likely—indeed more likely—that the confusion is Zeno's own. As a refutation of the view that time is composed of atomic quanta, it suffers from the short-coming that—as soon as the distinction between instant and interval had been drawn—the proponents of atomic quanta could object that, given that their quanta are of non-zero magnitude (that is not durationless), proposition 2 can be rejected. Nevertheless the importance of the paradox for the development of Greek thought about time remains. One of the two senses of 'now' in play in the argument is that of durationless instant, and although we should not ascribe to Zeno a clear explicit idea of that concept, his implicit use of it, in this paradox, may justly be considered to mark a stage in the advance towards the formulation and definition of that concept.

The Moving Rows argument, finally, has also been construed in two sharply opposing ways. Here two rows of bodies (As and Bs) are imagined as moving past each other, and past a stationary row (Cs), in opposite directions. In this situation each member of row A passes two members of row B for every one of row C and Aristotle reports the conclusion as being that half the time is equal to its double. Controversy turns on whether the rows comprise bodies of any kind, or whether the bodies in question are atomic units moving in atomic quanta of time. If the latter is the case, the point made by the argument is undoubtedly a more interesting one. Yet none of our ancient sources interprets the paradox in that way. Aristotle, in particular, refutes the argument simply by pointing out that it ignores the fact that the speed of a moving object is relative to what it is measured against, and in view of the absence of any contrary indication, we have to rely on his testimony.

If these interpretations are correct, the thesis that the four arguments form a highly sophisticated multiple dilemma fails: they attack not 'unit-point-atomism', but a variety of sometimes common sense views on motion. The importance of the arguments, however, remains. They posed problems concerning space, time and the continuum some of which were clarified by the work of later Greek philosophers, but some of which have proved suggestive far beyond the limits of the original context in which they were put forward.

Many of the themes we have so far considered recur—though often in a modified or developed form—in Plato. Thus in dialogues from the *Meno* onwards we find both mythical and non-mythical expressions of the doctrine of the immortality of the soul, which is connected, in Plato, with a key epistemological theory, that of recollection (*anamnēsis*), the method whereby knowledge of the Forms is attained, as well as with such ethico-religious doctrines as the need to cultivate the soul, the doctrine of rewards and punishments after death and the idea of reincarnation in other species of animals. In the *Phaedo* (70 c ff), in particular, the rebirth of souls is associated with a general theory that things come to be from their opposites. Just as stronger, for instance, 'comes from' weaker and vice versa, so not only do the dead come from the living, but also the living from the dead. Coming-to-be would cease unless 'like things going round in a circle' things turned back on themselves and went in the opposite direction (72 a, b).[26]

The doctrine of the Great Year, too, which is associated with the Pythagoreans, is alluded to first in the *Republic* (546 b) and appears again in the *Timaeus* (39 d) where it is defined strictly in astronomical terms as the time taken by the eight circuits of the heavenly bodies to accomplish their courses together.

In the context of his political philosophy, especially, Plato takes over and adapts earlier themes. The topic of periodic catastrophe—of the successive destructions or near-destructions of mankind—recurs in various versions. On the subject of the origin of civilization Plato not only presents his own ideas (e.g. at *Laws*, 676 a ff) but is also our chief source for the views of, for example, Protagoras who, in the Great Speech in the dialogue named after him (320 c ff), outlines a theory that puts special emphasis on the idea that all men have a share of *dikē* (justice) and *aidōs* (shame). The origin of civilization, the best state, and the decline of constitutions, all provide Plato with opportunities for arguing political and ethical theses. In many cases the framework of the discussions is a temporal one: yet their chief purpose is not to suggest would-be historical accounts or explanations, so much as to advocate particular political and ethical theories. In the *Republic* and *Laws* Plato does not concern himself so much with the future, as with the ideal. Even though the decline of constitutions in *Republic* VIII and IX is cast in a quasi-historical mould, it is essentially analytic and evaluatory in purpose.

The same is true to only a slightly lesser extent of Plato's use of the theme of the golden age or age of Kronos. In the *Politicus* (268 d ff) we have a quite detailed version of the myth. In the age of Kronos natural processes were reversed: the heavenly bodies rose in the west and set in the east; men were not begotten but born from the earth, resurrected from the dead and buried in the earth; there was no war, no political constitutions, no possession of wives and children, no agriculture. The myth is explicitly introduced in order to help discover what true kingship is by considering the role of the 'divine shepherd' who is in complete charge of the world during the age of Kronos, and Plato gives the theme of the age of bliss a new twist when he suggests that it is only if men then devoted their abundant leisure to philosophy that they could be considered many times happier than men now.

In these and other cases Plato uses and modifies traditional ideas connected with time. But the notion of time also plays a fundamental role at the very heart of his metaphysics. In the philosophy of the middle period a fundamental contrast is drawn between the world of Forms and that of particulars, between the world of being and that of becoming. It is well known that Plato's Forms share many of the characteristics of Parmenides' One Being. They are intelligible, not sensible. They are not subject to coming-to-be or change of any sort. They are, too, in a more clearly defined sense than in Parmenides, eternal. Thus in the *Symposium* (211 a), for instance, the beautiful itself is described as 'always being' (*aei on*) 'and neither coming-to-be nor passing-away'. But the expression 'always is' by itself is not clear, for it can refer not only to what is eternal, but also to what is everlasting, that is to what was, is and will be. By the time we come to the *Timaeus*, however, Plato explicitly distinguishes between these two ideas, even though his terminology remains unstable, in that, for example, he uses the term *aiōnios* for both 'everlasting' and 'eternal'. At *Timaeus* 37 c ff he contrasts eternal being, of which neither 'was' nor 'will be' should be used and only 'is' is appropriate, with everlasting being, being through the whole of time. The model after which the created universe is made is eternal (*panta aiōna*). The created universe itself imitates the eternal model as far as it can, given its corporeal nature, and is everlasting: it was and is and will be 'through the whole of time' (*ton hapanta chronon*).

The universe is undoubtedly described as created in the *Timaeus*, but whether Plato intended his account of creation to be taken literally, or whether he gave his account that form merely for the sake of convenience in exposition, is a dispute that can be traced back to the generation of Plato's own immediate successors in the Academy. So far as time itself is concerned, Plato says that this comes into being with the created universe. The latter, however, presupposes pre-existing matter which is described as being shaken in the Receptacle of becoming before the Craftsman introduced order and created a cosmos. In his *Commentary on Plato's Timaeus* Taylor remarked on this that 'no sane man could be meant to be understood literally in maintaining at once that time and the world began together, and also that there was a state of things, which he proceeds to describe, *before* there was any world'.[27] But this is to miss an important feature of Plato's idea of time. For Plato, time is a matter of, indeed identified with, not just motion in general, but orderly, regular motion, specifically the motion of the heavenly bodies. Time is not just a measure of, or measured by, the movement of the heavenly bodies: that movement is time.

Taylor's objection appears, then, to be based on a misconception. Time and the created universe came into being together. There was no time before the created universe: that would, for Plato, be a contradiction in terms, for both time and creation depend on the introduction of order into disorder. On the other hand there can be a state of affairs before that order is imposed, 'before the cosmos came to be'. Two differences between Plato's view and our own common assumptions stand out. First, for Plato, as for many Greeks, time presupposes order. Secondly, where we might assume time to be a dimension within which creation takes place, for Plato it is part of creation, in the sense that it is itself created. Time is, as he puts it (*Timaeus* 37 d), the everlasting likeness, moving according to number, of eternity. It is by means of time—by existing through the whole of time—that the created sensible universe approximates, as far as its nature permits, to the immutable being of the intelligible model. Everlastingness is the nearest approach to eternity of which sensible things are capable.

The distinction between eternal and everlasting is not the only notable contribution that Plato made to the philosophical analysis of time. In the *Parmenides*, in passages where he considers how 'the one' participates in time, he distinguishes between being in time (where 'was', 'is' and 'will be' are appropriate expressions) and *not* being in time (141 d ff, 151 e ff), although the various uses of the latter expression are not systematically analysed. Then at 156 c ff he formulates the notion of the instant, that is a point in time that itself has no duration. Plato says of *to exaiphnēs*, literally 'the sudden', that it is 'in no time' (*en chronōi oudeni*). The proof of this point proceeds by considering the transition between rest and movement. In the moment of transition, which itself occupies no time, the object neither rests nor moves. This may be considered the first clear expression, in Greek thought, of the idea of the instant, but we should note that the idea is not yet applied generally, but presented in the particular context of the transition between one state and another.

Although Plato's contributions towards the clarification of problems associated with time are considerable, we have to wait until Aristotle for the first comprehensive, systematic philosophical analysis of time. Aristotle devotes the last five chapters of *Physics* book IV to the subject. The discussion is subtle and tightly argued and no attempt can be made here to do more than merely identify the most important points. As usual, his treatment begins with a survey of earlier views and a statement of the difficulties they present. He mentions and rejects three views of time in turn, namely the identification of time (a) with the movement of the universe (where it is likely that he has Plato chiefly in mind); (b) with the heavenly sphere itself; and (c) with a kind of movement or change, where he observes, first, that the change and movement of each thing are only in that thing—whereas time is everywhere—and secondly, that whereas change and movement may be fast or slow, time itself cannot be, for fast and slow are themselves defined by time. Nevertheless he accepts a close association of time with movement or change and rest. Time, he maintains, presupposes change or movement. He remarks that when the state of our minds does not change, or we do not notice it changing, we do not recognize that time has elapsed. When the difference between two 'nows' is not recognized, the interval does not seem to be time. It is, in fact, by recognizing before and after in change that time is apprehended. So although without time change could not take place, without change time could not be recognized.

The formula he arrives at (*Ph.* 219 b, 1 f) is that time is the number of movement in respect of before and after. It is 'in respect of before and after' since we apprehend time only when we mark distinctions within movement, and this we do by recognizing a before and after. And it is the 'number' of movement not in the sense of abstract number (that by which we count) but in the sense of what is counted. Time is, then, that in movement which is numbered, or that in virtue of which movement is numerable.

Aristotle provides a clear statement of the view that time is a continuum and presents an intricate analysis of the 'now'. Time, movement and length, as magnitudes, are all continua, and they are all infinitely divisible. But if time is both continuous and a succession, what account is to be given of the 'now'? The difficulties are put in the form of a dilemma in *Physics* IV, Chap. 10. If the nows are always different, there is a problem. How can any now cease to be? It cannot cease to be in itself. Nor can it cease to be in the 'next' now (for if time is a continuum, the nows are not next to each other, any more than two points on a line can be said to be next to each other); nor yet can it cease to be in any of the infinite intermediates between it and any other given now. On the other hand if the nows are not different, but the same, nothing would be before or after anything else, and there would be no time.

The ensuing discussion elucidates the now by means of two analogies, especially, those of the moving body and the geometrical point. He suggests (*Ph.* 219 b 22 ff) that in the continuum of time the now corresponds to the moving body in the continuum of movement. It is by means of the moving body that we recognize before and after in motion: so analogously it is by the now that we recognize before and after in time. As movement is the flux of the moving body, so time is the flux of the now. Yet there is, of course, one crucial disanalogy between the two cases—and one that is skated over in Aristotle's discussion—namely that the moving body is clearly recognized as a single thing.

Time is not only continuous in virtue of the now, but also divided by it, and here the use of the second analogy, that of the geometrical point, enables him to draw some distinctions that are basic for the clarification of the paradoxes of Zeno. The now is no part of time—time is not composed of nows—any more than the points are parts of the line or the line composed of points. The now has no extension, that is no duration, but is rather the limit (*peras*) or boundary (*horos*) of time. Developing a point already anticipated by Plato, Aristotle explains that in the now as strictly defined—that is as the instant—a body neither rests nor moves, for both rest and movement require duration.

Although he rejects the identification of time with the movement of the heavens, this is, he agrees, the measure of time *par excellence*. Natural rectilinear movement—the upward motion of light, and the downward of heavy, objects—is, he believes, irregular (they accelerate as they near their 'natural place') and it cannot be continuous. He denies the possibility of movement in a straight line to infinity in what he holds to be a finite universe. The only uniform, regular and continuous motion, and the only one, therefore, that can be, and is, everlasting, is natural circular motion, the motion of the heavenly bodies. Against what he represents as being Plato's view, he maintains that neither the heavens, nor time, can come, or cease, to be. At *Physics* 222 a 29 ff, for example, he argues that time will not fail on the grounds that movement cannot fail, a thesis he establishes in *Physics* VIII mainly on the basis of an analysis of causation.[28] There he denies that there can be a 'first' or a 'last' change. Any movement, as the actualizing of a potentiality, presupposes the existence of something capable of undergoing the movement and of something capable of bringing it about, and these must either have come into being (which implies an earlier change) or have pre-existed (and that also requires a change to bring them into a relation in which the one acts upon the other). In either case there must be a change before the alleged 'first' change, and by a similar argument he shows there can be no 'last' change. Movement is, then, everlasting, and he goes on to argue that the prime cause of movement is a mover that is itself unmoved. Time, therefore, takes us to the centre of his theory of causation, and eventually to his theology, for the unmoved mover is identified as god.

In line with his general methodological principle to examine earlier views to see where they may correspond to the truth, he mentions and reinterprets traditional ideas in a variety of contexts. Thus at *Physics* 223 b 24 ff he refers to the views that 'human affairs form a circle' and that 'time itself is thought to be a circle' and explains the latter in terms of the doctrine that time is measured by the circular motion of the heavens. Elsewhere he adapts the idea of the Great Year when, in explaining inundations affecting different parts of the earth, he suggests that the seasons may be subject to fluctuations, a 'great winter', for example, bringing excessive rains (*Meteorologica* I Chap. 14). Against those like Anaximander and Empedocles who had argued that there had been substantial changes in living species (Empedocles spoke of the birth of 'oxen with the heads of men' and maintained that it was the creatures with the best suited constitutions that happened to survive), Aristotle held that the species of animals have always been the same. Yet he agrees that human society has developed, giving his own theory about its origins in *Politics* I Chap. 2, while he showed his awareness of the importance of the historical development of political constitutions by initiating a series of no less than 158 studies of particular states. Nevertheless his conception of social change is a closed one, of rise and decline, not open-ended, of continuous progress towards the future. Although he does not accept the extreme view that time is repeated in the sense that what recurs is numerically the same, a version of the idea of recurrence appears in his often stated belief[29] that all the arts and philosophy, and indeed all opinions, have been discovered not once, but an infinite number of times, in the past.

Aristotle's philosophy of time, like so many other aspects of his thought, was enormously influential. Yet it was criticized and modified or rejected as often as it was accepted. Thus Strato, the third head of Aristotle's own school, the Lyceum, already objected to the idea that time is a number, on the grounds that number suggests a discrete quantity. The Stoics, too, whose cosmology incorporated a version of the belief in the Great Year in the doctrine of the periodic return to the state of *ekpyrōsis*, or pure fire, agreed with Aristotle that time is a continuum and infinitely divisible, but rejected his identification of it as the number of movement. Both Zeno of Citium and Chrysippus described time as the interval of movement and introduced into their definitions the notion that the function of time is to measure swiftness and slowness.[30] On the question of the 'now', especially, the Stoics were at odds with Aristotle. For him, as we have seen, the now is defined strictly as the instant and conceived on the analogy of the geometrical point, but the Stoics rejected this conception and insisted that the now has the same character of being an interval of movement as time as a whole. Where Aristotle had been unclear on aspects of the relation between the present and the past and future, the Stoics, in line with their conception of the now, saw the present as extended, part of it being future and part past. Thus according to a report in Plutarch they 'do not admit a shortest time and do not concede that the now is indivisible . . . , but that which anyone might assume and think of as present is, they say, partly future and partly past'.[31]

While the Stoics worked out a thorough-going doctrine according to which time, place, matter and motion are all continua, the opposite view was maintained by Epicurus, for whom all of these were discontinuous and composed of indivisible magnitudes. In general his physics owed much to the fifth-century atomists Leucippus and Democritus, although what we know of their views on time does not suggest that they considered it to be composed of atomic quanta. Epicurus, however, evidently applied atomism to time as well as to matter and place. In the *Letter to Herodotus* he distinguishes 'times that are perceptible to reason' (the atomic quanta) both from 'sensible times' and from the 'smallest continuous times' (these last being, it seems, the shortest period during which a general tendency of motion manifests itself).[32] Sensible time can, then, be analysed—beyond the limits of what we can perceive—first into the smallest continuous times and then into the ultimate indivisible units. Whereas movement gives the appearance of continuity to the senses, it must ultimately be analysed in terms of discontinuous units, the traversing by the atoms of indivisible units of space in indivisible units of time—differences in the speed of perceptible objects depending on the aggregation of the movements of large numbers of atoms all moving at the same speed but in different directions.

On the problems of time and space, matter and motion, the Stoics and the Epicureans adopted diametrically opposed positions. Yet this is far from exhausting the controversies on the topic of time in and after the Hellenistic period. At one extreme various expressions of the unreality of time are found in, for example, the sceptical tradition. Sextus Empiricus, for instance, records a series of antinomies relating to time, for example that it is neither divisible nor indivisible, in *Outlines of Pyrrhonism* III Chap. 19, 136 ff, and *Against the Physicists* II Chap. 3, 169 ff. On the other hand late antiquity also sees new constructive and speculative approaches to the problem of time, and the work of two thinkers, Plotinus and St Augustine, must be mentioned especially.

Plotinus devotes *Ennead* III. 7 to an extended discussion of time and eternity. This begins, analytically, with a survey of earlier views and it presents an extended critique of Aristotle, against whom Plotinus argues that time itself is not a number nor a measure, although he agrees that it is, no doubt, incidentally a measure of movement. To say that time is the measure of movement, he writes (III. 7, 9), is to say what time measures, but not what time is. But after analysis and criticism Plotinus turns to give his own ideas on time, drawing on Plato, especially, but going a good way beyond him. As in Plato himself, the topic of time takes us to the centre of Plotinus' metaphysics.

First he accepts from Plato the distinction between time (*chronos*) and eternity (*aiōn*) and the idea that the former is in some sense an imitation of the latter. Plotinus insists that it is not enough merely to characterize time: its essence must be grasped, and to do this it must be located in the hierarchy of being. Below Unity or the One comes Intellect or Real Being, and below this again Soul. Eternity is neither the intelligible substance itself, nor rest in the intelligible world. Rather it is the life of the intellect, at once whole, complete and without extension: clearly he would deny, what we would hold to be self-evident, that life implies temporal duration, a 'before' and 'after'. As Parmenides had said of his One Being, and Plato of his Forms, so Plotinus writes concerning eternity that neither 'was' nor 'will be' are to be said of it, only 'is': it is all together now, life without change, abiding in the same in itself (III 7, 3).

While eternity is the life of the intellect, time is the life of the soul as it passes from one stage of actualization to another. Time is produced by the world-soul when it produces the sensible world in imitation of the intelligible one. Plotinus expresses how this happens in a vivid image in III 7, 11:

> as, from a quiet seed the formative principle (*logos*), unfolding itself, advances, as it thinks, to largeness, but . . . instead of keeping its unity in itself, squanders it outside itself and so goes forward to a weaker extension; in the same way Soul, making the world of sense in imitation of that other world, . . . first of all put itself into time, which it made instead of eternity, and then handed over that which came into being as a slave to time, by making the whole of it exist in time.[33]

Time is the product of the spreading out (*diastasis*) of life. As in Plato, eternity is the model of which time is the imitation. But whereas for Plato time is the means whereby the sensible world approximates as far as it is able to the intelligible model, in Plotinus the emphasis is rather on time as the product of the degeneration of the soul, of its 'going forward' to a 'weaker extension'.

St Augustine marks at once an end and a new beginning. The influence of Greek thought, particularly of Plato and the Platonic tradition, is strong in, for example, his use of the distinction between intelligible and sensible being. Yet his Christianity introduces important new perspectives. For Augustine God creates the world not, like Plato's Craftsman, by bringing disorder into order, but by making the world, both spirit and matter, from nothing. But as in Plato, God makes time *with* the world. To the question of what God did before he created the world, Augustine replies that there was no before: before those times that God created, there was no time.

As for time itself, Augustine confesses himself baffled: 'what is time then? If nobody asks me, I know; but if I wish to explain it to someone who asks me, I do not know' (*Confessions* XI Chap. 14), but he pursues the inquiry persistently, frequently calling on God's help, in book XI of the *Confessions*. He firmly denies that time is the motion of the heavens. Even if the heavenly bodies were to cease to exist, time could be measured by the potter's wheel. He cites the biblical case of the standing still in answer to Joshua's prayer (Joshua 10 12 ff) —while time continued—to suggest that time is independent of the movement of the heavenly bodies and he asserts that time is not the movement of any body (XI. 23–24). His own approach to the problem is distinctively psychological. The past exists now, he says, in the sense that it exists as the present image, or memory, of the past event, and so too does the future, as the present anticipation of future events (XI. 17–18) and so there is a present time of past things, one of present, and one of future things (XI. 20). The soul has, then, the power of stretching itself out into the past and the future. But not only is it in the soul that times are measured, but time itself, he concludes, is a certain *distentio*, stretching out or extension, of the soul.

Finally, Augustine's thought must be contrasted with that of all the Greek writers we have discussed on a second fundamental point, and that is in his attitude towards the past. For the Christian, the belief in the incarnation colours, indeed determines, his whole understanding of the past. As we saw, a sense of the extent of the past begins to be developed among the Greeks from the fifth century B.C. Yet those who saw time as stretching back into an indefinite, or indeed an infinite, past, viewed the history of the world as essentially uniform and repetitive. For the Christian, however, the birth of Christ is a unique event. History is now viewed in terms not of repetitive cycles, but of epochs, and the importance of this, in introducing a quite new attitude towards the history of the world and to man's place in it, would be hard to exaggerate. Our survey has been rapid, but we may now attempt to take stock of some of the more important characteristics, and dominant trends, of Greek thought on time. First there is, we must repeat, no such thing as the Greek view of time. The very variety of ideas and approaches, both within and outside philosophy, must be not only given due weight in itself, but also acknowledged to be one of the essential features of the Greek contribution. Outside philosophy, Greek epic, lyric and tragedy, especially, are rich in myths, images and symbols for time and temporal phenomena. The study of time, in many instances, takes us to the study of the writer's whole conception of life and death, man and nature, the human and the divine. The topic of time is often the vehicle for the expression of the writer's profoundest reflections on the human condition, and the visions of time we can document in Greek literature are as complex as those reflections are subtle and original.

Within philosophy, and from the very beginning of philosophical writing, there is an intense debate between competing views on the nature of time itself and on a whole series of related cosmological and ethical questions, on whether the universe is created or not, whether it is the product of design or chance, on the nature of the soul and on free will and determinism. So far as the West is concerned, philosophical debate in general originates with the Greeks, and we should not forget that they take the credit for being the first to have realized and explored the possibility of subjecting common assumptions concerning time to scrutiny, of evaluating alternative views and arguments, in short of seeing time as a philosophical problem.

History and science both contributed to the opening up of new perspectives. We noted the contrast that Herodotus implies between his own and Hecataeus' sense of the depth of the past (p. 125). Knowledge of such effects as erosion and the silting up of rivers was already used in the fifth century B.C. to suggest theories concerning long-term changes in the surface of the earth, as also was the evidence from the existence of fossil sea-animals inland (noticed, for instance, by Xenophanes).[34] Astronomy contributed not only to a greater understanding of the vast size of the universe (in the fourth century B.C. Aristotle is in no doubt as to the minute size of the earth compared with the surrounding heavens) but also to the determination of the periodicities of the heavenly bodies.

Precise estimates of the lengths of the seasons begin to be made in the fifth century, and some half dozen corrections to the determination of the length of the solar year are recorded from that and the next three centuries. Thus Hipparchus in the second century estimates the solar year as $4\frac{4}{5}$ minutes less than $365\frac{1}{4}$ days, and the lunar month at about 29 days 14 hours 44 minutes $2\frac{1}{2}$ seconds, and he was also responsible for discovering the longest astronomical periodicity known to the ancient world, the phenomenon known as the precession of the equinoxes: he estimated that the equinoctial points are displaced in relation to the fixed stars at the rate of not less than 36 seconds of angle a year.[35]

Yet this positivistic picture must be qualified by at least two important

19. Stobaeus, *Ecl.* 1.18.1; cf. Aristotle, *Ph.* 213 b 22 et seq.; Simplicius, in *Ph.* 651.26 et seq.; Aetius II.9.1.
20. Simplicius, in *Ph.* 732.30 et seq.
21. Aristotle, *Ph.* 252 a 5 et seq., 31 et seq. See especially U. Hölscher, 'Weltzeiten und Lebenszyklus, eine Nachprüfung der Empedokles-Doxographie', *Hermes*, No. 93, 1965, p. 7–33; F. Solmsen, 'Love and Strife in Empedocles' 'Cosmology', *Phronesis*, No. 10, 1965, p. 109–48; J. Bollack, *Empédocle* (3 vol.), Paris, Éditions de Minuit, 1965–69. D. O'Brien, *Empedocles' cosmic cycle*, Cambridge, Cambridge University Press, 1969.
22. The literature on Zeno's paradoxes is immense. H. D. P. Lee, *Zeno of Elea*, Cambridge, Cambridge University Press, 1936, provides text and translation. Two recent general discussions, with extensive bibliographical notes, are: W. K. C. Guthrie, *A History of Greek Philosophy*, Vol. 2, p. 80–101, Cambridge, Cambridge University Press; and G. Vlastos, 'Zeno of Elea', article in *Encyclopedia of Philosophy* (edited by P. Edwards), Vol. 8, p. 369–79, New York, Macmillan and Free Press, 1967.
23. P. Tannery, *Pour l'Histoire de la Science Hellène*, p. 255–70, Paris, Gauthier-Villars, 1930 (lst ed. 1877) 2nd ed.,; Cf. also V. Brochard, *Études de Philosophie Ancienne et de Philosophie Moderne*, 2nd ed., Paris, Vrin, 1926 (lst ed. 1912).
24. G. J. Whitrow, *The Natural Philosophy of Time*, p. 135–52, London, Nelson, 1961.
25. W. D. Ross, *Aristotle's Physics*, p. 75, Oxford, 1936.
26. In this passage we find both a cyclical and a to-and-fro image, apparently treated as equivalents.
27. A. E. Taylor, *A Commentary on Plato's Timaeus*, p. 69, Oxford, Clarendon Press, 1928.
28. At *Ph.* 251 b 10 et seq., Aristotle argues the converse of 222 a 29 et seq., namely that movement is everlasting since time is.
29. *De Caelo* 270 b 16 et seq.; *Meteor.* 339 b 27 et seq.; *Methaph.* 1074 b 10 et seq.; *Pol.* 1329 b 25 et seq.
30. Stobaeus, *Ecl.*, 1.8.40 and 42; von Arnim, *Stoicorum Veterum Fragmenta* I.93, p. 26 and II.509, p. 164.
31. Plutarch, *De comm. not.* 41, 1081 c (*SVF* II.519, p. 165).
32. Paras. 47 and 62. See, e.g. D. J. Furley, *Two Studies in the Greek Atomists*, p. 121 et seq., Princeton (N.J.), Princeton University Press, 1967.
33. Translation of A. H. Armstrong, Loeb Classical Library, Vol. 3, 1967.
34. Hippolytus, *Ref.* I, 14.5–6; see W. K. C. Guthrie, *A History of Greek Philosophy*, Vol. 1, No. 2, p. 387, Cambridge, Cambridge University Press, 1962.
35. On Hipparchus, see, for example, Ptolemy, *Syntaxis*, III.1, IV.2 and VII.2.
36. e.g. Vitruvius IX.8.4 et seq.
37. One may contrast an approach via the distinction between tensed and tenseless statements.

BIBLIOGRAPHY

CALLAHAN, J. F. *Four views of time in ancient philosophy.* Cambridge (Mass.), Harvard University Press, 1948.

CONEN, P. F. *Die Zeittheorie des Aristoteles* (Zetemata 35). Munich, Beck'sche Verlagsbuchhandlung, 1964.

FRÄNKEL, H. *Wege und Formen frühgriechischen Denkens*, 2nd ed. Munich, Beck'sche Verlagsbuchhandlung, 1960.

KNEALE, W. C. Time and eternity in theology. *Proceedings of the Aristotelian Society*, New Series 61, 1960–61, p. 87–108.

LEYDEN, W. VON. Time, number, and eternity in Plato and Aristotle. *Philosophical quarterly*, no. 14, 1964, p. 35–52.

MOREAU, J. *L'espace et le temps selon Aristote*. Padua, Antenore, 1965. (Saggi e testi 4.)
ONIANS, R. B. *The origins of European thought*. Cambridge, Cambridge University Press, 1951.
OWEN, G. E. L. Plato and Parmenides on the timeless present. *The Monist*, no. 50, 1966, p. 317–40.
ROMILLY, J. DE. *Time in Greek tragedy*. Ithaca (N.Y.), Cornell University Press, 1968.
VERNANT, J. P. *Mythe et pensée chez les Grecs*, 3rd ed. (2 vol.). Paris, Maspero, 1971.
VIDAL-NAQUET, P. Temps des dieux et temps des hommes. *Revue de l'histoire des religions*, no. 157, 1960, p. 55–80.

THE VIEW OF TIME AND HISTORY IN JEWISH CULTURE

André Neher

One of the most fertile contributions of the Jewish mind to universal culture is not merely that, at the level of the superior existential values, it has associated time with space in such a way that Israel's vital space has been described as having been reduced to its pure duration (P. Masson-Oursel), but also that it has fitted time into a constructive historical dimension.

The Jews as the 'builders of time' (Abraham Heschel), constrasted with the Egyptians or the Greeks, who were builders of space, the Romans who were builders of the state and of the empire, the Christians as builders of heaven . . . the definition is appealing and accurate, but it must be set in its proper perspective and we should not be surprised if it extended to conceptions that are sometimes contradictory. Is not the very history of the Jewish people—this many-thousand-year march through the most multifarious of times—a unique paradox, a challenge to all sociologies and to the clockwork rigidity of their laws? Not surprisingly, this challenge recurs in the Jewish people's conception of time and history in their universal significance.

The point of departure must obviously be Genesis, the biblical narrative of the Creation which simultaneously relates two births, that of the cosmos and that of time.

Different interpretations have stressed what seemed to be essential in the thinking about origins presented in Genesis. At the beginning was the Spirit, at the beginning was the Word. . . . However, the very term with which the account begins, *bereshit*, indicates that what seemed essential to the narrator of Genesis was not what was at the beginning, but the fact that there was a beginning. *Bereshit* does not mean 'at the beginning', but 'in a beginning'. The creative act occupies a period of time. God begins to create, and he spreads creation over seven days. The primordial element is 'time' itself. Creation was manifested in the appearance of time.

This time is entirely new. That is the significance of the verb *bara*, which designates the creative act. Throughout the Bible this verb is reserved for God. Only God can 'create', i.e. bring forth in a sudden and sovereign manner. Creation expressed as *bara* is indeed *ex nihilo*, since it is a break with all that went before. The anterior is inexistent by comparison with the *novum* that is creation.

These first indications would suffice in themselves to raise the problem of the origins of being in a way that is radically different from that of myth. If all forms of human thought originally had a common bent, we are here in the presence of one of the great partings of the ways which disrupted for ever the primeval unity and guided the adventures of the mind in diametrically opposed directions. And at the very heart of this rending, an almost insurmountable divergence appears in the approach to and interpretation of two facts which are external to human thought but without which it can neither conceive itself nor exercise its power over things: time and space.

The dialectic of time and space overshadows human thought in all its processes. Every religion, philosophy and civilization confers on it a special meaning. From the primary sense of an opposition between the mobile and the stationary a scale mounts up to the great polarities of happening and being, dispersion and identity, the provisional and the eternal. Of all ancient peoples, the migratory and conquering Semites, who had a very turbulent history, were the first to become aware of the divergent functions of time and space. For their history, a record of expansion and will to power was woven into the fabric of time, while space remained for them an insuperable boundary, a barrier to the torrent of history. Political power grew with time, but on the frontiers new territories were for ever appearing and they had to be conquered. So long as the empire did not stretch to the uttermost ends of the earth—and the sky—history was but a figment of the imagination. As a result the metaphysical conceptions of the Semites are haunted by space. While risking their existence in time, they could not see it as the supreme reality; eventually time was always conquered by space: the Tower of Babel never reached the sky and so the eye could never take in the whole of space at a single glance. Hence space was consigned to the realm of the sacred. It surfaced, in deified guise, in the symbolism of the great astrological, agrarian and political rituals, each of which reflects in miniature the set of conceptions by means of which the Sumerians, the Babylonians, the Phoenicians, the Canaanites and also the Egyptians attempted, through religious ritual, to conquer space, in real history their master. We know the debt of the Greek mind to the Semites and the Egyptians. But the Greeks grasped the intelligible which lay behind the tangible. They conserved not the actual rites but their meanings; in renewed form, the explanation and exploitation of space were revealed in philosophy and science, both of which were initially spatial and geometrical. Throughout the whole of its evolution, Greek philosophy bore the mark of this origin. Time, in its strong and true meaning, was never perceived as a reality in Greek philosophy, for which the world remained essentially cosmos, a changeless and orderly universe, a regular and numbered motion, space.

Viewed in this way, history could hardly be anything other than an account of past events, a collation of anecdotes that may be of interest to the mind but are valueless as a clue to the individual or collective destiny of mankind. For the Semites, whose life was one of movement, conquest and expansion, history was a majestic procession of dynasties. For the Greeks, who were less adventurous, it was an intellectual curiosity, a logical investigation or an exercise in rhetoric. Alone among the systems of thought of antiquity, Hebraic thought thoroughly dominated space, raising human time to the level of a history that was unique, fertile, bursting with meaning and a challenge to the very destiny of man. By a maieutics worthy of Socrates, though applied not to the generality of the human mind but to the singleness of human existence, the Bible was able to bring forth a 'philosophy' from history.

While the term 'philosophy' should not be applied to the Bible except with extreme caution, the fact remains that no other term so neatly captures the biblical conception of history as 'philosophy', so much so that even today the term 'philosophy of history' is always followed by a more or less implicit reference to the Bible. Modern thinkers who, since Hegel, have employed both the term and the notion, all know that its origin is biblical, and one of them (Benjamin Fondane) goes so far as to say that they found their philosophy 'ready-made' in the Bible. One might add that they could not have found it in the Greeks, for the rift between Hebraic and Greek thought is nowhere more sharply and emphatically demarcated than in the sphere of history.

It is not immaterial, therefore, that the Bible should open with Genesis. With a single stroke Genesis sweeps aside the spatial obsessions which had cluttered Oriental systems of thought with complicated myths and their ritual extensions and which had decisively slanted Greek thought towards the classical, non-historical forms of philosophy. It is no accident that, at turning points in the dialogue between Jerusalem and Athens, between the Bible and philosophy, in the age of Philo or Origen and at the time of Maimonides and Saint Thomas Aquinas. Genesis remained the touchstone in the ultimate argument. For Genesis embodies the rejection of space, the espousal of time, as a result of which biblical 'philosophy' will always be alien to Greek philosophy. All the dramatic conflicts of space, which recur endlessly in the Semitic and Hellenic religions and philosophies were compressed by the Hebrews into a single moment: Creation. The concept of creation subsumes all the problems of space, which are thus resolved at a stroke. The Semitic cosmogonies are accompanied by a theology; in the nascent world the gods are born: there is a problem of divine plurality, which multiplies, instead of reducing, the created spaces. According to the Hellenic explanation the birth of the world is attributable to the reciprocal action of two forces: matter and energy, content and form. The problem of the world remains the problem of being, and the encounters of space and time scatter the problem throughout history. The Hebraic concept of creation takes being for granted: if nothingness gives way to something, then something will give way to everything; the problem is no longer one of being but of becoming. Life does not illustrate the victory over nothingness: it is its consequence. In a beginning, time was set in motion, and ever since then history has been moving forward irresistibly.

Structurally, the Bible gives the impression of being the highway of this history. Its narrative parts recount the lives of men whose chief function was to keep the highway open, to clear it constantly. The nomadic life, which is so characteristic of biblical sociology and which is the lot of whole groups of the Hebraic community, such as the Levites and the Prophets, so characteristic too of the ethics of the Torah, is none other than a permanent and concrete expression of the rejection of space, a fierce determination to allow neither human psychology nor institutions to crystallize or to ossify. By contrast with Plato's Republic, which chooses philosophers to be the vigilant custodians of the public weal, the care of the Biblical City is entrusted to the makers of history.

But biblical thought goes even further. Over and above humanity, which is wedded to history and whose existence is reflected in the Bible, an intelligence is at work in history, trying to define its meaning. What is original about Hebraic thought is not merely that it ascribes creation to a single God, but that it established between this God and the world created by Him a historical, not a mythical, relationship. This historical relationship, the 'Covenant', implies two equally important consequences. One is the transcendence of God, the other His immanence. In the biblical conception there is no contradiction between God and the world, but a contradictory situation on the part of God with regard to the world. God is both near and far, outside the universe and omnipresent within it. He is both being and becoming.

God's transcendence arises from the fact that nothing of what is created is contemporaneous with God. Since the whole of Creation took place in the time of history, none of its elements existed in the non-time of God. God's externality in relation to His Creation is truly absolute, and this absolute will return at the end of time. When history comes to an end, Creation will disappear: only God will remain in His non-time. In eschatological terms, the notion of the 'end' echoes the cosmology of the 'origin'.

But whereas Creation is not contemporaneous with God, God is contemporaneous with His Creation. The universe is not a parenthesis within God. He penetrates and permeates it, without however identifying Himself with it. This is the biblical 'panentheism', which has rightly been interpreted as the original Hebraic response to the transcendentalism and pantheism of philosophies. In the story of Genesis, 'panentheism' fluctuates between two expressions, each of which has its own value and significance. The first concerns the 'Spirit' of God; the second His 'Word'. The 'Spirit' of God moved upon the face of the waters, which themselves cover the chaos and darkness of the void: this is the vision of the second verse of Genesis. It acknowledges a confrontation between God and matter; the waters 'face' the Spirit. Created matter is amorphous, opaque, massive, immobile. Facing it, the Spirit is in motion, and this motion is gentle, light as a caress; it watches over sleep and calls to waking life. The image suggests that the Spirit of God embraces the world without, however, entering into it. It is the 'Word' which effects this entry. In the third verse, God speaks and the 'Word' is ingrained in the world, becomes incarnate in the thing created. Each new 'Word' of God evokes a new phase of Creation. The 'Word' of God accompanies Creation. It is the rhythm of Creation.

The created world is not severed from God like some carelessly flung projectile: God and the world watch each other; though contradictory, they are face to face, the unified and moving 'Spirit' as opposed to multiplicity and torpor. The mute and peaceful coexistence evoked by the second verse of Genesis is the more remarkable in that the partners are implacably antagonistic entities: matter and spirit, darkness and radiance, immobility and motion, disorder and unity. This verse puts the encounter between God and the world in terms of an encounter between God and man, in which the imperishable and the perishable know each other through confrontation with the 'Spirit', just as God and the world, the Creator and the created, contemplate each other in confrontation with the 'Spirit'. Upon the emergence of the 'Word', the confrontation ceases to be mute and becomes a dialogue. The world responds to the 'Word' of God by creating itself, by 'becoming', just as man responds to the 'Word' of God in a 'becoming'. Creation no longer 'faces' God but docilely follows the movement of the 'Word' advancing, adding one segment of becoming to another as it is created, one day to another. Through the 'Word' a 'history' of Creation takes shape, its fabric receiving and absorbing in turn the great contradictory forces: light and darkness, heaven and earth, earth and water; then the cosmic and stellar rhythms; finally, living beings, from the plant world to man.

Thus the relationship of God to the world is not mythical; it is historical.

How does the Bible refer to history? The initial terminology revolves round the word *yom*, meaning day. The 'words' or 'deeds of the days'—*divre hayyamim*—mean history in the sense of narration. The 'days of old'—*yemot olam* (literally: 'the days of the world')—define history in the wider sense of becoming (Deut 32:7). This terminology is supplemented by another, a companion form based on the word *toldot*, which is translated by 'generations' and literally means 'children'. Thus conceived, history is composed of an intimate and endless lineage, which links fathers to children and, inversely, children to fathers. The expression *shenot dor va-dor*, 'the years of many generations' [literally: ' . . . of generation and generation'], is synonymous with *yemot olam* meaning history, and Deuteronomy (32:7) uses the two terms in parallel, thus showing that they are identical.

This dual terminology is used in the story of Genesis. In Chapter I, Creation is divided into seven 'days'. What meaning should be ascribed to this term? In the first place, we should note that the word has three different senses in this chapter of Genesis. In Verse 4, day is identified with light, or rather is the name of light. *Yom* therefore has a cosmic significance in this context; it is one of the elements in the great pair of contradictory forces light-dark. In Verse 14, the same word *yom* has an astronomical sense; it refers to the full cycle of the day, from sunrise to sunrise. Everywhere else, in its appearances at the end of the different stages in the story of creation, the word *yom* has yet another meaning: it designates a period, one moment linked to another, following it and announcing the next. It is in this sense that the Bible later uses the word *yom* for the connecting links of history. It is immaterial that the seven days of Creation are abnormal in that they are not equally divided in relation to the sun. They are not days in the astronomical, but, as it were, in the chronometric sense. They suggest the mobility of time, its forward movement, in short, history. The seven days are no more mythical than is the act of Creation itself. They are the first in a succession of days which will henceforth punctuate the life of Creation. The subject of the biblical discourse is not prehistory, but the beginning of history.

The second chapter of Genesis gives up the step-by-step approach and reduces the work of Creation to a single day, *beyom assot* (2:4). The same verse, however, points out that the story of Creation is that of the *toldot* of the heavens and of the earth. This is the other term used to refer to history. The day on which heaven and earth were created was a historical day; it was the beginning and setting in motion of subsequent history, which will be marked by the rhythm of the *toldot*, the 'generations' (5:1).

Thus the same language refers to both the period of Creation and to subsequent periods. The origins of the world are not concealed from human intelligence, which has no need to seek for them elsewhere, in a dimension attainable only by transcending its own condition. They are perceptible and comprehensible in history itself, of which they are the emanation. To remain in touch with the origin, man has no need to transcend his history in order to accede to a mythical dimension; by accepting and abandoning himself to it, he finds in his own history the continuation of the origins. This is the deeper meaning of Creation in the biblical economy. Being history rather than myth, the Creation does not weigh upon biblical religious thought; it does not force it to escape or seek refuge in rites or in a doctrine of recurrence. It does not place behind man a nagging anxiety which he must overcome. On the contrary, it bids man to advance into his history, of which it is the liberating source. Biblical man, plunged into the flow of history, discerned its direction; knowing the origin behind him, he realized that he was advancing towards a goal.

The canonical structure of the Bible reflects this economy. The dual terminology of 'days' and 'generations', used by the biblical narrator to characterize the creation of history and its development, is also employed for the culmination of history. The *reshit yamim*, the 'beginning of days' has its counterpart in the *aharit yamim*, the 'end of days'. The 'days' of history have a beginning and an end. In the same way, the 'generations' of history advance towards a goal. In keeping with the symbolism of the expression *toldot*, the end is here described metaphorically. There may be faults or breaks in the chain of generations, but the final redemption consists precisely in repairing the rents and restoring the fabric to wholeness. This is the thought expressed in so many words in the chapter containing the final vision of the prophet Malachi (4 :6), the last canonical prophet of the Bible: 'And he shall turn the heart of the fathers to the children, and the heart of the children to their fathers.' The role of the divine messenger is reparative: to restore the fallen links and permit a continuous and progressive reading of the sequence of generations. Continuity and progression: these are the features of the historical time made possible by the biblical interpretation of Creation.

But the Jewish view of time and history is not led astray by these soothing prospects. Without abandoning its basic optimism or denying its biblical sources, in particular the theme of the Creation, it reaches out to a beyond more vibrant with anxiety, to a sort of antithesis which questions the thesis and puts it in the form of a query rather than a response.

As we have just seen, Jewish thought is aware of the final catharsis, the plenitude at point Omega, which gathers to itself the fragments and failures of what went before and reunites them in a pattern that is at last eternal, as a magnet orders iron filings in a magnetic field; but this awareness is dreamlike and nostalgic rather than dogmatic. Jewish thought knows there is a key to history which gives meaning to the whole; but as soon as the essential is at stake, it suddenly remembers that sometimes—and perhaps for ever—this key is lost or rather that it constantly changes hands between the two partners of the Covenant: God and man, with the result that radical uncertainty runs through the length and breadth of history. Time is not a majestic flow from a beginning towards an end: it is an unending series of leaps. History is not a continuous progression: it is an eternal improvisation.

This disturbing prospect is traced back by Jewish thought to the origins, in the entrails of time, to the moment when the convulsive effort occurred which was to bring forth the world. Within the strict logic of Genesis, the account of the Creation, it discovers the illogical. In the regular rhythm of the whole, it perceives surprising irregularities. For the conception of a universe created of a piece, in all its parts, it substitutes the vision of a world in which there are lacunae, blanks, and conversely, additions and excesses. Finally, it is conscious of the fact that, far from submitting to the divine Word, some creatures offer resistance to it, are refractory and thus provoke deviations, rebellions and crises. Plunging even deeper, it dares to penetrate the mystery, to discover, with stupefaction but without complacency, that far from having been thought out and accomplished according to a pre-established plan, this work had sprung from a state of total unpreparedness, displaying throughout its execution the alternately disappointing and stimulating signs of improvisation.

Indeed, according to rabbinical exegesis (Bereshit Rabba 9 :4), the world did not spring from God's hand all at once. Twenty-six attempts preceded the present Genesis, and all were doomed to failure. The world of man issued from the chaotic womb of this previous wreckage, but bears no guarantee: it, too, is liable to failure and may return to nothingness. 'If only this one holds!', *Halway sheyaamod* exclaims God as He creates the world, and this wish echoes through the subsequent history of the world and mankind, emphasizing from the outset that our history bears the imprint of total insecurity.

Moreover, in the biblical universe, there is no point Omega, for the simple reason, first, that there is no point Alpha. The Hebrew Bible begins not with the first letter of the alphabet, but with the second, *Bet-Bereshit*. History does not begin with Genesis; it is the Parousia of a history which is already mature, which carries within it the remains, the wreckage perhaps, but also the vital germs and above all the irretrievably lost realities of the preceding Alpha. No point Omega can claim to be the culmination of the sum total of history because, at the other end, the only reference point is a second point: the point of origin will always elude it; also perhaps because Alpha will not, and cannot, appear until after Omega. From A to Z, biblical history in the Jewish conception remains open. A is not the beginning, but what went before. And Z is not the end, but the opening. The great Jewish affirmation is that Omega is neither the end nor the centre, nor is it the decisive turning point. The last letter of the Hebrew alphabet is *tav*, which indicates the 'second person future', thus laying hold of man who is summoned towards an infinitely open future. A meta-Omega always remains a possibility, of which no one can foresee or foretell the new fascination. This is to say that Omega may possibly never come, just as, at the further extremity, Alpha never appeared. At the opposing doors of history, the entrance and the exit both remain free. Genesis and Exodus are infinite and eternal risks. And so are life and death—the Genesis and Exodus of individuals and communities alike, at every moment of their history.

The secret and the mystery of these risks are to be found in 'one of the most terrifying notions invented by the strict and terrible logic of Jewish theology: the freedom of man' (Hermann Broch).

By creating man free, God brought into the universe a basic element of uncertainty, that no divine or divinatory wisdom, no mathematics, not even prayer, can foresee, forestall or combine in a pre-established movement. Man born free is improvisation made flesh and history, the absolutely unforeseeable, the boundary with which the guiding forces of the plan of creation enter into collision, without anyone being able to say in advance whether the boundary will allow itself to be crossed or whether, through the power of obstruction it presents, it will constrain the creative forces to turn back, jeopardizing in their ebb the plan of creation as a whole. Free man represents the divine watershed: henceforth, the upper waters, separated from the lower, live their own life.

Jewish thought perceives the moment at which this divine risk is born in the curious apostrophe: *naase adam*, 'Let us make man', in Verse 26 of the first chapter of Genesis. Whom is God addressing at this solemn moment of deliberation when the project of man seems unrealizable without the co-operation of some other force with the creative force of God? Is he addressing the angels, the world or himself? Without rejecting any of these hypotheses *a priori*, Jewish tradition reaches the conclusion that the divine appeal is addressed to man, to this potential Adam embraced by the divine project but able to arise only through co-operation between man and God. 'Let us make man', together —you as man, I as God, and this covenant founds for ever thef reedom of man whom it has made for ever the partner of God.

From then on, the successive and dramatic stages, of history, in its first manifestations, are moments in the initiation to freedom. It is as though God were tempting man, forcing him to temper his freedom like hardened steel. It is as though God were seeking to test the creature on whom He had just bestowed freedom, endeavouring by passage through the crucible to toughen him still further, to weld him even more closely to his freedom. The great danger was that of reaching the stage where man and his freedom became one, and that thereupon—with all the inevitable consequences—man would be debarred from ever partaking of the nature of either angel or beast. In the illuminating comment of Maimonides, the great challenge was that freedom should become the physical law of man, not just potentially, but in deed; that this freedom invented by God for man should really and truly envelop him, that it should daily live within him, that it should accompany him in his thoughts, his passions and his history, and that in future he should be governed by a single constraint only—that, precisely, of being free. In the cosmos, where every creature has its own law which it must follow to the exclusion of all others, the law of man is to be free: in the infinite landscape of Creation, he represents the reserve of liberty. Indestructible, protected from all forces but its own, this reserve can survive indefinitely by itself, in peaceful isolation.

It can also overflow, at any time, break through the barriers, explode, threatening to invade creation to the end of time and to the boundaries of space, to annihilate or sublimate it, to snatch it from God in a brutal gesture or to return it to Him in an absolutely new dawn, to offer it for damnation or redemption. And God takes upon himself the risk, the great risk, of entrusting to man and to man alone the die of this fearful choice, in the sense that He calls man to account, that from Adam to Abraham and Moses He initiates, breaks off and resumes the tenuous thread of dialogue, that in Ernest Bloch's fine expression He expects men to be the 'helmsmen of history'.

In Judaism, one might say, the view of time and history has a musical structure. It is perceived in the style of a fugue, the major theme of which is that of 'what may be', for by bestowing on man the heady gift of freedom, the Creator tipped the time scale of 'what is' towards what 'may be'.

To begin with, what 'may be' is in the minor key; it is pained scepticism, aching uncertainty, the pessimism of solitude. Everything is possible, but 'it may be that nothing' will come to pass. It is Jonah's bitterness at God's repentence: all his preaching and all his words had predicted the destruction of

Nineveh, yet Nineveh was saved. And still more seriously, it is the cry of pain at the suddenly perceived boundary between the possible and the real, between the dream and its accomplishment, between the intention and the act. You may have done all that is required to set the ethical process in motion, to ensure that evil-doing is punished and virtue rewarded, that evil gives rise to evil and good to good; you will never be able to prevent a grain of uncertainty from blocking or smashing the mechanism. You may harness the whole of human and divine energy and apply it to the conquest of justice and peace, you may make a fresh start on building a better world, but you will never be able to avoid the accident or inadvertence which will bring your efforts crashing to the ground like a house of cards and set the world adrift. You may proclaim the City of Light of the Messiah, but you can never discount the expression of doubt voiced by both God and the prophet to the effect that it is all too good to be true. All too good . . . and maybe . . .?

Conversely, overlaying the previous theme of the fugue, comes 'what may be' in the major key. Indeed, everything may be, anything is possible, nothing is too abominable to appear in the world and history, or too sublime to materialize in mind and deed. The universe is the infinite field of the possible, a forge in which any spark may be struck at any moment, in which any industry may produce any manner of atomic sword, but in which will-power may also transmute any manner of sword into a ploughshare. 'What may be', in the major key, represents power, in Hebrew *koah*, the unfathomable reserve of Being, the inexhaustible reservoir of unused forces, which no dream prevents, or can prevent us from seeing used tomorrow. 'What may be', in the major key, is the triumph of Jeremiah over Cassandra, of God over Jonah, of man over the Messiah. For Cassandra cannot bear the failure of her prophecies; if Troy does not fall, Cassandra is defeated. But Jeremiah prophesies the misfortunes of Jerusalem only to *fail* in his prophecies, to see 'the potential existence' of Jerusalem gain the upper hand and the failure of his word rise up, *de profundis*, in a psalm of hope. It is the very lesson given by God, at the gates of Nineveh which was saved by repentance, to Jonah, whose soul longed for the automatic certainties that had been shattered by the tempestuous fugue of what 'may be'.

It is also the triumph of man over the Messiah. *Aharit hayamim*, the biblical term designating the end of time, does not refer, in its true sense, to the ultimate point of history, but to the period following the end. The end, too, shatters, dissipates, comes to grief; but it is under the victorious pressure of a hope which has not lost its impetus at the end; it has acquired new strength by plunging into the inexhaustible reservoir of Being, found a new lease of life. In the final wreckage of each of its failure, time discovers new territory. And throughout the whole fugue, history is nothing other than the abounding harmony of dissonances stretching to infinity.

APPENDIX

Empirical apperceptions of time in Judaism

From the origins to our own time, the astronomical measurements of which our Jewish people has safeguarded the tradition, have remained immutable with the result that we have never been obliged to alter our calendar in any way whatsoever, whereas other peoples have been forced to do so seven times already. I say this not by way of apologia or because I am myself a Jew; the most eminent of astronomers, from antiquity to the present age, that is, from Hipparchus up to Copernicus, Tycho Brahe and Johann Kepler, marvel at this unique phenomenon of a calendar so meticulously worked out that it has managed to endure, unchanging, for thousands of years.

The author of this statement, David Gans (1541–1613), must have been all the prouder to place it in the introduction to his astronomical work *Nehmad Venaim*, composed around the year 1600, for his ears still echoed to the peals of bells with which, a few years previously, on 4 October 1582 to be precise, all the churches of the Western world had greeted the introduction of the Gregorian reform. By the will of a pope, Gregory XIII, Western Christendom had aged eleven days in a night, for the day following that memorable fourth of October had been proclaimed the fifteenth of the same month.

Eleven days! While the mere fact of reform was startling enough for a Jew accustomed to the stability of his own calendar, the total of eleven days by which Gregory XIII endeavoured—in vain incidentally—to correct Julius Caesar's errors, must have strengthened his inner conviction that science was decidedly no appanage of Athens or Rome but was at one with Jerusalem. For the theme of the eleven days, as we shall see in a moment, is the very cornerstone on which the immutable Jewish calendar is built. And it had taken the Gentiles a millennium and a half before they finally discovered the virtues of this theme; even then, they applied it in an apparently absurd way, like so many quacks, at a point in human time where it could bring temporary relief, but not in the age-old manner of the Jewish Sages, at the precise spot where time, no longer dominating and sweeping man off his feet, became his docile servant and the balanced instrument of his existence.

Balanced? It is no exaggeration to use this term if, at least, as we shall in the following pages, we confine ourselves to the world of biblical man, and limit our comparative study to the three major religions which sprang from the Bible and to the civilizations which they moulded: Judaism, Christianity, Islam.

While not wishing to oversimplify, we find that one fundamental difference is self-evident, placing balance firmly on the side of the mother religion. The Christian calendar, a legacy of the Graeco-Roman world, took the solar cycle as its basis. The Moslem calendar, a product of the Oriental environment, is tied to the orbits of the moon. Judaism, on the other hand, being situated between Athens and Babylon (if not in the flux of history, at least by reason of its biblical birth place), builds its calendar on a daring but durable bridge between sun and moon.

But before explaining why and how the Jews achieved this synthesis, we should point out that in the scale which keeps the year in balance with the months, the Jews managed to incorporate the two primary elements in the measurement of time, i.e. the day and the week, likewise in a most original way, and yet without upsetting the equilibrium.

Me-erev ad erev (Lev. 23:32), 'from even unto even', that is how the Jewish day is counted, in accordance with the very principle of creation, which places the evening before the morning: 'And the evening and the morning were the first day' (Gen. 1:5) (literally: 'And it was evening, and it was morning, one day'). According to the account in Genesis, six days passed in this way, none of them bearing a name, for their distinctive characteristic is that they lead up to the seventh day, the seal and culmination of the divine task. And the seventh day, preceded by its procession of the six days, forms with them the Jewish week.

This is the point of departure for the Jewish way of measuring time. It is straightforward in its division of the day and of the week. It is immutable, for it is rooted in the account of Creation. It is original in the importance it accords to the previous eve, to the precedence of the night before the day. All Jewish festivals bear the stamp of feverish preparations during the preceding day, followed at sunset, with the appearance of the first stars, by a sudden transformation, a transition from activity to relaxation, from the profane to the sacred. Nightfall is a solemn, fervent, joyous occasion. Communion with others, first at the synagogue and then round the family table, robs the night of its terrors. The evening celebration becomes a hymn. And certain introductory eves, such as that of every seventh day, the Seder of Passover or Yom Kippur, the full twenty-four hours of which are devoted to prayer and fasting, have a poetry and a magic that are most moving. The rising of the sun merely prolongs this atmosphere until dusk, which is seen as a leave-taking and also as ushering in the challenge of a strenuous new day. It is as though the daily rhythm itself was reversed by the spacing of the three prayers from even unto even; the evening prayer, the morning prayer and the afternoon prayer. It is not the cock-crow which awakens the Jew; rather, on the previous evening, he will already have sung a psalm to the human and cosmic day. Being anonymous, the days are void of the mythological or astral influences with which their names are imbued in the non-Jewish calendars. They are drawn towards the seventh day, which alone has a name: *shabbat*, 'rest', the concentration of human activity in a purifying nucleus, a pivotal moment in which spent energies are absorbed and new life is breathed into them for the future.

But the sabbath is not just a weekly event. It permeates the entire fabric of time, building up into a temporal pyramid structured round the figure seven.

Each seventh year is a sabbatical year, during which the fields remain untilled, debts are remitted, slaves are set free and the balance of agricultural and social life is restored. Upon the completion of the cycle of seven sabbatical years, i.e. forty-nine years, the sabbath of the fiftieth year is celebrated: the jubilee year, the redeeming power of which is even greater than that of the sabbatical year. All outstanding claims are combined and settled by the restoration of alienated land to its original owner. After having been estranged from his heritage, man rediscovers himself, in his primordial identity.

Thus time is measured in cycles, with its origin in Creation and its nodal points in the 'reversions' which are staging posts on the way to fulfilment. It is an arbitrary measurement, since it is independent of the cycles of nature. Each individual and each human community choose their own sabbath. Should you be lost in the desert or the polar regions, out of touch with other Jews, or should you have forgotten what day of the week it is, then all you need to do is choose a first day for yourself and count up to the seventh, which will be your sabbath. The Jews of New York and Tokyo celebrate the sabbath with a twenty-four hour time-lag; nowadays, by studying the time-tables of the major air lines, a traveller could plan a round-the-world trip which would be, for him, one long sabbath. Like the desert nomad, he would still be expected to appoint his own sabbath, break his journey and consecrate his 'seventh day' to rest and to God.

The Jewish Sages, however, decided to introduce an element of stability into this arbitrary system, a standard measure, and this standard sabbath is no longer related to the dimension of time, but to that of space. It is the sabbath of the Holy Land, *Erets Israel*, Palestine. It alone may be said, in the metaphysical sense, to count, and just as Jews the world over turn towards Jerusalem when they pray, so the Jewish soul leans towards the sabbath of Jerusalem, the twenty-four hours of which constitute the absolute sabbath, just as the prescriptions of the sabbatical year and the jubilee year are valid only within the limits of the Holy Land.

And so, little by little, we have progressed from the day and the week to the measurement of the year, to which we shall now devote our attention.

It is here that we come face to face with the eleven days (to be exact, ten days and 17/90 of an hour) which represent the difference between the annual solar cycle and the twelve monthly orbits of the moon, which by rights should constitute a year. The Jews used these eleven days not as part of one of the two systems, either the solar or the lunar year, but as the hinge between them, thereby introducing into men's lives, with equal intensity, the contradictory demands of day and night, of the ever-radiant orb and the inconstant satellite, of the year and the month.

The basis of the Jewish year is the lunar cycle: 'This month shall be unto you the beginning of months: it shall be the first month of the year to you.' This biblical verse (Exod. 12:2) has permanently combined in one breath, within the Jewish consciousness, the notion of the 'lunar month' (*hodesh*) and that of the 'year' (*shana*). It has also linked these two ideas to the theme of Exodus, the escape from Egypt playing the role, in Jewish history, of a second and new creation. And it is this creative force, this perpetual passage from emptiness to fullness, this eternal *Passover* which guarantees that the waning is but a stage on the way to rebirth, that the Jews perceived in the symbol of the lunar phases, of which they discern the geometrical projection (as it were) in their own history. The moon is the foundation of the Jewish year because it introduces a meta-natural rhythm into the rigidity of nature.

But this meta-nature neither overshadows nor spurns nature. Like the soul, it must be sought in the body, the physical stability of the world, whose most evident symbol is the astral endurance of the sun; unchanging in its brilliance and its course around the zodiac, it holds together all metaphysical vagaries, encloses them and gives them their true significance.

Consequently the year is also solar, and has been so ever since the Bible spoke of the four seasons (*tekufot*) and associated the cycle of festivals with the seasons. How could the Passover be always celebrated in spring, Pentecost at harvest time, Tabernacles 'at the year's decline', if the lunar year alone held sway, with its lag in relation to the solar year? Twelve lunations comprise a year only if the eleven-day gap is made up within a cycle which allows nature to support supernature, as the tree nourishes a graft.

The means by which the Jews reconciled the lunar and the solar years remained, until the fourth century of the Christian era, purely empirical. They were based on observation, which had three facets: the very wide variety of spheres the phenomena observed; an acute sense of the need for internal coherence; and the use, in the final analysis, of scientific reference points which later made it possible to change the mobile empirical system into a fixed astronomical system.

Let us begin with the variety of the phenomena observed. The moon completes its revolution round the earth in 29 days, 12 hours, 44 minutes and 3 seconds. Consequently, to determine the precise moment of the 'new moon' (*neomenia*), i.e. the lunar zero, its 'birth' (*molad*) in Hebrew, testimony was needed from intelligent and reliable observers distributed at various points throughout the territory, who could record the moon's appearance during those fleeting seconds when it is visible, each month after sunset, in the first phase of its ascendant arc.

Nor were abstract dates assigned to the solar seasons. For a predominantly peasant people, spring and autumn had a practical meaning. Spring could come early, autumn late. The attention of observers was focused on such outward signs of nature, just as, for the balanced life of the population, it took economic factors into account: drought or excessive rainfall might lead to food shortages, speculation, social inequality or even injustice. Winter would sometimes destroy the roads, cut the bridges, damage the ovens for baking unleavened bread, all of which were needed by the pilgrims who set off from distant places to celebrate the Passover in Jerusalem. The lambs and pigeons which the pilgrims brought to sacrifice at the Temple would be born later than usual. When observers reported facts of this kind, they were taken into account in establishing the link between the synodic month and the seasons.

It was obviously necessary to bring all these different observations together in a synthesis and to have the conclusions weighed and established by a central body, with the power and authority to impose it on the people as a whole. This authority was vested in one man: the *Nasi*, spiritual leader of the Jewish people during the period of the Second Temple and after the destruction of the Temple, a function he combined with that of president of the Sanhedrin, for as long as this supreme court existed in history. But this authority was not vested in the Nasi out of respect for his person or function. Something else, some higher power, caused him to be the supreme arbiter, and this something, this fulcrum of the scales, one side of which held the lunar month and the other the solar year was the Land, the Holy Land, *Erets Israel*, and its capital Jerusalem.

Many talmudical texts describe the picturesque two-way movement which, every month and every year, brought testimony to Jerusalem and sent back the decisions towards the most distant Diaspora.

Every month, on the thirtieth day, a flurry of observers hastened from all over the territory to testify before the court at Jerusalem that they had seen the new moon. Mounts were lent to the aged. Guards were provided on dangerous routes. Sometimes whole families took to the road, communities, clusters of people. Since the testimony of two men of mature years was sufficient, Rabbi Aqiba one day attempted to turn back the procession at Lod, for no further witnesses were required. But Rabban Gamliel forbade him to block the way so as not to discourage observers for the following month. However large it might be, the crowd was joyfully received at Jerusalem, well fed and housed in a roomy inn, while the testimony was thoroughly scrutinized by the court. When the observations were received in good time on the thirtieth day, it was solemnly proclaimed Rosh Hodesh, first day of the following month. If night had fallen before the court could give its ruling, Rosh Hodesh was postponed to the following day.

And then the return flow began: the transmission from Jerusalem to the communities of Palestine and Diaspora of the fixing of Rosh Hodesh. To begin with at least, this was done during the night following the thirtieth day by the kindling of torches. At the top of the Mount of Olives, a sentry lit a torch attached to a long cedarwood pole. He swung it back and forth until he caught sight of another torch-bearer lighting his cedarwood brand on a hilltop further to the east, towards the horizon. And in this way the light signals advanced in the direction of Babylon, where the majority of Jews of the Diaspora lived. As soon as they caught sight of the signal on the high ground of the horizon towards the west, each of these exiles would climb to the roof of his house and wage a torch, with the result that on the night of Rosh Hodesh the whole of Mesopotamia appeared to the final sentinel posted with his torch on a mountain top like one vast firework display.

The Samaritans, so it is said, marred this happy celebration by themselves lighting torches on the hilltops of Gerizim and Ebal, at a time when the court at Jerusalem had decided to postpone Rosh Hodesh by one day. At some unspecified period of the Second Temple, therefore, use had to be made of a different, less spectacular means of communication. Messengers were sent out from Jerusalem to the communities of the Diaspora to bring the news of the fixing of Rosh Hodesh on the thirtieth day. Unlike the chain of torches, these messengers obviously could not reach all the Jews of Babylon in a single night. Many communities lived beyond the outer zone that was accessible by a twenty-four hour march. This had important consequences for the Jewish calendar: whereas in the vast 'urban zone' of Jerusalem traversed by the messengers Rosh Hodesh was celebrated as in Jerusalem itself, beyond this zone the first day of the month was fixed automatically on the thirty-first day of the preceding synodic month, which also led automatically to a general slippage of the Festivals, whether celebrated, like Rosh Hashana, on the first month of the Tishri, or like Yom Kippur on the 10th of Tishri, the Passover on the 15th of Nissan, Tabernacles on the 15th of Tishri or Pentecost on the fiftieth day after the day following Passover. It was agreed that, for this too distant Diaspora, the festivals would be celebrated for two days instead of the single day laid down in the Bible. This is the origin of the 'Second festive day of the Diaspora', which allowed the Jews of the Diaspora to be at one, give or take twenty-four hours, with their brethren in Jerusalem and its 'urban zone'.

It seems likely, moreover, that this more complex system had been introduced before the Samaritans and their ruses. The outward spread of the Diaspora from the period of the Second Temple, and particularly after the destruction of the Temple, had made it necessary. For while the accidents of physical geography made it possible to send messages between Jerusalem and the Babylonian Diaspora by torch telegraphy, how could the Jews of the Diaspora of Egypt, Greece, the Ionian Islands, Italy, Provence and Spain be informed of the exact date of Rosh Hodesh unless by messages that were bound to take a long time to transmit? The system of the 'two-day benefit of the doubt' must also be a very ancient one.

Thanks to this to-and-fro movement of observation and decision, whatever the means of communication, the months of the lunar year followed one on the other with a duration varying between twenty-nine and thirty days, while the Jewish people, scattered throughout the Mediterranean Basin, celebrated Rosh Hodesh and the Festivals in harmony with the Palestinian motherland and the Torah which emanated from Zion, Jerusalem, or, at least after their destruction, with the Torah emanating from *Erets Israel*, the Holy Land, centre of the world.

The same rhythm applied to the solar year. The eleven-day gap between the eleven synodic months and the sun's passage through the zodiac had to be made up, which required the intercalation of an additional lunar month approximately every three years. There was obviously complete freedom to make this intercalation at other than three-yearly intervals, so long as the balance was restored by skipping a year or, alternatively, by bringing two intercalary years closer together. Here again, all depended on the agricultural, social and economic signs that trustworthy messengers transmitted to the Nasi. He would first collect the material, then convene his colleagues of the Sanhedrin and, once the decision for intercalation had been taken, it would be solemnly transmitted to all communities in a message from the Nasi. The Talmud (Tractate Sanhedrin IIb) preserves the text of one of these messages and how it came to be written:

Rabban Gamliel, seated on one of the steps of the Mountain of the Temple, addressed Yohanan the Scribe who was present before him, three letters being ready for drafting in his presence. Take a first letter, he said to him, and write this: To our brothers of upper Galilee and lower Galilee, may peace be upon you! We inform you that the time has come to tithe the olives. Then take the second letter and write this: To our brothers of the South, may peace be upon you! We inform you that the time has come to tithe the wheat. And now take the third letter and write this: To our brothers of the Diaspora of Babel, to our brothers of Media and to all the other communities of the Jewish Diaspora, may peace be upon you forever! We inform you that as the pigeons are still too young, the lambs too weak, and the spring very late, it has pleased us as it has pleased our colleagues to add thirty days to this year.

Side by side with empirical observation, made coherent by the Nasi's authority, a further element provided even greater coherence: namely a system of scientific reference points. Only scholars versed in astronomy were eligible for the office of Nasi and those chosen to assist him in determining the synodic and intercalary months. The Bible already refers to the existence of a sort of academy of specialists, whose members were recruited from people of the tribe of Issachar, which was dedicated to scientific research (whereas its brother tribe, Zebulun, went in for trading and supplied the academy with funds).

And the children of Issachar, which were men that had understanding of the times, to know what Israel ought to do; the heads of them were two hundred; and all their brethren were at their commandment (1 Chr. 12:32).

The talmudical sources are more forthcoming. Rabban Gamliel had a virtual laboratory at Jerusalem, even a sort of observatory, whose walls were lined with mathematical and astronomical tables. This is where, every month, he questioned the 'observer-witnesses', requiring them to compare their empirical observations with the diagrams and formulae he showed them. At a later date outstanding scholars appeared on the scene, who deserve a place among the astronomers of antiquity. Suffice it to mention Mar Samuel, head of the Babylonian talmudical Academy of Nehardea, who flourished half-a-century after

Ptolemy. 'The paths of heaven are as familiar to me as those of Nehardea' he was in the habit of saying, and he went down in history under the appellation of *Yarhinaa*, Samuel the lunar. All these men possessed what was respectfully known by the people as 'the secret of the *Yibbur*', the word *Yibbur* meaning the intercalation (literally, 'pregnancy') of the thirtieth day of the synodic month and of the supplementary month in the solar cycle. Basically, this involved knowledge of a body of astronomical data. The important point to note is that, in the final deliberations, these data invariably took precedence over purely empirical data. Because mathematical precision prevailed over empirical imprecision it was possible to reveal the 'secret of the *Yibbur*'.

In the fourth century of the Christian era, before the spread of the Jewish Diaspora and because of the risk of excessive discrepancies, not to mention schisms, the Nasi Hillel II took the decision to change the mobile empirical system into a fixed astronomical system, based precisely on the body of mathematical and astronomical knowledge stored up by the Jewish community over the centuries.

Rabbi Adda, a Jewish contemporary of Ptolemy, had drawn up a series of tables in such meticulous detail that they were used to establish the supreme Table, the *Luah*, a term used to this day to designate the Jewish calendar. Nothing has been altered in the Jewish *Luah* since Hillel II; nothing will be altered until the coming of the Messiah. The starting point is the fictitious date of birth of the moon and the sun, Wednesday (the fourth day of Creation) of the year of chaos, prior to the year in which, on the first day, Sunday, the Creator uttered the august first phrase: 'Let there be light!' Starting from this purely mathematical *molad*, there developed the mechanism of the lunar year, the solar year, and their conjunction in a synthesis typical of the Jewish way of measuring the year. Beginning with the month of the Exodus from Egypt (Nissan), the lunar year is a regular succession of a month of thirty days followed by a month of twenty-nine days, except for the ninth and tenth months which, in accordance with a calculation laid down in advance until the end of time, include one of twenty-nine days and the other of thirty, or both of twenty-nine days or both of thirty days. The solar year is caught up by the lunar year in the course of a nineteen-year cycle of which the third, sixth, eighth, eleventh, fourteenth, seventeenth and nineteenth include an intercalary month which always becomes before the month of Nissan.

Thus the Jewish calendar is built on structures that are simple and, at the same time, so strong that they have resisted time, arousing the admiration of scholars throughout the long Ptolemaic era, not to mention that of the post-Copernican astronomers, as illustrated by the text of David Gans cited at the beginning of this study.

Jerusalem, 1972

BIBLIOGRAPHY

BUBER, M. *Werke*. Munich, Kösel/Lambert Schneider, 1962.
HESCHEL, A. J. *Les bâtisseurs du temps*. Paris, Éditions de Minuit, 1960.
——. *Dieu en quête de l'homme*. Paris, Éditions du Seuil, 1968.
LEVI, L. *Jewish chrononomy, the calendar and times-of-day in Jewish law, together with extensive tables*. New York, Gur Aryeh Institute for Advanced Jewish Scholarship, 1967.
MAHLER, E. *Handbuch der jüdischen Chronologie*. Leipzig, 1916.
NEHER, A. *Amos, contribution à l'étude du prophétisme*. Paris, Vrin, 1950.
——. *L'Essence du prophétisme*, 2nd ed. Paris, Calmann-Lévy, 1972.
——. *L'exil de la Parole*. Paris, Éditions du Seuil, 1970.
ROSENZWEIG, F. *Der Stern der Erlösung*, 2nd ed. Frankfurt, 1930.

THE CHRISTIAN CONCEPTION OF TIME

Germano Pàttaro

Christianity is only concerned with time as related to other problems and yet it might be said that in some ways the problem of time constitutes the core element in Christianity's conception of itself. Moreover, its interpretations of time are so varied that differences of persuasion among the various forms of Christianity may depend on the concept that each one has of 'time'.

This observation should serve to highlight two points. In the first place, over and above the various schools of thought, it is important to discover the significance of 'time' by trying to single out, so far as possible, the basic conception. To do this, the New Testament must be taken as a starting-point in order to arrive at a common generalized notion on which all forms of Christianity agree. In the second place, it should be noted that the questions which arise in connexion with time are subordinate to the theme of history, of which they necessarily constitute one aspect.

The treatment of time must therefore satisfy both these requirements in a balanced way. We shall naturally be dealing here with the Christian philosophy of time, but the theme of history will be constantly referred to, since it forms the backdrop that is essential to an understanding of our subject.

Let us note to begin with that in early Christian literature time is linked to the theme of the ages of the world.[1] The subtle variations of this concept generally relate to the history of salvation, which is divided into four successive periods, namely the age of natural law, the age of the Mosaic law, the age of grace and the age of glory.[2] This division, in its anthropological aspect, enables the author of the letter to Diognetus to speak of the '*Tertium Genus*', i.e. the Christian race, which is chronologically the last, after the pagan race and the Hebrew race.[3] And we do find in holy scripture the idea that the history of the world is unfolded in various stages the progress of which is linked to the notion of God's close alliance with Adam, Noah, Abraham and Moses.[4] This alliance or covenant runs through history and re-emerges with David,[5] who inaugurates the new and final age, namely that of the new David.[6] Christ, who is the new and last David, initiates the time in which all promises are fulfilled: the time which marks the transition from slavery to freedom,[7] from wrath to grace,[8] and from image to reality.[9] The time of Christ is final, it is an actualized, usable time which must follow its course. Luke calls it the time of the nations, Peter the time of conversion, while Paul describes it as a tension within which the Body of Christ is formed and which enables the Son to increase it as a kingdom which he will return to the Father.

These interpretations show that in the consciousness of Christianity there is a certitude that man and mankind experience the active intervention of God in regard to them. This intervention should be understood not in the cosmological sense, as an intervention affecting things, but in the anthropological sense as an intervention in the history of man.[10] Stated more explicitly, this God is the God of the patriarchs, the God of Abraham, Isaac and Jacob, and thus in the profession of faith which the Israelite makes during the sacrifice, he is not proclaiming the marvels of creation but the *mirabilia Dei* which God has accomplished for the people.[11] The prophetic eschatology[12] is never reduced to a symbolism, as would be done by a gnosticism transcending events, furnishing those who possess the key with an interpretation which would be without any meaning so far as time is concerned. The typology of the prophets and the allegory resulting from it spring from historical facts[13] and are so closely linked with them that eschatological hermeneutics is not always able to grasp the transition between the fact which takes place and what it prefigures. For that reason the interventions of God are anticipatory manifestations of the judgement he passes on men, a judgement which is accomplished already in the world.[14] In this sense, historical consciousness is able not only to open up the present to the future but also, as it were, to give effective meaning to the present in the light of the future which will come to pass as a result of God's certain intervention. This means that the *mirabilia Dei* are not meta-historical: they take place within the history of the world and succeed each other in an order which explains its destiny and over-all meaning.[15] While eschatology is often a certitude about the past, a return to the happy days of the exodus or of David which will finally be accomplished on the last day, it is more often and perhaps basically the promise of the new David, the new Temple, the new Jerusalem, the new Covenant.[16] In other words, the consummation promised by eschatology draws the past towards a future whose end, which will be at the same time the end of the world, will constitute the culminating point of all past history.[17]

A number of important conclusions clearly emerge from the foregoing. The first is that in the religion of the Bible, the interpretation of history radically precedes that of time and the latter derives from the former.[18] Furthermore, history is bound up with time and is subject to it in that it follows the internal thread of its movement.[19]

The second conclusion is that history has a meaning. This implies that time also has a meaning, defining as it does one of history's essential characteristics. The governing principle of Christianity is thus to be found within history and along the axis of time. This is an important point, since Christianity's conception of itself is often judged by meta-historical parameters which are closer to the a-temporality of philosophy than to the historicity of the Bible.[20]

The third and last conclusion is that there is a reciprocal relation between time and history that begins with Christ who, in the history which he fulfils and inaugurates at one and the same time, appears at a particular moment defined as the 'fullness of time',[21] in accordance with a plan that God has laid down in advance 'to be put into effect when the time was ripe'.[22]

The time for Christ and of Christ is thus a datable and open time; it lies within human events and can be classified according to the rhythm of the ages. Christ is said to have come 'in the reign of Caesar Augustus'.[23] In other words, the advent of Christ—or rather Christ as advent—is such that the time in which it occurs prepares for the advent of Christ by flowing in the direction of Christ,[24] who belongs to that time.[25] Furthermore, it leads time to its fulfilment: being fulfilled in Christ, it in turn belongs to him.[26]

This last conclusion introduces us to the heart of the problem that concerns us. Christ is first and last, both in relation to men and in relation to things,[27] and what he did constitutes a standard of comparison for everything and every man that has been, is or will be. Christians therefore take Christ as the point of departure in interpreting the whole succeeding ages of the world.[28] It therefore seems appropriate to consider the problem of time from a threefold point of view: first, by juxtaposing it to eternity; second, by examining how it may be said to be continuous in relation to a fixed event in whose light it can be interpreted; and third, by studying the division of time in order to discern the logic of the relations which bind together the various moments of its unfolding.

Linear time

It seems clear that time as conceived by the New Testament must be considered a continuous succession of moments, and thus line is the figure that best illustrates its continuity.[29] Christian time is said to be a linear time. This may be understood in contrast to the Greek conception of time which is diametrically opposed to the Christian revelation. The Hellenic world conceived of time as circular: unable to escape its own movement, time is enclosed in an endlessly repeating circuit offering no way out. To the endlessly repeated movements of men and things in this circuit no possible meaning can attach.[30] In this view, the future is not a form of liberation, which cannot take place as a transition from the past to the future but only by going from 'here' to 'elsewhere'.[31]

The result is to drive one towards a mystical self-discipline,[32] of a spatial type, where the 'elsewhere' in which one is liberated is situated 'beyond' time and outside 'time';[33] but such self-discipline is only for the individual.[34]

Christianity, on the contrary, attributes the maximum potentiality to time. Christian history is not in time despite time. It conceives of time as a liberation. Thus the past always appears as a possibility of the future and what takes place is always in expectation of its 'afterwards' as a real possibility. We can therefore neither flee nor escape from it, for it is the authority without which nothing that is historically significant takes place. This means that events are not rendered vain by time, but on the contrary that they give it its significance and its orientation. That is why the years must be counted from the birth of Christ—an event which is dated by time and which dates time. The fact that the Christ-event took place is therefore such that the entire past and the entire future take their own orientation from Christ. Similarly, the fact that the past and the future are the terrain on which human history unfurls is such that it is absolutely impossible to imagine the Christ-event outside their schema.[35] Time can no longer efface what has happened; for the same reason it cannot efface itself.[36] Thus it is for Christians the historical fact of Christ's work of salvation that confers value on time and also precludes any asceticism which would seek to escape it. Christianity is therefore incompatible, on the one hand, with the metaphysical interpretation which devalues time and replaces it by the dimension of 'here' and 'elsewhere'[37] and, on the other hand, with the historicist interpretation that empties history of its content for the sake of time because it does not allow us to pick out any key event that may serve to interpret the transition from past to future.[38] Christ is both the end-point and the goal of history,[39] and time is the condition that makes this twofold assertion possible.

Thus neither time nor history can be considered separately. Any abstraction is incompatible with Christianity. The Pauline πλήρωμα[40] proves this to us in the form of a dialectic between two terms which act upon one another without ever excluding one another. Similarly, when the author of the Epistle to the Hebrews speaks of the 'City of Heaven', he defines it as the future Jerusalem and the word 'future' means that beginning with any today, Christians already 'look forward to' it.[41] This city is now present because it is future and belongs to the temporal series of events. This is confirmed by the fact that the tendency to deny any meaning to time in history found its ultimate expression in the heretical gnosticism of the Valentinian type,[42] where we find again the Greek notion of a time which renders everything vain. Thus gnosticism eliminates the human reality of Christ, with a Docetic tendency that robs the Incarnation[43] of its historico-temporal dimension by simultaneously rejecting the Old Testament which, by the same logic, is no longer regarded as a historico-temporal prophecy of the Father's covenant with mankind, fulfilled in Christ.[44] In addition, it rejects eschatology as a vision of time as operative and a generator of tension, and sees in the Parousia (Second Coming) a transition from time to eternity similar to that from 'here' to 'elsewhere'.[45] If indeed we examine

Christian writings from this standpoint, to see where and in what respects there is a narrowing in the scope of New Testament eschatology,[46] we see how eschatological thinking is depleted to the extent that Christianity comes under Greek influences. It is not so much a question of the increasingly obvious remoteness of the Parousia which modifies from within the significance of the Christian expectation, as of the influence of a different concept of time which, lending support to a spatial view of history, seems to make the future less significant.[47]

This last observation enables us to note how much the Christian notion of eternity, considered as a modality of time, differs from the Greek conception. The Hellenic world and its philosophy provide an alternative vision of eternity,[48] in accordance with the dichotomy which deprives the past-future opposition of all significance and focuses the 'here'–'elsewhere' opposition instead. The New Testament ascribes no meaning to 'the absence of time',[49] whereas this, on the contrary, is what eternity seems to consist in according to neo-Platonism. For the early Christians, time and eternity were not opposites. When John, in the Book of Revelation,[50] has the angel say that there will no longer be χρόνος, he is not implying the absence of time but the end of all delay, which amounts to stressing the density of time. The Epistle to the Hebrews removes all doubt in the matter for, like Revelation, it states: '... he that shall come will come, and will not tarry';[51] in this context the reference is to Christian expectation conceived of as a time of patience. Culmann has had occasion to point out, after a close analysis of the language of the New Testament, that eternity—which must be regarded as an attribute of God—is an infinite time. Stated more clearly, what is called 'time' is nothing other than a fraction, limited by God, of the unlimited duration of God's time.[52]

This is to be understood in the light of the nature of the Gospel message, seeking as it does to reaffirm the uniqueness of the history of Salvation, in relation to which there can be no spatial equivocation concerning time. Furthermore, New Testament exegesis is now in a position to asseverate that the word αἰών[53] expresses both eternity, viewed as unlimited time, and historical time considered as limited time. For God, as for man, by virtue of the uniqueness of the history of Salvation, time and eternity are united through a linear relation that is ever closer.[54] Naturally, eternity is not time and the distinction must be kept, but no longer as an opposition. The fundamental idea is linked to the profession of faith regarding the omnipotence of God in so far as that omnipotence makes God 'the eternal', for it is he who was in the beginning, is now and ever shall be.[55] That is why it was said that time, which emanates entirely from God and depends on him, must also form part of God's 'duration'.

The difference between time and eternity apparently lies in the juxtaposition between a particular time and a limitless time. The expressions referring to limitless time relate to its extension before and after. The statement in the First Epistle to the Corinthians[56] in which Paul speaks of the wisdom of God 'which was ordained before the ages' is not concerned with an eternal wisdom lying outside time but with a wisdom that precedes the time experienced by man. The Old Testament tradition lies in the same stream and the distinction that it makes between 'present time' and 'the time to come', αἰών οὗτος, αἰών μέλλων,[57] confirms the special way in which it understands, from the linguistic and conceptual points of view, the relationship between limited and unlimited. When 'this present world' is described as 'evil',[58] this does not break the thread: what is meant is that the opposition between this present time and the time to come is attributable to sin—not that sin itself stems from the temporal condition, but from the men who live in it and partake of it. The reference to original sin as a beginning is consequently linked to the history of a time and not to the time of that history.[59] Essentially therefore it is the notion of limit which distinguishes the two αἰῶνες.

If we were to attempt to portray the matter in diagram form, we could take as a central point the αἰών οὗτος which begins with the Creation and ends with the Parousia, and then locate in relation to it the αἰών ἐκ τοῦ αἰῶνος, the time which stretches away without limit before the Creation and, at the other extremity, the αἰών μέλλων. Paul's expression,[60] 'the end of the ages' means that with Christ, the time devoted to awaiting him is ended, the final time being henceforth inaugurated in him for ever. Paul's judgement is purely qualitative and does not modify the point of view characteristic of the New Testament.

A few observations will help to clarify this aspect of Christian thought in regard to time.

The first relates to the time which precedes the 'present time', what Protestant theology calls the time of God's 'rest'.[61] The beginning of John's Gospel seems to imply a radical 'before' situated beyond time and distinct from it, which would justify an interpretation favourable to eternity. A more attentive exegesis, however, shows that the expression 'in the beginning' must be read in relation to the Creation, which has its ontological antecedent in the reality of God: it is in God that the Creation must be understood as the principle of the αἰών οὗτος in which history as it concerns man begins. That history is the key to our interpretation: it is already present in God and it is in him that it prepares itself for man.[62] So far as revelation is concerned, the interesting aspect of this dimension which goes back to God by transcending the 'present-time' lies in the fact that it is always spoken of in relation to God's plan. Similarly, when Paul speaks of the time that will follow the Parousia when 'God will be all in all',[63] it is always in relation to that plan that the biblical word unfolds.

The second observation concerns the radical future: apocalyptic eschatology, both in the Gospels and in Paul, speaks of the future in a strictly temporal sense.[64] This is not because literary language expresses itself through a series of recognizable signs and ages counted in years, in the manner peculiar to the genre in question: in this connexion Bultmann may be justified in calling, in the name of a new approach to hermeneutics, for reduction (*epoche*) of the cultural forms linked to the cosmological universe of time.[65] Rather is it because the αἰών μέλλων is already actualized at the 'present time', a time which, because of Christ, has already begun? Thus what is situated after already exists before, i.e. in time, and not only beside or beyond time, because Christ's judgement is already at work in the time which we are living.[66]

The third observation has to do with a comparison between the αἰῶνες based on the fact that 'future time' is not a mere re-impression of 'past time' which is situated beyond, at the beginning. The future is not a passive authentification of the past in an inert history which, returning on itself, destroys itself; if this were so, time would be like a film run backwards in which the beginning and the end become indistinguishable. The future, starting from Christ, is 'a new path of life',[67] so much so that its unfolding opens on a 'what we shall be has not yet been disclosed'.[68] That is why the αἰών ἐκ τοῦ αἰῶνος is the time that preceded the Creation, during which the history of our salvation was prepared; the αἰών οὗτος is the time which unfolds between the Creation and the Parousia, in which that history is entirely fulfilled; and the αἰών μέλλων is the time which consummates the new and final Creation and leads it to its fulfilment. Thus the first and last times are not the same, while the second is the locus of the first as well as containing the seeds of the third. In this way, the linear reading of time presented by the New Testament revelation seems plausible and well founded.

Time and times

This general view of time makes it necessary to inquire into the meaning of the internal times which unfold following the line of the three αἰῶνες, in other words to ask ourselves whether there are not individual times which may be regarded as having a particular status.

The way in which John the Evangelist proceeds when he studies the work and mission of Jesus Christ is significant in this regard. He observes that all Christ's action is directed to a precise moment of time which Christ calls the hour for which he has come. Christ sees in that hour the time in which his mission must be accomplished. Its importance is decisive: every other moment of his life is subordinate to that hour and to that day, and is interpreted in relation to them.[69] The linguistic use of the word ὥρα obviously refers not only to a chronological time but also to what must take place at that point in time. The location in time is however determinant, in the sense that what must happen will happen at that moment and neither before nor after. The Evangelist indeed is at pains to dwell on that hour, since it belongs to Christ and no one can share it with him. It is absolutely original and constitutes 'the time' which co-ordinates and unifies 'the times' of his life. It is the 'central hour' in which everything is fulfilled and which gives meaning to everything. It is the 'hour' of his death[70] which thus becomes the 'hour' *par excellence* of Christ and all biblical history. Here is another unit of measurement for all temporal comparison. Its excellence derives from the fact that it has been fixed by God.[71]

John's words are not isolated nor do they reflect only the point of view of the Fourth Gospel: they form part and parcel of the general line of thought which begins with Christ's preaching and is developed in the Synoptic Gospels and in the Epistles of the Apostles. The language here is different from John's and is characterized by the predominant, though not exclusive, use of the thematic expression καιρός which corresponds, substantively at least, to the ὥρα of the Fourth Gospel. When used in non-biblical language, this expression usually means a time that is fixed inasmuch as it is the active and passive occasion of an event which is considered significant, and by reason of which the time is called καιρός, either from the chronological point of view, because it is the time itself which is excellent, or from the anthropological or historical point of view, because its significance depends on what happens, or from both points of view together, which gives it the maximum semantic content. The New Testament uses the term καιρός in this sense, but reinforces it with two elements, the weaker of which refers to the third aspect mentioned—which is the prevailing one in the linguistic concepts of the New Testament texts—relating to the peculiarly biblical nexus of time and history, whereas the stronger[72] and the more singular one makes the καιρός and the καιροί depend upon God's direct decision and choice in their regard. Thus the fourth use of καιρός, so far as its origin and its intention are concerned, is equivalent to the Johannine ὥρα. In short, the καιρός is time determined by and for an event decided upon and chosen by God for a precise purpose.

The καιρός is thus a key word for the general hermeneutics of the New Testament and, in particular, for a real understanding of the concept of time in the Bible.

The fundamental καιρός is Christ with his life and his work. This is the indication given by Paul,[73] who thus expresses the word of the Father which is manifested in Christ through his preaching. In the same way and with the same expression the Apostle Peter defines the whole earthly life of the Master. Furthermore, Jesus, himself, according to the testimony of the Synoptic Gospels, personifies in his passion and death the fundamental and central καιρός of his life. This is, in any case, part of what is meant in the Easter text of Matthew[74] where Jesus, describing the last events of his life, says: 'My time is at hand.' But more broadly, the Gospel message situates the various καιροί in the single exhaustive discourse concerning the Kingdom, which is said to be 'at hand' not in the spatial sense but in the eschatological-temporal sense.[75] The Kingdom as καιρός unfolds in a series of particular events the first of which is linked to the fact that Christ is come into this world, whereas the others, which form a more or less well articulated succession, are the announcement of the Glad Tidings to the oppressed, the healing of the sick, the defeat of the devils and, lastly, the victory over the world and its covetousness. Their link with the Kingdom makes of these times, which have been rendered significant by their redemptive efficacy, the καιροί directed according to a Messianic logic towards the καιρός of the death and resurrection of Christ. Through these times there runs a thread that makes them the histories of a history, the times of a time, dominated by all Christ's action. Furthermore, these καιροί can create no confusion because the logic which guides them is different from that which lends significance to the times decided upon by men. John's words, 'My time is not yet come: but your time is always ready',[76] imply that man's time, which comes from man, depends on him because it is in his hands. Every decision makes it timely, whereas the time of Christ does not depend upon a human decision but on the choice of God. What is at stake for Christ is not a moral time-limit established by human will, but a plan chosen directly by the will of God. The καιροί of Christ are therefore the times that are decisive for the history of God in this world. No one has power over these 'times', and their reality is marked by the impossibility of repetition which binds them irrevocably to God in such a way that they can no longer be emptied of their meaning or replaced.

It should be noted in this connexion that the definitive character of the καιροί of Christ stems from the fact that in them Christ exhausts the span of days assigned to him by his Father, but also from the fact that all the other times marked by God, while they may also be καιροί, depend upon the central, exclusive character of the Messianic times. It is in this sense that Peter localizes these times, all the times of prophetic history, when he states: 'This salvation was the theme which the prophets pondered and explored. . . . They tried to find out what was the καιρός . . . to which the Spirit of Christ in them pointed, foretelling the sufferings in store for Christ, and the splendours to follow'.[77] In this sense, the New Testament approach to καιρός implies a movement of history the internal times of which, gravitating round the καιρός, extend backwards, yet continue to depend upon the time marked and characterized by the action of Christ. This confirms what we said above with regard to the linear conception of time.

The same observation applies to future times. Thus the language used by John in the Book of Revelation refers to the end of the world as καιρός. The time of this end is assimilated to the καιροί of Christ, because it is also said to be 'at hand', an expression which perfectly describes the temporal condition of the Kingdom.[78] The discourse of the Synoptic Gospels adopts a similar standpoint, recalling that there are due times or seasons still to be fulfilled in regard to the history of Salvation whose fulfilment the Father will ensure because of Christ. The fate of Jerusalem is linked to the fact that it did not recognize the καιρός of Christ when he visited it.[79] The καιρός consequently has an eschatological dimension which owes its significance to its dependence on the 'time' of Christ. The future καιροί are thus characterized by the fact that they form a continuous strand of the same history and, fulfilled in themselves, they yet owe their fulfilment to the fact that they always form part of the Messianic times which are the times of the Kingdom and which belong to the time of Christ. Paul asserts this explicitly when he charges Timothy 'to keep the commandment unstained and free from reproach until the appearing of our Lord Jesus Christ . . . at the proper time, καιροῖς ἰδίοις'.[80] The future καιροί therefore depend on the past καιρός. 'Christ Jesus', says Paul again, '. . . gave himself as a ransom for all, the testimony to which was borne at the proper time, ἴδιοι καιροί.[81] Confirmation of this continuity may be had at least indirectly by noting that, in any event, even the καιροί of the future are not subject to man's decision but depend directly on the explicit will of God[82] to which man is subject when he lives the interval of time which separates him from the 'due time' in an active manner, characterized by the 'watchfulness'[83] which places present time at the disposal of God's καιρός.

This last observation then introduces the theme of the 'present time' which is the time situated between the καιρός of Christ and that of the last day. The New Testament affirms that the present time is also dominated by God's καιρός and relates to the condition of the Christian community in dependence on Christ its Lord. This community has an internal time, peculiar to it, because it is founded in Christ, dominated by his καιροί and perpetuated through its testimony to his work. Peter states that 'The time has come for the judgement to begin; it is beginning with God's own household'.[84] The time of the Church is the καιρός of judgement. In this sense, all Paul's preaching is concerned with the edification and fulfilment of this 'due time'. He professes '. . . the secret hidden for long ages and through many generations, but now disclosed to God's people, to whom it was his will to make it known—to make known how rich and glorious it is among all nations. The secret is this—Christ among you, the hope of a glory to come'.[85] The notion of καιρός is here expressed by the word νῦν in virtue of a terminological and lexical interchangeability vouched for by the affirmation: 'Christ among you.' The time of the Church is the time that begins at Pentecost, the αἰών dominated by the *maranatha*, by the invocation: 'The Lord cometh.'[86] It is the time of the eschatological waiting, which Paul calls also σήμερον, the present and now final 'today'.[87] It is the 'present time' which must be used to advantage. From this point of view, the whole burden of ethical injunction for this time would seem to entail simply an active disposition to prevent the καιρός of Christ from being in vain.

We may therefore draw the following conclusion about the relation between time and times: the key καιρός is that of Christ, within which there exist other καιρός that are differentiated, co-ordinated with one another and oriented according to the καιρός of his death.

In this connexion, there are still other καιροί that are defined and fixed by the will of God in the past as in the present and future. They are subordinate to the καιρός of Christ which integrates them as particular times in a single history, a stream of prophecy whose earlier reaches foretell it and later ones fulfil it.

These καιροί constitute the organic history of the Bible because they are the key times or segments of a time which unfolds in the direction of Christ and proceeds from him. In this sense, from a phenomenological and general point of view, this history is a short episode in the long history of mankind. It takes place within it, not beside it and, consequently, is conscious of being able to interpret from within the whole succession of human events, the times of which continue to be judged by its times.

Thus a double circle is formed: the first one groups round the 'time' of Christ a series of 'times' closely linked to Christ; the second groups all human time together and subjects it to the irrevocable judgement of bibilical history, so that, for Christians, time and history cease to be profane because they are subordinated to this irrevocable judgement.

Time and its internal tension

As we have seen, all times which are singled out as key times, and, more generally, all time, springs from the central καιρός of Christ and is therefore in a relation of continuity with that καιρός. This unifying process explains why the New Testament expresses the certitude that Christ is both 'the end point' and 'the goal' of history. This assertion is important; the relationship between the time of Christ and the other times must be clearly understood if we are to apprehend the dialectic which underlies it.

As we have seen, in the panorama of times presented by biblical tradition, the central time, which is present time, lies between the Creation and the Parousia, and the times before the Creation and after the Parousia may be defined in relation to that central time. On the linear continuity of this triple schema there is superposed, as a dynamic internal principle generating tension, another schema which establishes a division between present and future times. Present time coincides with the time that runs from the Creation to the Parousia and concerns our own history as men, whereas future time, that which still remains to be fulfilled, coincides with the ultimate time. The transition from present to future time takes place through the 'Messianic time',[88] a final point towards which all present time tends. In this classification of times, the qualifying element *par excellence* is the coming of the 'desire of all nations'[89] in whom are to be fulfilled the promises which God made to the Patriarchs and which were sealed by the pact of the Covenant. Consequently, for biblical tradition, the significance of everything that happens lies essentially in the future with the result that the centre of gravity of the entire time line is radically shifted ahead. The New Testament on the contrary, while it respects this view of time, offers a different interpretation of it, since it places the central point on which the significance of the unfolding of time depends, not at the frontier between present and future time, where the one is transformed into the other, but at the very heart of present time. The Christian consciousness recognizes that the transition from the old to the new 'eon' takes place in the time experienced by mankind, and it identifies it with the Messianic era which was accomplished with the coming of Christ. Christ's time is therefore the time of times and the καιρός of his death and resurrection becomes the key to the interpretation of the ages of the world.

The situation thus established is totally different from that contemplated by Hebraic tradition, in that the Messianic era can no longer be situated in the future; it lies now and for ever in the past, which is the past of Christ for all the future that comes after him. In this sense, although the biblical conception of time is preserved, Christianity is distinguished by its own radically different interpretation, one that is based not on time but on the division of time. Thus a seemingly formal distinction entails a different conception of history and reinforces the interdependence of time, events and their interpretation. This statement takes on its full importance when we consider, for example, the very nature of Christianity. In the Judaic view of time, Christianity would be no more than a heretical sect whereas, in fact, because of this different division of time, it takes Judaism to its end point, goes beyond it and transcends it.

What makes the Christian interpretation exceptional and singular is that it asserts that the καιρός of Christ, while it is situated in time and consequently forms part of time by becoming past, does not deprive the future of its own significance, so that the future is not reduced to a mere long drawn-out memory of the Christ 'moment–event'. If it were, the time after Christ would correspond to the time following the Hebraic Parousia. Although already definitively come, Christ remains the one who is still to come, since the 'last day' of present time is the 'day of the Lord' who will judge the αἰών οὗτος in order to open the definitive way to the plenitude of the αἰών μέλλων. For Christianity there is a Parousia that is still to be accomplished, so that the present still leaves scope for the past and the future, which give meaning to the time situated between the Christ who has already come and the Christ who is still to come. In the name of Christ, therefore, the Judaic interpretation which still places the accent on the future is both superseded—because Christ has 'manifested' himself—and maintained—because 'his coming' is still awaited. For Christians, the time that runs from the Creation to the Parousia is thus characterized, in an apparent ambiguity, by a dialectical tension between an 'already' and a 'not yet' which cannot be thought of separately, but are such that the first is the ground and condition of the second.

The very fact that all the New Testament literature was written after the death and resurrection of Christ and that it bases its own authority on these events shows implicitly that the authors were aware that they were shifting the time axis by referring to Christ in the past. The problem, however, is somewhat different: the question is whether it is Christ himself who assigns this value to time by placing this dual emphasis on it and subordinating the future to the past. All that we have said about the relation between each past and future καιρός and the καιρός of Christ shows that it is Christ himself who makes his time the yardstick for this dialectical, tension-generating division. All the sayings about the Kingdom are related to the theme of the 'Lord and Master' who has come and is going away to return on the 'last day' and ask for an account of what man 'has done' with what was given to him and the interest he should have earned on it.[90] Eschatology is thus not dominant in Christianity, as the school of Werner and Schweitzer claim. It is only one feature the significance of which concerns only Christ and what he has already accomplished. It is the very person of Christ which is the point of intersection where time enters into this dialectic, because it is in Christ that time finds its final plenitude and that the time of judgement is first actualized in the world.[91] His resurrection is the critical moment where the old αἰών is overcome and, while retaining its temporal identity, marks the beginning of the new αἰών. Christ is indeed the 'first-born' resurrected from the dead.[92] The early Christians were so conscious of this fact that the reality of the Resurrection constituted for them a subject linked fundamentally to faith and not to hope.[93] It is not hope that must be relied on to enter into the Passover and therefore into the new αἰών. If the future, and not the past, were the point round which time gravitates for Christians, it would be through hope that the awaited Salvation would be gained. This would produce a history whose καιροί would point to an ultimate καιρός, to the Messianic καιρός which, by the very fact that it was the last, would transform the time of expectation into a time without meaning throughout its entire duration. But if on the contrary hope is founded on faith,[94] it proclaims that the past of Christ is never absent of the arc of time and asserts its certitude that he is Κύριος of the entire future.

The objection that is generally raised to this is that the teaching of the Apostles is not explicit on this point. Careful exegesis however reveals that the eschatological outlook which seems linked to an imminent return of Christ is not invalidated because that return has not happened, but takes on a deeper meaning as soon as it is discovered that the duration of the time of expectation is secondary.[95] In any case, exegesis makes it clear that the certitude of the eschatological future always stems from the certitude of the past of the death and resurrection of Christ. John the Evangelist does not shrink from appearing illogical when, after stating that from the point of view of faith, judgement has already been given, he then states that the same sentence will be passed on the last day. He knows that time now depends upon the logic introduced by Christ. The theme of judgement indeed illumines all Christian eschatology, establishing an indissoluble bond between hope and faith because of the accusation brought by God against the world,[96] for it is the prophetic reality which announces the last judgement.[97] Paul himself, who believed that the interval between the Ascension and the Parousia would be extremely short, and even thought that he would still be alive on the day of judgement, later took a broader view of the notion of expectation,[98] and revealed that his thought was essentially linked not to the duration of the expectation, but to Christ's promise that he would return, which explains the interval of time between these two events.

It has still to be explained in what sense time that is past in relation to Christ is redeemed in him in such a way that the αἰών ἐκ τοῦ αἰῶνος is a time which already moves towards its καιρός. John's teaching about the Incarnation dovetails perfectly with Paul's. The age preceding the Incarnation is the time when God plans the Salvation that He wishes to offer the world through the action of Christ who is to come. The will of God and His precepts determined the entire action of the Passover.[99] The Creation itself is considered from this point of view, so that no time, even if we go back to God's immanent self-existence, can be thought of other than as a time willed and chosen by the Father for the Son.[100] Paul expressly states that it is only possible to speak of Adam in relation to Christ, Adam having been first in relation to him, whereas Christ is precisely the second Adam.[101]

It thus seems possible to draw the conclusions that follow. Christ is the Lord of all times, which he consequently unites in himself, and thus the past is fulfilled in him and the future is anticipated in him. This then confirms the assertion that Christ is the 'goal' and the 'end point' of history. That is why his disciples proclaim that all things are brought together in the Risen Christ.

Accordingly it may be said, without falling back upon a metaphysical or purely eschatological interpretation, that time has its centre at its end point, to which a strictly temporal value must be assigned. This καιρός must be considered in its chronological density. The future is therefore judged by Christ, not as a closed book, but in an active, creative way because it is the time in which, by his Resurrection, he has given the world the possibility of redemption from sin—the stigma of Satan, who has however already fallen from heaven.[102]

This sin which he has conquered is still at work in the world, as is the Prince of Darkness who was 'a murderer from the beginning'.[103] The course of time is therefore not yet finished and the present time can only be consummated at the moment of the second coming of Christ.[104] This time which was required by the οἰκονομία of God is entirely governed by it, and thus the time of man becomes the time of Christ and Christ becomes the centre of all history.

Ritual time

There exists for Christians a ritual reading of time within the framework of their liturgy. The liturgy must be understood as the totality of those acts whereby the Christian community celebrates the memory of Christ by proclaiming his coming, living his presence and prophesying his return.[105] Every liturgical ceremony is consequently an ἀνάμνησις, a καιρός and an ἔσχατον of the unique καιρός of Christ. The liturgy thus represents history as it is lived by Christians and as they express it ritually, in the twofold tension which links them to the time of Christ who has already come while at the same time turning them towards the time when Christ will come again, transforming their present into a καιρός founded on ἀνάμνησις and directed in turn towards the ἔσχατον. Hence the chronology of Christians has a particular characteristic which depends precisely on the ἀνάμνησις of the temporal acts of Christ.[106] It takes place in an annual cycle, within which there is a weekly cycle.

It should be noted that the ritualistic character of the Christian calendar is bound up with the acts which determine its rhythm, the significance of which depends on the way in which one interprets the nature of the καιρός, i.e. whether the accent is placed on ἀνάμνησις or on the ἔσχατον. This question of emphasis is so important as to be at the root of the diversity of denominations into which Christians are divided.[107] We must therefore present here the doctrine which transcends these divisions in order to get at the fundamental consensus in regard to the ritual chronology of time.

We have thought it advisable to follow the historical order in which Christians have arranged the chronological composition of sacred time, this order being in fact the same as that dictated by the essential significance of the events. We shall therefore consider first the weekly cycle, and then the annual cycle.

The Lord's Day

The Evangelists describe the life and actions of Christ as they took place according to the rhythm of the Hebraic calendar. Thus they state that Jesus arose on the Sabbath.[108] According to the Hebraic tradition which is the basis for the cosmogonic account in Genesis, the Sabbath becomes the first day,[108a] in the same way as the day on which God created light and separated it from the darkness wa the first day.[109] This term has been used to designate the day on which Christians meet to celebrate the Paschal rite of the Lord's Supper. This fact shows clearly that, in their liturgical ritual, Christians commemorate the day of the Resurrection as the first day of the week. In other words, Christians consider that the day on which they meet to 'break bread' in order to celebrate the Eucharist of the Death and Resurrection is the first day of the week. This clarification helps us to understand that the value of this day does not spring from the fact that it was the first day of the Judaic week but depends on the Christian ritual. Christians in the Hebraic world must have realized almost immediately that they could not make the new requirements of Christianity fit in with the Sabbath tradition of the Hebrews.[110] Since they had a totally different reason for their gathering, they had to choose another day to celebrate the Lord. Thus was established the tradition of the 'Lord's Day', the κυριακή ἡμέρα,[111] which the Romans translated by the expression *dominicus*(*a*) *dies*, or simply *dominica*.[112] This reference to the Κύριος indicates that on that day Christians celebrate the Christ who has become Κύριος through his Resurrection.[113] It should be noted in this connexion that the κυριακή or *dominica* is the only day differentiated by Christians in the series of days of the week that was first Judaic and then Graeco-Roman. That means that this day has a determining and decisive character. It must indeed be regarded as the day on which Hebraism is superseded, in such a way that if Hebraism is the religion of the Sabbath, Christianity is the religion of Sunday.[114] The Sabbath is to the Law what the κυριακή is to Grace. The day of the Resurrection marks the transition from one Testament to the other, the New Testament superseding the Old. It is in this sense that the κυριακή has acquired a unique status in both Eastern and Western Christian traditions. Language also reflects this choice that has been adopted in all linguistic areas with the exception of the Semitic which has kept the term *Sabbath* and the Germanic which has taken the words *Sonntag*, 'Sunday', etc. from the planetary calendar.[115]

These names bring us to a delicate matter, that of the amalgamation of the weekly chronology of the Christians and the weekly calendar of the Greeks and Romans, organized as it was, according to a planetary scheme that gave the days of the week the names of the five planets known at the time (Mars, Mercury, Jupiter, Venus and Saturn), to which they added the names of the luminaries, the sun and the moon. The names of the days showed so clearly that each day came under the influence of a planet that ritual prayers were recited as an invocation sacred to the planet of the day.[116] Without going into the many questions of history and chronology which arise in this connexion, it must be stated that the intrinsically religious character of the pagan week has always given pause to Christians, because they feared a syncretism[117] which, at least formally, could always give rise to a certain confusion, especially at the level of popular manifestations.[118] For this reason, despite the coincidence of the κυριακή with the 'day of the sun', Christians have been unable to adopt that term. A few limited attempts however were made in this direction, because it was easy to transpose these two names through analogy, by referring either to the tradition of Genesis which presents 'the first day of the Lord' as the day on which 'there was light', or to the Resurrection which readily lent itself to metaphors linked to the symbolism of light[119] mingled with the themes of the new life and joy. These attempts were abortive because of a fear of the inevitable syncretism that would result, as we have seen, not from linguistic usage but from the contamination to which religion would implicitly be exposed.

The final acceptance of *dominica* as the Christian day *par excellence*, the permanent beginning of the week, took place as part of the process that began with Constantine's Peace and ended with Valentinian and Theodosius.[120] Under Constantine this day devoted to worship of the Lord also became an established day of rest on which all work ceased,[121] a characteristic which it kept when it became part of the traditional calendar throughout the Christian world. It should likewise be noted that the particular and exclusive attention given to the κυριακή, by virtue of the sacred mystery which it symbolized and which led to its being considered as 'the day' *par excellence*, had no effect on the names of the other days of the week which, at the popular and civil levels, continued to be based on the planetary terminology. At the liturgical level, however, their generic names were kept because of the possibility of syncretic contamination. Thus the days were considered to be 'feasts' (in Latin, Italian and Spanish:

feria; in French: *férie*). Those were numbered from the first to the sixth, reserving for the seventh day the name *Sabbath*, taken from the religious world of the Old Testament, with which the Christian community stands in a relationship, at once of continuity and discontinuity.

The liturgical year

In the first century, the weekly rhythm based on the κυριακή broke up the ritual year into a succession of weeks in which only Sunday was singled out as something special. From the second century onwards, however, the year was little by little subdivided to meet the liturgical requirements which gave rise to characteristic periods in the year likewise based on the Paschal καιρός of Christ.[122] Thus a particular week gradually came to stand out from the others. It was called 'Holy Week' because it is the week in which, recalling chronologically the acts accomplished by Christ ,[123] Christians commemorate his death and resurrection.[124] The Resurrection is celebrated by the Catholic Church, the Reformed Church and the Anglican Church on the Sunday following the March equinox. This date has an ideological explanation: the Christian Passover, as we have already seen in connexion with Sunday, marks the radical transition from the economy of the Old Testament which is that of the law to the economy of the New Testament which is that of Grace. Consequently, it is impossible to celebrate the Christian Passover in the context of the Hebraic Passover, even though Christ celebrated the new Passover in that framework.[125] The underlying religious motivation is determinant and explains the major controversies to which its date has given rise.[126] The desire to celebrate successively in time the mysteries of the passion, death and resurrection of Christ has thus led to the determination of three successive moments which correspond to the moments experienced by Christ, namely the Thursday, Friday and Saturday preceding Easter Sunday which constitute the basic triduum of the whole Christian calendar.[127] In the dynamics of the καιρός of Christ, these days, which are defined as 'holy', lead to the great vigil of Saturday night which merges into the dawn of Resurrection Sunday. This 'night' marks the high point of the Christian liturgical year, because it unites in a single movement the reality of the Cross with the reality of the Resurrection[128] and constitutes the focal point which determines the logic of the other liturgical times.

This liturgical καιρός of course has no didactic and hence external meaning. It exerts a stimulating effect through an ethical and figurative representation of the acts of Christ. On the basis of the καιρός, a time chosen and willed by God, Christians regard this moment as a critical and operative time, a moment in which the Christ of the past transforms the Christian community and, even if it is subject to the laws of αἰών οὗτος, causes it to live henceforth in αἰών μέλλων. It is therefore a time which transforms time because of the events which take place in it. It is called the 'due time'.[129] And just as the moments in the life of Christ are those in which his καιρός, the ὥρα which becomes the νῦν for Christians, is prepared and then accomplished, so the celebration of the triduum and Easter Sunday entails both a time of preparation and a time of accomplishment, though the time considered does not lose its underlying continuity. There exist then two other significant periods the first of which, called 'Lent', is linked to the καιρός of the death and Good Friday which it prepares by 'penance and fasting', whereas the other, the so-called 'Paschal time' or 'time after Easter', is linked to the καιρός of the Resurrection and the 'Sunday' *par excellence* which it manifests as part of the 'victory of the risen Christ'.

The period of 'Lent' has a history. Starting from the original nucleus formed by the 'three holy days', it was extended backwards until it included, from the sixth century onwards,[130] seven Sundays before Easter and provided an opportunity for an inner pilgrimage, and later a daily one, which makes this period the time of 'conversion'.[131] Christians undertake to pattern their lives during this period on the model of Christ who lived his life according to the rhythm of the καιροί which led to the central and final καιρός of his Death and Resurrection, with stress laid on the Lord's Passion. It is for this reason that Lent is a period of penance. It is the period in which 'the old man gives way to the new man' according to the mystery of 'death'.

Similarly, the time 'after Easter' is made up of the fifty days which separate the Resurrection from Pentecost. Originally this was a uniform time, devoted to the permanent celebration of the Mystery of the Resurrection, contemplated and presented in all its redeeming aspects. The internal structuring of this period only came later with the determination of meaningful stages which were still part of the actual movement of Easter.[132] One period became particularly outstanding, namely 'the octave' which follows Easter Sunday and ends on the next Sunday. It is referred to as '*in albis*', a period devoted to the time of Christ who 'appeared' after the resurrection, the time of his 'glorious manifestation'.[133] Also prominent is Pentecost Sunday, the day on which the Christian Church celebrates the 'descent of the Holy Spirit', sent by Christ as a gift to the Church to be his witness among men. It is from the 'Holy Spirit' that the Church receives its mission of announcing the resurrection to the world. Pentecost is thus pre-eminently the day of the Church because it is the day on which Christ celebrates his continuity in history by making the Church an eschatological community in which the 'Kingdom' is perpetually fulfilled and in which the αἰών οὗτος is transformed into αἰών μέλλων.

Alongside this weekly and annual chronological cycle of Easter, there grew up, towards the end of the third century and the early decades of the fourth, another chronological cycle, the time of the 'Nativity' and the 'Epiphany',[134] which became a permanent cycle throughout the Church.[135] Its emergence was due, at least originally, to apologetic and ideological considerations. The 25 December in Rome—and the 6 December in Egypt—were marked by the celebration of winter solstice rites in honour of the *Natalis Invicti*. The conviction grew slowly that it was desirable and necessary to confront the pagan myth of the birth of the sun with the Christian reality of Christ, God who had come into the world as a sun that would never set.[136] The birth of Christ was thus the ritual nucleus whereby these two dates were given their specific character and raised above their pagan significance.

This measure had become urgent because the celebration of the *Sol Invictus* was much emphasized and very widespread, inspired as it was by the cult of Mithras and, more generally, that of the sun. The apologetic concern is explained by the political ideology of Constantine who sought to bring about a synthesis between these two events or at least to make them compatible. It was this emperor who decided that Sunday should be set aside for rest both as the 'day of the Lord' and as the 'day of the sun'.[137] For that matter, the transition from the *Natalis Invicti* to the *Natalis Christi* was justified, at least indirectly, by several Messianic indications.[138] The choice of the dates is thus an ideological, not a chronological, question.

It should be noted here that the word *Natalis* (Nativity) formed part of the terminology of vital statistics as well as the political vocabulary. From the point of view of civil status, the term applied to birth, whereas in the political sense it referred to the emperor's holidays (*fastes*). In this latter aspect, it belonged to the rhetoric of the court and its purpose was to exalt the important anniversaries of the ruler.[139] Christians, on the contrary, gave it its first meaning in their religious vocabulary, designating by the term *Natalis* the day of baptism which marked the second birth that 'came from heaven' according to God's will.[140] As applied to Christ, this term took on its full civil and religious meanings. The day of the 'Nativity' became the day on which men commemorate the birth of the Son of God to man, on which they glorify him because God thus manifests himself to the world, and on which they celebrate his life-giving bounteousness because through his very birth he causes men to be reborn to God by making them sons of his Father.

This last idea suggests that the Nativity of Christ also implies Easter, in so far as the καιρός which transforms the αἰῶνες resides not in his coming into the world but in his death and resurrection. In this connexion, the Western concept of Christmas overlaps the Eastern concept of Epiphany and, despite its different connotations, is identified with it. Linguistic usage relating this ritual feast is also significant. In the civil and religious vocabulary of the Greeks and Romans, the term Epiphany designated the political and military holidays of the sovereigns; it also designated the appearances or manifestations of gods to men.[141] These two meanings were used in the New Testament[142] and widely incorporated in ritual expressions. Thus from a single concern two Nativity traditions grew up, differing in emphasis despite their basic similarity. The two feast days were therefore kept and in due course exerted an influence on one another when the Epiphany came to be accepted by the West and Christmas by the East. However, Christmas places the accent on the birth of Christ, whereas the Epiphany emphasizes the presentation of Christ to the world.[143] Let us also note that, at least at the level of popular devotion, the Mystery commemorated has been and is to some extent lessened, in so far as it is considered an accomplished καιρός which is on the same level as the καιρός of Easter, whereas in the deeper sense of all liturgical and ritual tradition it depends on the Paschal καιρός. Thus, when Christians celebrate the Nativity of Christ to glorify his coming, they are celebrating their own rebirth rather than the birth of Christ, even if the former depends upon the latter, viewed and interpreted in the light of 'Holy Week'. Thus, also, the seasonal ceremonial of the Nativity is closely linked to the Easter ceremonial on which it is utterly dependent.[144]

This being so, it is understandable that the time of Christmas was later extended backwards, since this feast called for preparation during a ritual period leading up to it. This period, called Advent, is subject to the same internal logic as governs the ritual of the two feasts for which it prepares. Actually, from the linguistic point of view, the Latin word *adventus* translates the Greek word παρουσία which is the lexical equivalent, at least in its political connotations, of the word ἐπιφανία.[145] In pagan ritual language, the term *adventus* signifies the theophany whereby God manifests himself to the faithful in his temple[146] and, by a natural lexical transposition, it easily took on a similar meaning for Christians. In this last sense it essentially expresses the time 'of the coming of the Lord', either through the act of the Incarnation or on the day which is to be the 'last' day of the world because it marks the consummation of the αἰών οὗτος. Advent is thus the season in which are fulfilled the Messianic times considered as the beginning which will henceforth always coexist with the αἰών μέλλων. Hence it is the eschatological time *par excellence*, even though it had an element of ascetism and penance originally. In the various ritual traditions, the liturgical texts used for Advent are those of the expectation of the Messiah, or those of the major prophecies,[147] or those of the Annunciation.[148] Here too, the internal logic governing this time in all its aspects links its ritualistic expression as a whole to the Paschal καιρός, because it is Christ who, through his Death and Resurrection, has initiated the Messianic times and the eschatological expectation of the final transition to the αἰών μέλλων. We may recall that, from the chronological point of view, Advent lasts four or five weeks before 25 December, according to the liturgical traditions.

'Ember days'

Christians attribute a sacred character to four periods in the liturgical year called 'Ember days' which are linked, at least in their deeper meaning, to all liturgical times but are conceived of as periods of penance and hence marked by ritual fasting of an ascetic nature. Each Ember day period is made up of a series of three days, namely Wednesday, Friday and Saturday,[149] the first two of which have always been considered ritual fast days.[150] Chronologically, Ember days occur as follows: the first, in the first month (March), gradually became identified with the first week in Lent; the second, in the fourth month, coincides with the first week after Pentecost; the third, in the seventh month (September), falls between the sixteenth and seventeenth Sundays after Pentecost; the last, in the tenth month (December), is part of the third week in Advent. Since these periods correspond to the different seasons of the solar calendar, they are referred to by the name of the season. We may add that this reference to the cycle of the seasons is not unrelated to the place that the Ember days have in chronology, their origin obviously going back to the ritual blessing of nature performed in a culture of a rural and agricultural type. Thus the period of the fourth month corresponds to the *feriae messis*, that of the September equinox to the *feriae vindemiales*, and that of the week before the winter solstice to the *feriae sementinae*.[151] This original significance has remained in the traditions and customs of popular devotion and has been partially kept in the liturgical texts which describe the content of the *actiones sacrae*. But under this relationship, the origins of which go back to pre-Christian traditions, both Judaic and pagan, there lies another, or rather two others, in connexion with the liturgical cycle of which Ember days constitute high points. The first is a relationship with the community, since the Ember days are periods of commitment not only to fasting but also to the practice of prayer and alms-giving. Thus this time is always devoted to God and to the service of our human brethren, in an unceasing refrain essentially characterized by the exercise of charity. The other is a relationship with nature which is the 'house' that God has given to man, where he lives by Divine Providence, and the Ember days are used to transform these gifts into a permanent offering of adoration and gratitude addressed to him by all Creation.[152]

Conclusion

In the first place, the certitude that time is useful and opportune clearly belongs to the conscious tradition of Christians; for them time is not an inert thing nor is its course a simple chronological unfolding without aim. Time is the internal rhythm of a history which unfolds between the two poles of the two Advents of Christ, the one which took place at the time of Palestine and the one which will take place with the 'close' of the 'last day of the world'. It is a time in which we 'come from' in order to 'go towards'. It is the time in which a faith justifies and gives rise to a hope which transforms time and all the events that take place in it in order to transform them into an expectation fraught with meaning. Moments within time are therefore the stages of a journey in which Christians 'walk before the Lord' in an 'exodus' of the present αἰών to the future αἰών. These stages introduce the Christian to the reality of Christ, in such a way that his ἀνάμνησις becomes a καιρός charged with ἔσχατον.

Secondly, the linear time characteristic of the New Testament outlook unfolds progressively, and without break of continuity, to the rhythm of the κυριακή of Easter, which draws all other time to it in an ever open spiral, so that the liturgical year becomes the transition of all human history to a perpetual becoming.

Thirdly, the protagonist of this time is not man in his individuality but the whole Christian community, the people of God who raise themselves up to the πλήρωμα of Christ. Time is therefore not a movement which regulates the life of the individual in his privacy, but a rhythm in whose thread are manifest the *mirabilia Dei* on behalf of his People. Thus the liturgical times are not a didactic, exalted way of recalling the καιροί of Christ; they are the very rhythm of a community which, in celebrating the *Mysteria Christi*, manifests itself to mankind by living and showing forth the transformation which Christ brings about in it. Hence the times of the Church, like the 'leaven' of the Gospels, are what cause the already transcended αἰών οὗτος to rise in order to release the 'seed' of the αἰών μέλλων already present in human time because of Christ.

NOTES

1. A. Luneau, *L'Histoire du Salut*, p. 37–76 (in particular the bibliographical section: III, p. 20–1), Paris, Beauchesne, 1964.
2. Saint Irenaeus, *Adversus Haereses*, IV, 25, in: Sources Chrétiennes Series, No. 100, Vol. II, p. 704-11, Paris, Éditions du Cerf, 1965.
3. Epistle to Diognetus, I, 1, in: *Bibliotheca Sanctorum Patrum* I, Vol. III, p. 124.
4. A. Luneau, op. cit., note No. 1 above, p. 37-45. Cf. Genesis 1:1–2, 5:1–6; 6; 12; 19–20.
5. H. Cazelles, *Les Livres des Chroniques*, p. 31, Paris, Éditions du Cerf, 1954, cf. Book of Samuel 16; Amos 9:11; Hosea 3:5; Isaiah 9:1–6.
6. Jeremiah 30:9; cf. Jeremiah 23:5–6; 33:15–17; Ezekiel 34:23–4; 37:24–5.
7. Epistle of St. Paul to the Galatians 4:1–7; cf. Hosea 14:2–9; Ezekiel 16:59–63; Gospel acc. to St. Matthew 5:17–19; Epistle of St. Paul to the Romans 3:31.
8. Epistle of St. Paul to the Romans 1:16–26; 8:1; Acts of the Apostles 17:30.
9. Epistle of St. Paul to the Colossians 2:17; cf. Epistle to the Hebrews 8:5; 10:1; First Epistle of St. Paul to the Corinthians 10:6.
10. G. Lambert, 'Création dans la Bible', in: *Nouvelle Revue Théologique* (Louvain), 1953, No. 75, p. 252–81; cf. Joshua 24:16–8.
11. Deuteronomy 24:5–10; cf. 6:20–4; Joshua 24:2–13; Exodus 19–24; Leviticus 26.
12. J. de Senarclens, *Le Mystère de l'Histoire*, p. 140-225. Geneva, Éditions Roulet, 1949, cf. Isaiah 24:1–15; Jeremiah 11:9–13.
13. S. Amsler, 'Prophétie et Typologie', in: *Revue de Théologie et de Philosophie* (Lausanne), 1953, No. 3, p. 139–48, cf. Hosea 2:14–15.
14. A. Feuillet, 'Le Messianisme du Livre d'Isaïe', in: *Revue de Sciences Religieuses* (Strasbourg), 1949, No. 36, p. 182–228, cf. Daniel 12:1–3.
15. Isaiah 2:2–4; 42:1–6; 45:14–16; cf. Amos 9:11–15; Gospel acc. to St. Matthew 24–25; First Epistle of St. Paul to the Thessalonians 5:13–18.
16. Isaiah 46–9; Second Epistle of St. Peter 3:13; Revelation 21:15. Isaiah 2 and 41; Ezekiel 40–8.
17. Second Epistle of St. Paul to the Corinthians 3:12–18; cf. Gospel acc. to St. Matthew 25.

18. R. Niebuhr, *Foi et Histoire*, p. 49-65, Neuchâtel and Paris, Delachaux et Niestlé, 1953.
19. O. Culmann, *Christ et le Temps*, p. 13–19, Neuchâtel, Delachaux et Niestlé, 1947.
20. ——, p. 43–8.
21. Epistle of St. Paul to the Galatians 4:4; cf. Gospel acc. to St. Mark 1:15.
22. Epistle of St. Paul to the Ephesians 1:10.
23. Gospel acc. to St. Luke 2:1; cf. 3:1.
24. J. Guillet, 'Thème de la Marche au Désert dans l'Ancien et dans le Nouveau Testament', in: *Revue de Sciences Religieuses* (Strasbourg), 1949, No. 36, p. 161–81. Cf. Exodus XXXVI, 20 et seq.; Isaiah 41:8–20; Epistle of St. Paul to the Hebrews 22:7–8.
25. O. Culmann, op. cit., note No. 19, p. 13–15, cf. Gospel acc. to St. Matthew 1:1–17; Gospel acc. to St. Luke 2:23–38.
26. Gospel acc. to St. John 1:11; cf. Gospel acc. to St. Matthew 21:38.
27. Epistle of St. Paul to the Colossians 1:17–21; Gospel acc. to St. John 1:3; First Epistle of St. Paul to the Corinthians 8:6.
28. O. Culmann, op. cit., note No. 19, p. 11–12.
29. ——, p. 13–14; 21–2; 26–42.
30. H. Ch. Puech, 'La Gnose et le Temps', in: *Eranos Jahrbuch, 1951*, Vol. XX, p. 59–67 and 60–3, Zurich, Rhein Verlag, 1952.
31. O. Culmann, op. cit., note No. 19, p. 26 et seq.
32. J. Sivadjin, *Le Temps, Étude Philosophique, Physiologique et Psychologique*, Vol. 1, p. 15 et seq., Paris, Hermann, 1938.
33. H. A. Wolfson, *Philo: Foundation of Religious Philosophy*, Vol. I, p. 115–37, Cambridge (Mass.), Harvard University Press, 1947.
34. O. Culmann, op. cit., note No. 19, p. 37–8.
35. ——, p. 57–65 and 86–123; cf. Gospel acc. to St. Matthew 11:1–6; Gospel acc. to St. John 3:18–21; 12:31–2.
36. R. Niebuhr, op. cit., note No. 18, p. 207–24.
37. E. A. Lévi-Valensi, *Le Temps dans la Vie Morale*, p. 45–57, Paris, Vrin, 1968; O. Culmann, op. cit., note No. 19, p. 43–77.
38. R. Aron, *Introduction à la Philosophie de l'Histoire*, p. 17–44 and 284–90, Paris, Gallimard, 1938.
39. J. Héring, *Le Royaume de Dieu et sa Venue*, p. 184–218, Neuchâtel, Delachaux et Niestlé, 1959; P. Lengsfeld, *Adam et le Christ* (French trans.), p. 124–30, Paris, Aubier, 1970; cf. Epistle of St. Paul to the Galatians 4:4; Gospel acc. to St. Mark 1:15; Epistle of St. Paul to the Ephesians 1:10.
40. H. Schlier, *Lettere Agli Efesini* (Italian trans.), p. 115–19. Brescia, Paideia, 1965; L. Cerfaux, *La Théologie de l'Église suivant St. Paul*, p. 250, 272–5 and 310–11, Paris, Éditions du Cerf, 1965; cf. Epistle of St. Paul to the Romans 11:25; Epistle of St. Paul to the Ephesians 1:23; Epistle of St. Paul to the Colossians 2:9; First Epistle of St. Paul to the Corinthians 10:26.
41. O. Culmann, op. cit., note No. 19, p. 38; A. Luneau, op. cit., note No. 1, p. 217–18; cf. Epistle of St. Paul to the Hebrews 11:10 and 16; 12:22; Epistle of St. Paul. to the Galatians 4:26; Revelation 4:1.
42. F. Sagnard, *La Gnose Valentinienne et le Témoignage de Saint Irénée*, p. 628 (the words: αἰών and αἶῶνες), Paris, Vrin, 1947.
43. J. Liebaert, *L'Incarnation*, 1) *Des origines au Concile de Chalcédoine* (French trans.), p. 53–7. Paris, Éditions du Cerf, 1966; cf. H. Ch. Puech, *Le Manichéisme*, Paris, Civilisations du Sud, 1949.
44. E. Ammann, 'Marcion', in: *Dictionnaire de Théologie Catholique*, IX, c. 2009–24.
45. F. Sagnard, op. cit., note No. 42, p. 518–19.
46. O. Culmann, op. cit., note No. 19, p. 56-123; cf. H. M. Feret, *L'Apocalypse de Saint Jean*, Paris, Corréa, 1943.
47. ——, p. 42, No. 2.
48. F. Amerio, 'Eternità', in : *Enciclopedia Filosofica*, Vol. II, c. 1099–101, Florence, San-

soni, 1968; J. Guitton, *Le Temps et l'Éternité chez Plotin et chez Saint August in*, Paris, Vrin, 1959.

49. H. Sasse, αἰών, in: Kittel (ed.), *Theologisches Wörterbuch*, I, p. 204–7.
50. Revelation 10:6; cf. 12–11; 16:17; 21:6; Daniel 12:7.
51. Epistle of St. Paul to the Hebrews 10:37; cf. Habakkuk 2:3.
52. O. Culmann, op. cit., note No. 19, p. 44.
53. H. Sasse, op. cit., note No. 49, I, p. 200–7; K. Barth, *Die Kirchliche Dogmatik*, Vol. II, I, p. 685–8. Zollikon/Zurich, Evangelischer Verlag-Flamberg Verlag, 1940.
54. O. Culmann, op. cit., note No. 19, p. 37–41.
55. Revelation 1:4 and 8; 4:8; cf. Epistle of St. Paul to the Hebrews 13:8.
56. First Epistle of St. Paul to the Corinthians 2:7; cf. Epistle of St. Paul to the Colossians 1:26; Epistle of St. Paul to the Hebrews 3:11; Gospel acc. to St. John 1:1; 27–24.
57. H. Sasse, op. cit., note No. 49, p. 201–3.
58. Epistle of St. Paul to the Galatians 1:4; cf. Epistle of St. Paul to the Ephesians 2:2.
59. P. Schoonenberg, *Dal Peccato Alla Redenzione* (Italian trans.), p. 20–7, Brescia, Queriniana, 1970. A. M. Dubarle, *Le Péché Originel dans l'Écriture*, Paris, Éditions du Cerf, 1958.
60. First Epistle of St. Paul to the Corinthians 10:11.
61. O. Culmann, op. cit., note No. 19, p. 45–6.
62. First Epistle of St. Paul to the Corinthians 2:7; cf. Epistle of St. Paul to the Colossians 1:15–21; A. Darlap, in: *Mysterium Salutis* (Italian trans.), Vol. I, p. 139–60. Brescia, Queriniana, 1967.
63. First Epistle of St. Paul to the Corinthians 15:28; cf. 5:23; 11:3.
64. J. Moltmann, *Teologia della Speranza* (Italian trans.), p. 33–91. Brescia, Queriniana, 1970; H. Fries, in: *Mysterium Salutis*, op. cit., note No. 62, Vol. I, p. 289 et seq.
65. R. Bultmann, *History and Eschatology*, Edinburgh, The University Press, 1957; A. Malet, *Mythos et Logos*, p. 59-75, Geneva, Labor et Fides, 1962.
66. Gospel acc. to St. John 16:8; cf. 12:31; 16:33; Epistle of St. Paul to the Colossians 2:14–15. H. U. von. Balthasar, in: *Mysterium Salutis*, op. cit., note No. 62, Vol. VI (1971), p. 179–80.
67. Epistle of St. Paul to the Romans 6:4; cf. 7:6; Second Epistle of St. Paul to the Corinthians 5:17; Epistle of St. Paul to the Galatians 6:25; Epistle of St. Paul to the Colossians 3:10; Epistle of St. Paul to the Ephesians 4:13–14.
68. First Epistle of St. John 3:2; cf. 2:28; Epistle of St. Paul to the Colossians 3:4.
69. H. U. von Balthasar, op. cit., note No. 66, p. 238–41.
70. ——, p. 238–9.
71. Gospel acc. to St. John 7:6; 17:1.
72. G. Delling, καιρὸς, in: Kittel (ed.), *Theologisches Wörterbuch*, III, p. 456–65.
73. Epistle of St. Paul to Titus 1:3; cf. Epistle of St. Paul to the Romans 16:25–6; Epistle of St. Paul to the Colossians 1:26.
74. Gospel acc. to St. Matthew 26:18; cf. Gospel acc. to St. Luke 21:36.
75. Gospel acc. to St. Matthew 3:2; 4:17; 10:7; cf. 13:18–51; R. Schnackemburg, in: *Mysterium Salutis*, op. cit., note No. 62, Vol. V, p. 375 et seq; J. Alfaro, in: ibid., p. 815 et seq.
76. Gospel acc. to St. John 7:6.
77. First Epistle of St. Peter 1 : 11; cf. Daniel 9:24–6; Gospel acc. to St. Luke 24:26; Acts of the Apostles 3:18.
78. Gospel acc. to St. Luke 19:44; cf. Gospel acc. to St. Matthew 3:2 and 4:17.
79. Gospel acc. to St. Luke 19:44; cf. 1:68 and 78; Daniel 9:4.
80. First Epistle of St. Paul to Timothy 6:14–15; cf. 2:6; Epistle of St. Paul to Titus 1:3.
81. First Epistle of St. Paul to Timothy 2:6.
82. Gospel acc. to St. Mark 13:32; cf. Gospel acc. to St. Matthew 24:42–4 and 25:13; Gospel acc. to St. Luke 13:39; Revelation 3:3.
83. Gospel acc. to St. Luke 17:26–7 and 34–5; cf. Gospel acc. to St. Luke 12:39–40 and

42–6; Acts of the Apostles 20:31; First Epistle of St. Paul to the Corinthians 16:13; First Epistle of St. Paul to Timothy 5:6.
84. First Epistle of St. Peter 4:17; cf. Ezekiel 9:6; Amos 3:2.
85. Epistle of St. Paul to the Colossians 1:26–7; cf. Epistle of St. Paul to the Ephesians 1:18 and 3:16.
86. B. Botte, in: *Noël, Épiphanie, Retour du Christ*, p. 25–42, Paris, Éditions du Cerf, 1967.
87. Epistle of St. Paul to the Hebrews 3:7 and 13:15.
88. Gospel acc. to St. Luke 4:18–19 and 21; cf. Gospel acc. to St. Matthew 11:5–6; Isaiah 11:1–10; 35; 61.
89. Hagga 2:8; cf. Isaiah 60:9.
90. Gospel acc. to St. Matthew 25:14–19; cf. Gospel acc. to St. Luke 19:12–15.
91. Gospel acc. to St. John 16:11; cf. Epistle of St. Paul to the Colossians 2:15; Epistle of St. Paul to the Hebrews 2:14.
92. Epistle of St. Paul to the Colossians 1:18; First Epistle of St. Paul to the Corinthians 15:20; Acts of the Apostles 26:23.
93. First Epistle of St. Paul to the Corinthians 15:17; cf. Acts of the Apostles 13:32–9.
94. Epistle of St. Paul to the Hebrews 11:1; cf. Epistle of St. Paul to the Romans 5:5 and 8:24; Epistle of St. Paul to the Galatians 5:5; First Epistle of St. Paul to the Thessalonians 2:19; First Epistle of St. Peter 1:21.
95. Second Epistle of St. Peter 3:8; Luneau, A., op. cit., note No. 1, p. 39–45.
96. N. Füglister, in: *Mysterium Salutis*, op. cit., note No. 62, Vol. V, p. 240–4.
97. First Epistle of St. John 2:18; cf. First Epistle of St. Paul to Timothy 3:1.
98. Second Epistle of St. Paul to the Corinthians 5:1; Epistle of St. Paul to the Philippians 1:23.
99. Epistle of St. Paul to the Ephesians 3:9; Epistle of St. Paul to the Colossians 1:26.
100. Epistle of St. Paul to the Colossians 1:16; First Epistle of St. Paul to the Corinthians 8:6.
101. Epistle of St. Paul to the Romans 5:13 et seq.; First Epistle of St. Paul to the Corinthians 15:45 et seq.
102. Gospel acc. to St. Luke 10:17–18; cf. Gospel acc. to St. John 12:31.
103. Gospel acc. to St. John 8:44.
104. Acts of the Apostles 1:7 and 11; Epistle of St. Paul to the Philippians 3:20–1.
105. First Epistle of St. Paul to the Corinthians 11:26; cf. Gospel acc. to St. Matthew 26:29; Gospel acc. to St. Mark 14:25; Gospel acc. to St. Luke 22:19, J. Alfaro, in: *Mysterium Salutis*, op. cit., note No. 62, Vol. V, p. 883–6; O. Casel, *Le Mystère du Culte* (French trans.), p. 21–89, Paris, Éditions du Cerf, 1964.
106. L. Bouyer, *La Vie de la Liturgie*, p. 231–42, Paris, Éditions du Cerf, 1960; R. Schulte, in: *Mysterium Salutis*, op. cit., note No. 62, Vol. VI, p. 17–9.
107. For the Catholics: P. Rado, *Enchiridion Liturgicum* (2 vol.), Rome and Fribourg, Herder, 1961. For the Orthodox: P. Evdokimov, *Orthodoxie*, p. 239–62, Neuchâtel, Delachaux et Niestlé, 1959. For the Protestants: R. Paquier, *Traité de Liturgique*, Neuchâtel, Delachaux et Niestlé, 1954. For the Anglicans: H. Field, *The English liturgies of 1549 and 1661, Compared with Each Other and with the Ancient Liturgies*, London, S.P.C.K., 1920.
108. Gospel acc. to St. Matthew 28:1; Gospel acc. to St. Mark 16:2 and 9; Gospel acc. to St. Luke 24:1; Gospel acc. to St. John 20:1 and 19.
108*a*. The Evangelists gave the name 'Sabbath' (μία, πρώτη σαββάτου) to the day of the Resurrection (even though it was the first day of the week) by analogy with the religious importance of the Hebrew sabbath, instead of inventing a new word for it.

A vestige of this is to be found, even today, in the Aramaic Christian tradition which refers to Sunday as '*ḥad bshabba*'. This explains the relation between the day of the Resurrection and the first day of Creation.
109. Genesis 1:5; A. Luneau, op. cit., note No. 1, p. 109–10 and 162–3.
110. H. Dumaine, article 'Dimanche', in: *Dictionnaire d'Archéologie Chrétienne et de Liturgie*,

Vol. IV, p. 900–5, Paris, Éditions Letouzey & Ané, 1907–53; B. Botte, in: *Le Dimanche*, p. 8–12, Paris, Éditions du Cerf, 1965.

111. W. Foerster, κυριακὸς, in: Kittel (ed.), *Theologisches Wörterbuch*, Vol. III, p. 1095–6; cf. Acts of the Apostles 1:10; Revelation 1:9–10.
112. Tertullian, De Corona 3:4, in: *Corpus Christianorum* 2, p. 1043; 11:3 in: ibid., p. 1058; P. Rado, op. cit., note No. 107, Vol. II, p. 1088–90.
113. W. Foerster, op. cit., note No. 111, in: Kittel (ed.), *Theologisches Wörterbuch*, Vol. III, p. 1088–94.
114. Ignatius of Antioch, Magnesii 9:1, in: *Bibliotheca Sanctorum Patrum* I, Vol. II, p. 106.
115. P. Rado. op. cit., note No. 107, Vol. II, p. 1089; B. Botte, op. cit., note No. 110, p. 14.
116. E. Schürer, Die Siebentägige Woche im Gebräuche der Christlichen Kirche der Ersten Jahrhunderte, in: *Zeitschrift für Neutestamentliche Wissenschaft*, p. 25–7 and 20–2, Berlin, 1905.
117. C. Barlow (ed.), *Martino de Braga. Opera Omnia. De Correctione Rusticorum*, p. 189–90, New Haven (Conn.) Yale University Press, 1950.
118. Saint Augustine, in: Psalms 61:23; in: *Corpus Christianorum* 29, p. 792.
119. Maximus of Turin, Homily on the Pentatench I; in: *Patrologie latine* 57, c. 371; cf. Ignatius of Antioch, Magnesii 9:1.
120. E. Dublanchy, article 'Dimanche', in: *Dictionnaire Théologique Catholique*, Vol. IV, c. 1311–13.
121. Eusebius of Caesarea, Vita Constantini IV, p. 18-20, in: *Patrologie Grecque* XX, c. 1165–8.
122. First Epistle of St. Paul to the Corinthians 5:7. J. A. Jungmann, *Eredità Liturgica ed Eredità Pastorale* (Italian trans.), p. 388–91, Rome, Morcelliana, 1963.
123. L. Duchesne, *Origines du Culte Chrétien*, p. 247–8, Paris, De Boccard, 1925.
124. L. Bouyer, *Le Mystère Pascal*, Paris, Éditions du Cerf, 1960.
125. cf. note No. 105.
126. G. Fritz, 'Pâques', in: *Dictionnaire de Théologie Catholique*, Vol. XI, c. 1948–54.
127. L. Bouyer, op. cit., note No. 124, p. 71–371; P. Rado, op. cit., note No. 107, Vol. II, p. 1188–217.
128. ——. p. 375–449.
129. C. Vagaggini, *Il Senso Teologico della Liturgia*, p. 214–30, Rome, Paoline, 1957.
130. E. Vacandard, 'Carême', in: *Dictionnaire de Théologie Catholique*, Vol. II, c. 1724–34.
131. J. Leclercq, *La Liturgie et les Paradoxes Chrétiens*, p. 114–32, Paris, Éditions du Cerf, 1963.
132. O. Casel, *La Fête de Pâques dans l'Église des Pères* (French trans.), p. 89–129, Paris, Éditions du Cerf.
133. R. Cabié, *La Pentecôte, l'Évolution de la Cinquantaine Pascale au Cours des Cinq Premiers Siècles*, p. 238–56 and 222–37. Tournai and Paris, Desclée, 1965.
134. L. Duchesne, op. cit., note No. 123, p. 271–81.
135. B. Botte, *Les Origines de Noël et de l'Épiphanie*, Louvain, 1932; P. Rado, op. cit., note No. 107, Vol. II, p. 1111–17.
136. O. Culmann, *Noël dans l'Église ancienne*, p. 29–36, Neuchâtel, Delachaux et Niestlé, 1949.
137. cf. note No. 121; B. Botte, op. cit., note No. 110, p. 24–5.
138. Malachi 4:2; Gospel acc. to St. John 8:12; O. Culmann, op. cit., note No. 136, p. 33–6.
139. H. Stern, *Le Calendrier de 354*, p. 76–9, Paris, 1953.
140. L. Bouyer, *La Vie de la Liturgie*, op. cit., note No. 106, p. 249–52.
141. B. Botte, op. cit., note No. 135, p. 68–76; J. Lemarié, *La Manifestation du Seigneur*, p. 48–51, Paris, Éditions du Cerf, 1957; cf. Epistle of St. Paul to Titus 2:11 and 13.
142. J. Daniélou, in: *Noël, Épiphanie, Retour du Christ*, op. cit., note No. 86, p. 66–84.
143. B. Botte, op. cit., note No. 135, p. 77–88; C. Mohrmann, *Epiphania*, p. 8–13, Nimwegen, 1953.

144. L. Bouyer, op. cit., note No. 106, p. 257; X. Weiser, 'Le Folklore de l'Avent et de Noël', in: *Maison Dieu*, No. 59, 1959, p. 104–31.
145. J. Hild, 'L'Avent', in: *Maison Dieu*, No. 59, 1959, p. 10–25.
146. Thesaurus Linguae Latinae, I, p. 837.
147. P. Rado, op. cit., note No. 107, Vol. II, p. 1107–9.
148. J. H. Dalmais, Le Temps de Préparation à Noël dans les Liturgies Syrienne et Byzantine, in: *Maison Dieu*, op. cit., note No. 144, p. 25–7.
149. G. Morin, 'L'Origine des Quatre-Temps', in: *Revue Bénédictine* (Maredsous, Belgium), 1897, p. 337–46; P. Rado, op. cit., note No. 107, Vol. II, p. 1099.
150. P. Rado, op. cit., note No. 107, Vol. II, p. 1096–8.
151. Saint Leo, Sermo 12:3, in: *Patrologie latine* 54, c. 170; 17:3, in ibid., c. 185; 20:3, in ibid., c. 189; 79:1, in ibid., c. 419.
152. G. Morin, op. cit., note No. 149; J. Janini, *San Siricio y las Cuatro Temporas*, Valencia, 1958.

MOSLEM VIEWS OF TIME AND HISTORY

An essay in cultural typology

Louis Gardet

Appendix The empirical apperception of time among the peoples of the Maghreb

Abdelmajid Meziane

Working hypotheses

Depending on the point of view one adopts, one may speak of Moslem culture as one, temporally and spiritually, or as many—Arab, Iranian, Turkish, Indian, etc.; many though these different aspects may be, however, and despite their 'regionalism' (*iqlimiyya*), there is nevertheless a number of common lines of force running through them all. This unity-diversity dialectic will be constantly borne in mind throughout this study.

Islam aspires to and, indeed, possesses universality. Moslem values have over the centuries been expressed through the medium of Persian, Turkish, Urdu and Malay. But it is from an Arabic book, the Koran, that they ultimately derive, and it was in Arabic that they were first formulated and developed. To say this is not to deny, for example, the Greek, Iranian, or Indian influences which will also have to be borne in mind. Some of these influences, in Iran or in the Indian sub-continent for example, impregnated the natural behaviour and culture of those peoples, while others, the Greek influence for example, were welcomed, and even sought, as a 'foreign' contribution which continued to inspire philosophers and men of learning; but they always merged with the basic Arabic-Moslem elements which took them over, reshaped and reoriented them. There is surely an analogy here with the present situation with regard to the scientific and technological values of modern Western civilization.

It follows that if we wish to get to the experiential reality, to explore it deep into a people's subconscious, there is no practical alternative to considering the Arabic vocabulary relating to time. This will be our first line of approach. We shall then attempt to identify the specific nature of the Moslem vision or visions of time and its evolution, both in terms of the dominant teaching (Sunnism) and in terms of a number of other interpretations. These multiple references will perhaps provide some indication of how the question stands in modern times. In a final section, we shall briefly mention the possible connexions between this apperception of time and the view of history.

The Arab-Moslen world: its vision and experience of time

VOCABULARY (AND GRAMMAR)

The Arabic words relating to time belong to the language of the pre-Islamic period. With one exception, they were all absorbed into the vocabulary of the Koran. We shall now attempt to identify, as far as this is possible, their original (pre-Koranic and Koranic) meaning.

Zamān is the most general term denoting time, and is used not only in the ancient chronologies but also in grammar, astronomy (and astrology) and philosophy. It belongs to the general Semitic lexicon but is not used in the Koran. The root evokes the idea of that which is chronic ('to be chronically ill') or ancient. *Zamān*, time, can also mean 'period' and 'season'.

Ān signifies the present moment, now; *al-ān*, 'today' (the root evokes an idea of calmness). It frequently occurs in the Koran in the sense of 'now' (e.g. 2: 187, 4: 18, 8: 66, etc.) and in one passage (72: 9), has the meaning of 'immediately'. It can also mean 'season'.

Ḥīn denotes a specific time, a fixed moment or period. It also means 'period' or 'season', but in a more restricted sense than *zamān*. A word derived from the same root, *ḥīnan*, means 'one day'. The root (*ḤYN*) implies the idea of misfortune, adversity, death. The Koran uses the word *ḥīn* in the sense of moment of fixed period (2: 36, 7: 24) period of time (76: 1), 'for a while' (10: 98, 12: 35), 'until a certain time' (21: 111), etc. *Kull ḥīn* means 'at all times', i.e. 'in every season' (14: 25).

Waqt is the main word denoting a point in time.[1] It seems originally to have competed with *zamān* (which subsequently became the principal term indicating astronomical time). The predominant idea in the root is that of an appointed time or moment. In three verses at least the Koran uses the word *waqt* with eschatological implications: the Day of Judgement is called 'the Day of the Time (*waqt*) Appointed' (15: 38, 38: 81; cf. 56: 50).

Mawqit and *mīqāt* (pl. *mawāqīt*), nouns of place from the same root *WQT*, stress the notion of localized time. They are most frequently used in two ways: (a) *Mawāqīt* often has the sense of 'points of reference in time'. The new moons, says the Koran (2: 189) are *mawāqīt* or, in other words, fixed points of reference; and the *mawāqit al-ḥajj* are the appointed times and places where the pilgrims to Mecca gather to perform certain acts; (b) *Mīqāt* evokes the idea of the spatio-temporal limits of a great event—a memorable 'rendezvous' such as the gathering of the 'sorcerers' in the presence of Pharaoh (26:38). But in most instances it refers to a 'meeting with God' such as the 'communion' of Moses with God 'which lasted forty nights' (7:142; cf. 7:143, 155) and, above all, the 'time appointed for all' to come together before God for the Last Judgement (44:40, 78:17). Lastly, the participle *mawqūt* means fixed or set, as of the prayers enjoined on believers 'at stated times' (4:103).

Dahr combines two principal ideas: (a) duration, prolongation, an indeterminate period of time; (b) the vicissitudes of fortune to which man is subject. *Dahr*, unlike *zamān*, *ān*, *ḥīn*, or *waqt*, cannot refer to the idea of 'season' (a given period of time). It seems that the Arabs in pre-Islamic times felt *dahr* to be a force of which man is not master, a sort of blind and oppressive *fatum* (cf. 45:24). Some pre-Islamic texts tended to personify *dahr* (cf. Kronos), but it was not worshipped. The Koranic teaching was opposed to this notion of blind omnipotence. In one *ḥadīth*[2] admitted to the canon by Bukhārī and cited by Ṭabarī (Commentary on the Koran, 45:24), God, according to the Prophet, affirmed: 'I am *dahr*', implying there was nothing reprehensible therein, but the dominant tendency rejected the identification of God and *dahr*, which was regarded as a divine attribute only by certain literalists.[3]

As a means of clarifying and drawing a distinction between the ideas in question one may divide them as follows: *zamān*, time (sometimes a synonym of *al-ayyām*, 'the days'); *ān*, present instant,' now'; *ḥīn*, fixed moment or period; *waqt*, a particular point in time; *mīqāt*, a memorable encounter; *dahr*, duration.

In grammar. In the Semitic languages, tense centres not on the act and the state of the agent, as in Indo-European languages, but on the action itself.[4] There are no past, present and future (although these concepts are distinguished), but a 'perfect' for completed action (which broadly speaking encompasses the past in all its forms), and an 'imperfect' for uncompleted action, whether present or future.

On the basis of the Greek classifications, the grammarians called the 'perfect' *al-māḍī* (the 'past'), and called the 'imperfect' *al-muḍārī*' (the 'similar'). The 'future' (*al-mustaqbil*) is the imperfect which is shown to be future by the insertion of particles or by the context.[5] In spite of outside influences, this basic semantic structure was to continue to inform the mode of thinking of Arabic speakers and, to a lesser extent, of non-Arabic speaking Moslem peoples since the Arabic language is sacred and remains the only 'liturgical' language of Islam.

ARAB PRESUPPOSITIONS: THE MEASUREMENT AND SCANSION OF TIME

The birth of Islam in the seventh century represents both a continuation of the past and a break with that past. There is no doubt that Islam has its roots in an embryonic Arab culture of which we have, unfortunately, only a fragmentary knowledge.

The ancient Arabs, nomads, merchants of the caravan routes, inhabitants of the oases, attached the greatest importance to the phases of the moon. The 'day', *yawm*, begins in the evening at moonrise—probably a general Semitic feature (cf. the Hebrew 'day'). It should be noted that in Arabic moon, *qamar* (which evokes the idea of 'whiteness'), is masculine, whereas sun, *shams* (implying the idea of 'brilliance') is feminine. The two luminaries together may be denoted by the dual form of *qamar*: *al-qamarān*, literally 'the two moons'.

It appears that the calendar was originally a purely lunar one, divided into twelve months each of twenty-eight days. But some two centuries before the Hegira, according to the mathematician and geographer Al-Bīrūnī,[6] the Arab lunar year became solilunar through the empirical intercalation of a thirteenth month every two or three years—the *nasī'* (which has the primary sense of delay, deferment). The year was regarded as beginning in autumn and was divided into three, four or six seasons determined by the condition of pastures and harvests. Because of the rule-of-thumb system employed, however, this solilunar calendar proved somewhat inaccurate and it soon got out of step with the solar calendar. In the early years of Islam, the year no longer began in autumn but in spring.

Thus the rhythm of time was marked principally by the phases of the moon and also by the condition of the land under the twofold influence of the sun and the moon. The predominant idea was not so much one of continuity and perpetuity as of points of reference breaking up the *dahr* or oppressive duration. The principal reference point was the appearance 'at nightfall', at the beginning of each lunar month, of the 'first crescent of the lunar month' (*ghurrat al-hilāl*);[7] the twenty-eight 'stations', literally 'resting places' (*manāzil*), of the moon remained the very basis of the measurement of time.

In pre-Islamic times, the Arabs celebrated two great festivals combining religious elements with those of an agricultural festival, both centred on the pagan sanctuary of Mecca. The ceremonies of the *'umra* were performed during the month of *Aṣam*, or *Rajab* to use the later name (the Hebrew *Nisān*?). This was the spring festival 'during which the young animals in the herd were marked and the firstborn were sacrificed'.[8] The major festival was that of the *ḥajj*, the festival of the pilgrimage to Mecca, which made an entire month holy. It occurred at the end of the year, during the month of *Burak* (*Dhū l-ḥijja*). It seems originally to have been the autumn and harvest festival. However, as a result of the discrepancy which has already been referred to in the computation of the solilunar year, it moved to the spring where it vied in importance with the *'umra*.

The chronological pattern of which these monthly, seasonal or annual rhythms formed part was nevertheless also marked by contingent human events: the famous 'days of the Arabs', *ayyām al-'Arab*, celebrated memorable battles, anniversaries, good and ill fortune, for example the 'days of treason' around 585–91, or the 'Year of the Elephant' around 570.

THE IMPACT OF ISLAM

The teaching of the Koran and the 'tradition of the Prophet' (*sunnat al-nabī*) transformed these apperceptions of 'the age of ignorance' (*jāhiliyya*) into a constant reference to the almighty and merciful divine will. This resulted in a piecemeal vision of the succession of things, a sequence of 'instants' (*waqt*, pl. *awqāt*), which are the signs and spaces of God's intervention. Although, under the influence of the civilizations of Greece and Persia during the classical age and of Western civilization in the modern age, and the urgent promptings of social and economic requirements, praxis has come to accept as a model the continuity and regularity of the succession of days, these influences by no means preclude incessant appeal to the discontinuous and inscrutable effects of the decrees of the Most High. The Koran refers to a 'divine time' which has nothing in common with earthly time, measured by reference to the heavenly bodies. For the eternity of God is not an undefined time but a mode of being the transcendence of which can only be glimpsed through the parables (*mithal*): as in the biblical image, 'a day in the sight of God' is equal to a thousand years (22: 47, 32: 5) or to 50,000 years (70: 4).

The calendar. Since Islam only the lunar calendar has been officially recognized: twelve months of twenty-eight days, each month being divided into four weeks, each week having seven days, each day beginning in the evening.[9] Muḥammad had abolished the old solilunar calendar and had prohibited the practice of intercalation (*nasī'*). The difference as compared with the solar year is about eleven days, thirty-three 'lunar' years being approximately equivalent to thirty-two 'solar' years. Thus in 1975, the *Hijrīya* year (dated from the Hegira in 622) was 1395.

In fact, certain traditions or practical considerations necessitated the maintenance of introduction of other calendars based not on the phases of the moon but on the solar rhythms of the seasons. Of these, the two most important are: (a) the Seleucid era, known as the 'era of Alexander', used in Iran, beginning in 312 B.C. and having a year and an intercalation similar to those of the Julian calendar; (b) the 'Coptic era', which dates from the triumph of Diocletian in A.D. 284. Furthermore, in Egypt under the Caliphate, a year dated from the Hegira but based on a solar rhythm was used for the payment of land taxes; and, in the seventeenth century, the Ottoman administration officially introduced a 'financial year' similar to the Julian calendar year which coexisted with the Hijrīya year. These practical compromises have, until our own times, remained very much part of the daily life of countryfolk, while in modern times the influence of the Gregorian calendar has been strongly felt among townsfolk. The fact that they were used to falling back on solar ('lay') calendars habituated the peoples of Islam to some degree of pluralism and relativism in the representation and measurement of time.

But the Moslem Community as such continued to use only the lunar system, for the moon[10] and, more especially, the Crescent, the new moon, was of particular significance in Moslem life. The Crescent (*hilāl*) is the symbol which appears on the flags of so many contemporary Islamic states. The full moon is associated with the idea of perfection: certain *ḥadīth*(*s*) and ancient 'professions of faith' state that, at the Day of Resurrection, God 'will be seen with the eyes like the moon of Badr', i.e. the full moon. But moonrise at twilight remains the most important moment. It was from moonrise on the first day of the first month of the 'lunar' year when the Prophet emigrated from Meca to Medina[11] that the first day of the Hijrīya era was determined during the time of the Caliph 'Umar I. The appearance of the new moon at the start of each lunar month, and particularly at the start of the month of *Ramaḍān*, must not be calculated astronomically (which the Moslems were able to do at a very early date) but actually observed by two 'witnesses of the instant'.[12] This rule is still in force. Only a minute Ismaili sect, followers of the Āgā Khān, recognizes astronomical computation.

Festivals. The festivals of the Moslem Community are exclusively commemorations of religious events. The pre-Islamic festivals of the '*umra* and the *ḥajj* were taken over, but were divested of their associations with the soil. Furthermore, the '*umra* is most frequently combined with the *ḥajj* in the act of pilgrimage prior to the sacrifice of animals which commemorates Abraham's sacrifice.[13] This commemoration of Abraham's sacrifice is the 'great festival' of Islam in the month of *Dhū l-ḥijja*;[14] the lunar calendar, which has the effect of continually moving this festival in relation to the 'lay' calendar, disassociates the festival completely from the seasons, which are determined by the movement of the sun. The second festival marks the end of the month of *Ramaḍān*, an occasion for collective rejoicing which lasts three days at the end of the fast. Each of the twenty-eight fast days is opened and closed by the setting and rising of the moon.

Throughout this period of fasting, the nights which mark the illustrious events of Islam are also commemorated: the night of the full moon, in commemoration of the battle of Badr, the first victory of the Prophet over the Meccan pagans and, more important still, the twenty-seventh night of the month which re-enacts, thus keeping it ever present, the sending down of the Koranic revelation. This is the *laylat al-qadr* (97:1), 'the night of destiny' in which 'the heavens are opened'. The Koran declares that the month of *Rajab* and the months of pilgrimage and fasting are 'sacred' (*ḥaram*) and that fighting is therefore forbidden at those times.

Minor festivals. The beginning of the Hijrīya lunar year which is the first day of *Muḥarram* and ten days later '*ashūrā* in commemoration of the martyrdom of Ḥusayn, Muḥammad's grandson; the birth of the Prophet (*mawlid*) which is generally accepted as falling on the twelfth day of *Rabi*' *I*, etc.

Lastly, it should be noted that the old solar festivals continue, in spite of the efforts of reformers, to be celebrated alongside the religious festivals with which they are even sometimes confused. Countryfolk, particularly in the Maghreb, recognize *yanā'ir*, the beginning of the year, according to the 'Coptic' and sometimes according to the Julian calendar. *Nawrūz* (or *nayrūz*), the first day of the Persian solar year, was for long an occasion of traditional popular rejoicing (the exchange of gifts, sprinkling with water, bonfires) in Persia, Iraq and Egypt and it is still a day of festivities in Imamite Iran.

But, with regard to Moslem festivals—the breaking of the fast and the sacrificial festival during the pilgrimage—it is true to say that the new crescent moon which rises at twilight 'marks the "opening" of a period of variable duration for the liturgical performance of required observances'[15] and only the five daily prayers at their set times throughout the day are connected with the stations of the sun. In fact, the rhythm of the day, thus marked by the five 'calls to prayer' which ring out in towns and villages and by the performance of the prayer itself, daily reasserts the importance for Moslem life not merely of the moon but of the moon and sun together. This is not in any sense a compromise with a solar calendar (or even a solilunar calendar); the stations of the sun divide into five the period between the setting of the moon at dawn and its reappearance at dusk. The ancient and oppressive power exercised by *dahr*, the 'unknowable duration', is negated by the surrender of self to the divine decrees (*qadar*). The *qadar* is the 'ordained measure' of things, for God is master of *dahr*. It is one of the most serious offences against the faith to affirm the existence of an eternal *dahr* independent of God.

Further developments

THE DOMINANT LINE

We shall consider first of all the subjective sense of time rather than the computation of the calendar or astral time. Attention should be drawn to two factors: First, experiential time is far less a duration which flows by than a discontinuous sequence of discrete moments. Moslem thinkers became aware of this at a very early stage and represented the spatio-temporal status of all contingent beings as one which is constantly established and re-established by a sequence of divine commandments which are themselves discontinuous. 'For the Moslem theologian,' writes Louis Massignon, 'time is consequently not a continuous "duration", but a constellation, "a milky way", of instants (just as space does not exist but only separate points).'[16]

In the early centuries of the Hegira era, certain theologians (*mutakallimūn*) developed this theme from an entirely occasionalist viewpoint (divine occasionalism): events follow each other in a particular habitual order willed by God and which God may at any moment suspend; second causes are not really efficacious. This is why any reference to a possible future should be qualified by the formula, *in shā' Allāh*, 'if God so wills'.

Second, this 'milky way of instants' is represented as a number of tangential points—points of contact rather than intersection—between human time and the eternity of the Most High. Consequently, each instant, by a motionless reversion to itself, tends to re-enact the original 'break' accomplished by the divine *kalima*, the creative Word which brings into being what must be, irrespective of any circumstances of time and space. The faith of Islam, as proclaimed by the Koran, which is the road to salvation, is the faith of Abraham; it is the great *mīthāq*, the 'covenant' granted by God to the human race before all eternity;[17] it is the ultimate testimony given at the Last Hour, at the Judgement. The events which mark a man's life, and the life of the peoples of the Community, retain their physical existence but their deepest reality (*ḥaqīqa*) is that of a tangential reminder of a Presence.

This, according to subsequent elaborations, was the true meaning to be attributed to *dahr;* not a duration which oppresses but the hidden secret of time, *bāṭin al-zamān.* In the words of a theologian of the fifteenth century, *dahr* 'is the permanent instant (*al-ān*) in which the divine Presence is extended; this is the secret of time and it embraces both that which was before eternity and perpetuity'.[18]

Ṣūfi elaborations. This definition by Jurjānī, in which many different influences are discernible, recalls a whole line of Ṣūfi interiorization. Ḥallāj, for example, had an acute sense of the instability and of the fluctuation of 'instants' in contrast with the perenniality of God: 'Behold this contingent being, turned aside as he is from the Creator of the whole fissure of time . . .'.[19] It is true that other texts by Ḥallāj measure metahistorical 'facts' such as the *mīthāq* (symbolically) in years. But as God is outside time and space, He cannot be bounded by questions of 'when' or 'where'. Thus, the instants which punctuate sequences of time must lose themselves in this immutability: 'post-eternity (*qidam*) means an end of fragmentation in accordance with number, and a disappearance of "instants" into divine everlastingness (*sarmad*)'.[20]

Waqt hence assumes its meaning of an 'instant' in which man becomes without past or future: 'when God descends into his soul, and makes his heart collected,' says Hujwīrī, 'he (man) has no memory of the past and no thought of that which is not yet come'.[21] And the *ḥāl*, 'spiritual state', is the 'ornament' of this pure instant 'as the spirit is of the body'. '*Waqt* has need of *ḥāl*, for *waqt* is beautified by *ḥāl* and subsists thereby'.[22] Junayd, who was the teacher of Ḥallāj, taught that the 'saint' (*walī*) should be 'the son of His instant' (*ibn waqtihi*), i.e. the 'instant of God', having neither before nor after.

In theologians such as Jurjānī or mystics like Junayd, Ḥallāj, Hujwīrī or Ibn 'Abbād, we find, here and there, highly elaborate developments in which Graeco-Persian influences may possibly, wittingly or unwittingly, intrude.

Nevertheless, time and the points at which it touches eternity continue to be seen against a background, numbered no doubt but discontinuous, of 'heterogeneous instants'.[22a] Time is less the measurement of movement than an indisputable sign of the impermanence of created things.

In conclusion, it should be noted that this subjective apperception and the Ṣūfi notion of a 'spiritual' instant certainly did not stop astronomical calculations and the measurement of time by the 'movement of the stars' from continuing. Astronomy, which was not at first distinguished from astrology, was at a very early date held in high regard in the courts of the Caliphs and the Emirs. It was an 'instrumental science' which was also necessary for the purpose of preparing the lunar calendar and determining the solar stations which govern the hours of prayer. There were some very famous astronomers in classical Islam, whose discoveries belong to scientific history. It was not as scientists but as philosophers that many of them expressed a Hellenistic view of temporal becoming.

SOME DIVERGENT LINES OF INQUIRY

The discontinuity of instants, derived from the apperceptions of the Arabs in ancient times, was thus predominant in the subjective experience of time in countries having a Moslem civilization; but it is clear that the over-all cultural development of these countries was by no means monolithic and that there was an interplay of different ideas therein. Is one to regard this as being due to the influence of the different ethnic groups and their traditions dating from pre-Islamic times? The answer is probably yes, although it would be unproductive—and arbitrary—to take any such identification too far.

It would be contrary to the facts to identify, as is sometimes done, Sunnism with the Arab world, and Shiism with (for example) the Iranian world or (to some extent) the Indo-Iranian world. It may be true that the Indo-Europeans belonging to Islam would be favourably predisposed towards the esoteric developments of Shiism. It should not be forgotten, however, that the first Shiites were Arabs and that great Shiite, Imamite and Ismaili texts were written in Arabic as well as in Persian and that Imamite Shiism did not become the official religion of Iran until the sixteenth century.[23] Rather than creating more and more divisions in terms of geographical areas, ethnic groups and national cultures, we shall be looking at the evidence provided by certain major schools of thought. We shall only in passing mention the *dahriyya* who believed in an eternal time which is not subject to the power of God. For the sake of brevity we shall limit our inquiry to two particularly important lines of thought.

Falsafa. This school included the great philosophers whose fame has come down through the centuries and whose thinking was steeped in Aristotle and Plotinus (the two being confused) and to a lesser extent in Plato, the Stoics and various apocryphal Greek philosophers. They include Kindī (an Arab), Fārābī (a Turk), Ibn Sīnā or Avicenna (a Persian) and, in the Maghreb, such thinkers as Ibn Ṭufayl and Ibn Rushd (Averroes). Their notion of time was Aristotelian in flavour. One example, taken from Ibn Sīnā, will suffice: 'Time (*zamān*) is the measure of circular movement considered from the point of view of anteriority and posteriority and not from the point of view of distance. Movement is continuous and therefore time is continuous'.[24] Instead of the 'milky way' of discrete instants we have here the Hellenistic-style notion of continuous time and space which is in keeping with the professed hylomorphism underlying it. Numbered time is the measure of the movement of bodies and the homogeneous succession of time is associated with their contingent nature. The rational soul (*nafs nāṭiqa*), which is a spiritual principle, is for its part referable to a stable measure which Avicenna calls duration, *dahr: 'Dahr* is that which expresses the relation of the stability of the soul with regard to time as a whole'.[25]

Such definitions are more or less common to the whole of *falsafa*. But it is only when they are seen in terms of that school's cosmology that they acquire their full meaning. For the *falāsifa*, the world has been contingent—and thus 'created'—from all eternity. There is no need for us to study here the work of 'interpretation' (*ta'wīl*) on which they embarked in order to reconcile this view of things with the Koranic texts. They came under attack from the doctors of Islam, jurists and theologians, and Ghazzālī charged that the theory of the eternity of the world was 'impious'; but such condemnations did not focus on the actual definition of time as the measure of movement and, like movement itself, continuous. When this definition was not presented as being connected with a 'necessary and intentional' emanation, it could compete with the experiential apperception of time as a discontinuous sequence of discrete instants. The influence of the *falāsifa* was a direct influence on intellectual circles. It is difficult to assess the extent to which it affected the ways of thinking of Sunni Islam.

Shiism. In fact, only the two great Eastern philosophers Fārābī and Ibn Sīnā really obtained a wide hearing within the Moslem culture and among the very people who opposed them. They both lived in a Shiite milieu which was not offended either by their emanatism or by the conclusion concerning the temporal eternity of the world which they drew from it. It is well known that the Shiites, 'the followers of 'Alī', whose beliefs centred upon the cult of the great Imams, his successors and heirs, developed the esoteric doctrine of the 'hidden meaning' (*bāṭin*) which is the only key to the truth (*ḥaqīqa*) contained in the verses of the Koran. Although the various sects of Shiism (Zaidite, Imamite and Ismaili) together form less than one-tenth of the present Moslem community, they have none the less had a profound effect over the centuries on many aspects of the culture of the Islamic countries. What have they to tell us on the problem of time?

Many Shiite works, subject to a number of different influences, put forward an emanatist view of the production of beings and hence a notion of time fairly close to that of the *falāsifa*. 'Time', writes the Imamite Mullā Sadrā Shīrāzī, 'is the measure which counts this passage (i.e. movement) . . . Movement is the eduction of this substance (i.e. a particular 'thing'), passing gradually from potentiality to actuality, and time is the measure of this eduction'.[26] But neither movement nor time can lead from the contingent to the eternal. The impermanence of the contingent being continues to be stressed: every existent has been preceded and will be followed 'by its own non-being in time'.[27]

Shiite esotericism, which in this respect is similar to the majority of Ṣūfi schools, particularly the 'Unity of being' schools, frequently draws a basic distinction between heavy, 'thick' time which measures the movement of corporeal beings and the 'subtle' time which measures 'spiritual movements', or between 'cosmic' (chronological) time and 'the time of souls'[28]—an incommensurable shift from the quantitative to the qualitative, the latter going beyond a 'duration' reminiscent of Bergsonian duration, to link up with 'the time of thy Lord'. Despite the incommensurability there are nevertheless symbolic affinities between them, for the world perceptible by the senses is merely the reflection, the imperfect and crude image of the spiritual world which precedes and governs it.[29]

It is in terms of the same movement of thought that one should understand the great meta-historical cycles (*dawr*) of Ismaili gnoses, to which we shall return later. They imply a notion of cyclical time which is moreover distinct from the Indian, Greek or Nietzschean notions. Indeed, these cycles are situated on a different plane of existence from that of the numbered time of bodies, and together with 'subtle time' symbolize spiritual durations. They are a projection of the transcendental imagination in which all things, by achieving perfection, return to the purity of their origins, a sort of counterpart, at the level of gnostic symbolism, of that 'motionless reversion to itself' which we mentioned in connexion with the discrete instant. The various currents of Shiite thought also regard time, even if it is without beginning or end, as emerging in the 'break' accomplished by the creative Word (*kalima*).

THE MODERN AGE

Over the centuries, therefore, the ideas put forward and the uses made of them have been very numerous. However, if we look not at the analyses of philosophers and scholars but at the everyday experience of ordinary people, we find that, against a background of continuity provided by the succession of seasons, the tasks of the agricultural calendar and the state of the pastureland, it is the fragmentation of instants and the relativity of temporal successions which constantly come to the surface.

Are the same dominant features to be found in the modern age? It would seem fairly safe to say that they are. One finds an apprehension of things both in their contingency and in their ultimate significance which is deeply rooted. It coincides with the meaning—and the experience—of temporal continuities, it becomes part of them, giving them direction and relativizing them.

But is it not likely that the intrusion of the modern world will bring about a new awareness of experiential time, one which is the same as that of the technically advanced West? This is certainly probable, at least initially and on a superficial level. Moslem culture is undoubtedly as receptive to modern influences as it was in earlier days to Greek, Persian and even Indian thought (and need one add that a culture which is loath to develop in isolation is, for that reason, all the more alive and all the more likely to bring forth riches of its own); it is quite likely, however, that this numbered and apparently continuous time will go on being used, against the background of the 'milky way' of instants, which has become almost an ingrained mental pattern.

One would need to be able to make a close study of contemporary Moslem literatures. It would probably be right to suggest that the treatment used by various Egyptian novelists or story writers, for example, in dealing with the everyday life of ordinary people in the countryside or in towns is imbued with this discontinuous and relativistic view of time. Is there not an echo of it, sublimated and mingled with many other influences, even in certain poems by that highly cultured man, receptive to all ways of thinking, who was not himself an Arab and did not write in Arabic, the Punjabi Muḥammad Iqbāl (1873 or 1876 to 1938)? A devout Sunni Moslem, invoking the celebrated Iranian Sūfī Jalāl al-Dīn Rūmī as his 'master' and capable of recognizing the greatness of such a writer as Ḥallāj, welcoming what the Shiite traditions had to offer, content to listen to the 'sages of India', inveighing against the materialism of a Western world which had lost its Christian faith and which he knew well, he did not hesitate to speak of the continuity, if not of time, at least of history unfolding in time.[30] Yet the apperception of temporality which sometimes emerges in his poetic works seems to be much closely related to the piecemeal nature of instants than to the measurement of a continuous movement: 'for the time which is allotted to thee has but the measure of a spark'—time both 'motionless and in motion' in which 'each of our instants announces eternity'.[31] And it was like a mirage that, one evening, Hegel's philosophical undertaking appeared to him—Hegel 'whose thought stripped eternity of the covering of the instant'.[32] Is this the influence of German idealism? Or is it, perhaps, a more direct resurgence of the 'subtle time' of the Shiites and the Sūfīs mingled with the atomism of the Ancients? 'Open your eyes on time and space', sings the *Djāvīd-Nāma:* 'each is but a state among the states of the soul', for it is 'through the oneness of the look' that 'atoms . . . become the sun'.[33]

Whatever the literary evidence may indicate, it must be recognized that a discontinuity composed of discrete instants, whereby the sense of homogeneous duration is made relative, is in no way at variance with modern life; indeed, it may be that this Moslem sense of the fleeting instant in its tangential relationship with the divine *sarmad* can provide new clues to the mystery or new responses to the anguish of experiential time as felt by modern Western man in introspection. It may be able to offer further extensions of, and fresh insights into, Bergson's 'duration', Proust's *temps perdu* and *temps retrouvé* or Heidegger's *Sein und Zeit*.

A discontinuous, piecemeal apperception of time does not, indeed, seem in any way incompatible with present-day scientific theories or models. More significant still, the temporal and spatial 'atomism' of early Moslem times might seem to be an anticipation, although not yet explicit, of the space-time continuum and of its relativity. Perhaps the poetic tribute paid by Iqbāl to 'the wise Einstein' is an indication of this.[34]

The view of history

The same Arabic word *ta'rīkh* means not only 'history' but also 'era, computation, date', or rather its basic meaning of 'epoch', 'date of a noteworthy event', extends outwards to cover 'chronicles', 'annals', and hence 'history' in all its accepted senses. In modern Arabic, the word *ta'rīkh* is used for history as one of the humanities.

NEITHER 'PROGRESSIVE HISTORY' NOR 'CYCLICAL HISTORY'

In broad terms, it would be correct to say that, in the specifically Moslem view of the world, there are 'histories' but there is no such thing as 'history'. The 'histories of the prophets' in the Koran all follow a simple pattern:[35] the proclamation from God, the rejection by the stubborn unbelievers and the punishment of the latter after the transcendental origin of the message has been proved. Men living in the *fatra*, the interval of time occurring between one prophet and the next, are plunged in the darkness of ignorance. The missions accomplished by the bearers of warnings and emissaries of God are discontinuous flashes of light, emanating from 'elsewhere', which pierce and illuminate this darkness. These missions also mark the 'fissures in time' by tirelessly calling to mind the 'covenant' existing from before eternity. The emissaries of God have the task of reiterating the original covenant and its demands. There is no progress in the revelation which is communicated, but rather elucidation and clarification of the same truth until the coming of Muḥammad. He is 'the Seal of the Prophets' (33:40), who, through a return to the restored faith of Abraham, puts an end to the intervals of temporal successions and sets the expectations of the Community upon the Last Instant, the Day of Judgement, *yawm al-dīn*.

In one sense, the life of the Community should be understood as a single 'day'. 'When the earth shall have only one day (var.: only one night) left,' says a *ḥadīth*, 'God shall prolong that day (var.: that night) so that a man of my family shall become sovereign.' For the devout Imamite, this refers to the expected coming of the 'hidden (*ghā'ib*) Imam'; for Moslems as a whole, it refers to the coming of the *Mahdī*, the guide of the last days who, before the Judgement, will lead the Community in the 'right way' (*hudā*).

Strictly speaking, this is neither rectilinear (progressive) history, nor cyclical history. Elements of both may be found, but they have been transposed in accordance with a synthesizing vision which retains its specificity. If one regards it as rectilinear history one must distinguish it from the Judaeo-Christian view of the divine scheme of things: the world had a beginning, and God will proclaim its end 'when the earth is shaken to her (utmost) convulsion' (99:1), 'when the sky is cleft asunder' (82:1), and 'all that is on earth will perish' (cf. 55:26). Thereafter there will arise another discontinuous, incommensurable 'instant' in which the dead will rise for judgement and retribution. In a sense this is cyclical history but it is not like that of India or Greece and even less like that of Nietzsche, for every temporal event circles back to its original perspective, which is also that of the Last Hour.

The foregoing outline mainly concerns Sunni Islam; the Shiite elaborations involve somewhat similar notions but they are conditioned by the esoteric gnoses of the 'hidden meaning'. In Imāmism, the time of prophecy, *nubuwwa*, leads on to *walāya*, the time of 'spiritual fidelity' which is that of the Imams. The hour of the prophet Muḥammad was when history reached its apogee. 'Immediately afterwards begins the decline, the close of day, the fall of the night of esotericism, the cycle of the *walāya*'.[36] Ismailism reverses the relationship: 'the world of prophecy', which is the present world since the creation of the first man, is a time of eclipse; it was preceded and will be followed by the 'unveiling of reality' illuminated by the splendours of the *walāya*. The Ismaili 'spiritual time' is thus divided into large alternating cycles of unveiling and eclipse, and follows a seven-year rhythm which recurs 'at all levels of being'.[37] The Last Hour is at the same time the Present Hour; the 'internal metamorphosis' will be the conclusion of history, transmuting the inadmissible today into 'spiritual resurrection'.[38]

THE MOSLEM 'THEOLOGY' OF HISTORY

Great as their impact may have been on Shiite and sometimes on Ṣūfi circles, it cannot be said that the gnoses of the hidden meaning and the many writings thereon have given the Moslem world as a whole a theology of history. Such a theology does, however, exist in a fairly clearly formulated form, and may be briefly summarized as follows.

Only the day of the 'covenant' before eternity and the Last Day, when the world ends, i.e. two meta-historical events, really transpierce time. Between these two decisive instants, the other 'days', which are demarcated by successive moonrises, are only the projection or prefiguration of the two instants: 'for the statute which they proclaim will come to pass only after a certain delay (*imhāl*), a certain time of tarrying (*labath*)'.[39] In historical terms, this 'delay' is a condensation of the notion of 'duration', 'the actual interval between two divine instants, the annunciation and the sanction'.[40] The sending of the prophets and above all the mission of Muḥammad are a special reminder of this.

In Islam, the 'theology of history' is drawn in two directions, that of optimism *ad extra* and that of pessimism *ab intra*. Optimism: the Nation of the Prophet, *unmat al-nabī*, will live until the Last Day, fulfilling its twofold earthly vocation of unity and universality. There have been and may be in the future times ('delays') of apogee followed by decline which, in its turn, heralds a renewal. Pessimism: faith as a witness, fidelity to the message received, will continue to deteriorate until the penultimate 'instant' of the world when the *Mahdī* will appear. The 'golden age' is not regarded as having occurred in a mythical time before time,[41] nor is it the age of Adam before the Fall. The 'golden age' of the Community is the age in which the Prophet of Islam and his Companions lived. It is the 'State of Medina', conceived not as the immutable prototype of all earthly cities but as the point of refraction in which every earthly city should be rooted. Subsequently, during the 'delay' which began with the Hegira and which will end, by a return to the origins, with the coming of the *Mahdī*, faith in the One God and obedience to His law will grow more dim except in the hearts of the faithful who have 'embarked in the Ark of Noah', as the commentators say.

It is here that the concept of *fitna*, which combines that of 'civil strife' and that of 'test', the supreme test of the believer, enters in. In the Medina period, only a few years after the death of the Prophet, there had already occurred 'the great *fitna*' which even set the Companions one against another. This culminated in the battle of Ṣiffīn, in which the main schisms came to a head. Armed conflict among believers is the principal and ever-present fear of the Community.

This kind of conflict is, however, predicted by a celebrated *ḥadīth* known as the *ḥadīth* 'of the saved sect' (*firqa nājiya*). The authenticity of this text was challenged by the Mu'tazilites (the oldest school of 'theology') and by such a recognized traditionalist as Ibn Qutayba. It is nevertheless included in the *Ṣaḥīḥ* ('reliable', 'sound') collection of Bukhārī, which is regarded as authoritative, and the great historian Ibn Khaldūn quotes it as valid. It runs as follows:

> What happened to the Children of Israel will happen to the Community. The Children of Israel split into seventy-two sects. My Community will split into seventy-three sects—one more than among the Children of Israel. All will go to hell except the one to which I and my Companions belong.

The 'saved sect' is attacked on all sides and constantly dwindles, but remains indestructible until the Day of Resurrection and is constantly 'helped to victory' (*manṣūra*) by God. For in every century of the Hegira, God creates a 'renewer' (*mujaddid*) to regenerate the faith of Islam and thereby to restore lustre to the earthly destiny of the Community. The notion of 'reform' (*iṣlāḥ*) is traditional in Islam and is constantly emphasized.

ANNALS AND HISTORY

Such, according to the Moslem faith, is the only true 'history', that inscribed by God, for those who have eyes to see it, in the 'fissures of time'. The Arab, Iranian and Turkish Moslem cultures have, however, had their own 'historians'. The predominant genre was for long that of annals or chronicles, some of which gave a day-to-day account of battles, reigns and memorable events. A very real gift for analysis and a scrupulous concern for objectivity are displayed in some of the annals—one only has to think of the most celebrated, for example, those of the Sunnite Tabarī or the Shiite Mas'ūdi.

Such writings are thus much less concerned with seeking out the laws of history than with recording and putting together the events. What is important above all else is that the event which has occurred in time should be attested by reliable witnesses and that their testimony should, in its turn, be relayed to us by a series of trustworthy intermediaries. From the quest for *ḥadīth(s)*, the establishment of sayings attributed to Muḥammad, developed *isnād*, the science of tracing back the traditions and the unbroken succession (*tawātur*) of authorities who have transmitted them, which go back as far as the Companions of the Prophet. But every event of which the memory has been preserved should be similarly substantiated.[42] Whether it is the rising of the crescent moon which begins and ends the month of *Ramaḍān*, or of a significant fact in human history, we are always brought back to the value attributed to authentic testimony—which was oral before it existed in written form. 'Historical criticism' is primarily a matter of verification, of *isnād:* the truthfulness of witnesses and intermediate authorities must be proved and it must be shown that each link in the chain could really have been in contact with the preceding link.

History, like time, does not 'unfold'; it is a discontinuous succession of experiential 'moments'; there are, it is true, apparent connexions between the successive moments, but the real significance of the succession remains wrapped in the motionless divine *sarmad* (and was to be projected by the Ismaili gnosis into the cycles of 'mytho-history'). The mystery of human freedom and responsibility does not relate to the 'course of history' but resides in the instantaneous divine creation of each act, which is not preserved in the being, a high-frequency alternating current, a separate and incessantly repeated surge of power from on high.

However, in the eighth century of the Hegira (fourteenth century), at the beginning of the decline of the classical age, there appeared a work which was to have a profound influence: the *Prolegomena* and the *History of the Berbers* by Ibn Khaldūn,[43] who has rightly been called the father of modern sociology. With him, the emphasis shifted from the establishment of authenticated chains of reliable authorities; 'the true object of history', he wrote, 'is to inform us concerning the social condition of man, that is to say concerning the social development (*'umrān*) of the world and concerning the phenomena which are naturally associated with it'.[44] In adopting this approach, Ibn Khaldūn was well aware that he was inventing a new method of analysis which he defines as follows: 'the study and verification of facts, the painstaking investigation of their causes, a profound knowledge of the manner in which events took place and of how they came to pass'.[45] This is no longer a 'theology' (and certainly not a gnostic theosophy as in Shiism), but a philosophy of history.

Ibn Khaldūn was a man of wide culture who was as familiar with Moslem religious science as with Greek philosophy and science and the positive science of his own time. Notwithstanding the criticisms which he made of them, the *falāsifa* had a significant influence on his thinking. However, his conception of history owes nothing to Herodotus, with whom he appears in fact to have been unacquainted; moreover, he unambiguously proclaims his Moslem faith, and the outlook described in our preceding paragraphs could easily be paralleled in the third part of his *Prolegomena*. This only makes the emphasis he places on the geographical, social, economic and cultural reasons for the facts which he examines all the more remarkable. It is not surprising that Western writers, struck by the directly sociological data and their material causes to which Ibn Khaldūn gives prominence, should want to judge him in Western terms, comparing him at times to Montesquieu or at others seeing him as a forerunner of Marx.

The truth is quite different. The real originality of Ibn Khaldūn within Moslem culture is that, instead of a circumstantial account of past events, he gives a sometimes analytical and sometimes dialectical analysis of social phenomena; instead of taking an extrinsicistic view of history, he endeavoured to make history intelligible. His inductive realism, far from being a repudiation of the 'Community of the Prophet' as he saw it after seven centuries of existence, stimulated in him an awareness which was for that very reason all the more exacting.

We might express the matter simply and concisely by saying that, in the short term, the method of Ibn Khaldūn, which is at the same time inductive and rational, led him to a cyclical and ternary view of historical events: every human society, every kingdom and every state goes through a period of struggle from which stability emerges; a time of stability and of climax, bearing within it the seeds of decline; and a time of decline foreshadowing (perhaps in other lands) further struggles and a new upturn. This was a kind of law derived by induction from the material, economic and social conditions which he observed. But these cycles are set in the heart of the fissures of time, those of the destiny of the human race from its creation until the Last Hour announced by God.

For each resumption of this progressive impulsion will be marked by a 'complete upheaval'. The social development 'of countries and peoples' rushes forward towards what Ibn Khaldūn himself calls 'a new creation', 'a renewed growth', and 'a new world'.[46] Perhaps, this spiral of history may seem like 'a continuous, collective movement, a truly inevitable development', as Muḥammad Iqbāl says.[47] Does this amount to an abandonment of the former apperception of time as being fragmented in and by its tangential relationship with the eternal *sarmad?* We do not think so, for this 'continuous' movement follows a spiral course[48] which, far from blurring the 'milky way' of discrete instants into homogenous duration, draws it along, glittering with its myriad points of light, visible signs of the divine Decrees, towards the Day of the 'Time Appointed'.[49]

The influence of Ibn Khaldūn on contemporary Moslem thought is undeniable. On condition that it is considered in its own context rather than through arbitrary transcriptions into Western terms, his work may provide a means of arriving at a view of history and of the world which will enable the Moslem historian of today to bring an original approach to bear on some of the most essential areas of research in the humanities.[50] Thus sublimated and consciously reassimilated, the lines of approach which have been outlined in very broad terms in these pages might make a positive contribution to universal culture.

APPENDIX

The empirical apperception of time among the peoples of the Maghreb

THE BROAD LINES OF THE INQUIRY

A study of the empirical apperception of time in the Moslem world as a whole would involve research covering a vast geographical area, extending from Africa to the East Indies. This would be beyond the capability of a restricted group of specialists, particularly since the reference to the 'empirical' aspect would entail research on the major variants of experiential time. We shall accordingly do no more than consider the apperception of time among the population of the Maghreb; but we shall try, as far as possible, to avoid making our study too ethnographically 'localized', an approach which would be, in the present instance, something of a danger for the research worker.

At the outset, the reader should be put on his guard against a number of possible misconceptions.

First of all, it should be pointed out that the empirical apperception of time among peoples which, for more than a thousand years, have lived under the influence of Moslem civilization, and which have also been in contact with other cultures and civilizations, cannot be entirely 'local'. The fact that we are on the lookout for an original set of assumptions does not mean that we must of necessity discover an outlook which is entirely *sui generis*. Even groups living in rural isolation draw a large part of their traditional culture, whether oral or written, from the world cultural heritage. Since the early Middle Ages hardly any localities have remained culturally isolated, and for this reason one can speak of a body of empirical knowledge which has been developed and experienced in common by population groups in constant movement and constantly intermingling. It is not therefore surprising, in small village or urban communities, to discover elements deriving from different cultures. In such circumstances, practical experience and religious conceptions, as well as scraps of scientific knowledge are mingled or superimposed one on the other and co-exist quite naturally. The empiricism, which at first sight may seem to relate only to rural matters, in fact interlocks solidly with the religious view which systematizes the apperception of time; both these spheres, in their turn, foster a receptiveness to the scientific knowledge which people are striving to acquire. Apperceptions of time among the ordinary people are therefore nourished from several sources, from the affective to the rational and from ancient agricultural practices to modern technology.

Furthermore, it is essential, as far as possible, to avoid over-emphasizing the distinctive characteristics of one group in relation to others. We therefore consider that there is no point in stressing the rhythm of agricultural activities to the extent of making it the built-in temporal pattern of peasant life, for the daily rhythm of religious life blurs this type of apperception. The town dweller, even though absorbed in his work, which obliges him to rationalize time, shares with the peasant those apperceptions which are determined by the religious consciousness, and is in any case fully aware of the rhythm of rural life.

Lastly, it would be artificial to presuppose any systematic separation between the notional and the real and suggest that empirical views of time were quite devoid of any abstract conceptions. The degree of interpenetration between experience and thought is immediately clear if one considers the strong tradition of idealization and the literary resources which are employed in the cultural heritage of the Maghreb to simplify the most abstract religious ideas.

Having drawn attention to the dangers of an excessive 'localization', we shall distinguish the three major categories into which the empirical apperceptions of time of the peoples of the Maghreb fall.

1. A religious apperception, ranging from the practical division of time to metaphysical conceptions adapted to the popular understanding.
2. An empirical view of time governed by the everyday needs of rural life.
3. A socio-historical conception with strong emotional overtones.

THE RELIGIOUS APPERCEPTION OF TIME

Islamic religion has the merit of imparting several kinds of temporal apperception. Believers are readily able to pass from a very practical level of experience to philosophical conceptions of varying degrees of complexity. Between, on the one hand, the division of the day into five times for prayer, clearly marked by the muezzin's call which is identical in towns and in remote villages, and, on the other, the conception of universal or divine time, there are various levels of concomitance from which the ordinary man draws certain elements of his culture.

At the practical level, it must be pointed out that communal life in traditional towns or in old pre-colonial villages is regulated by the religious division of time. Thus, the markets which are often held one after another in the same place, the meeting places for merchants, the hours of work of craftsmen or the times for watering crops are organized in hourly stages corresponding to the hours of prayer. A number of supplementary subdivisions are observed in order to achieve greater accuracy.

For example, in most old towns the dawn prayer indicates the time for setting up the cattle markets or markets for the sale of wool, fruit and vegetables from the surrounding countryside. The *sūq* (market) for certain essential commodities such as hides, copper-ware and second-hand goods is held in the forenoon (*ḍuḥā*) between eight and ten. *Ẓuhr*, noon, is the time of the midday meal and of the siesta after prayer. The early afternoon, *'aṣr*, is the time when the shopkeeper and craftsman resume work. The *maghrib*, or evening prayer, is the time for relaxation and for cultural activities; in the towns people listen to public addresses in the mosques, and in the countryside they attend the *jamā'a* (assembly). The determination of the hours of prayer involves a practical knowledge of the positions of the sun, a careful attention to changing shadows and the colours of the clouds, and observations of the night sky, the stars and the moon.

The religious calendar is a lunar calendar based on what is immediately visible in everyday life, and unheedful of the slower rhythm of the changing seasons. The religious authorities observe a very strict law in this connexion and always give priority to direct observation of the moon rather than to advance computations. It is on this basis that the annual festivals and the month of fasting (*Ramaḍān*) are fixed. The new moon must be visible to the naked eye and moonrise must be officially verified by eye witnesses. Groups of persons of all ages participate in these observations at twilight after noting the setting of the moon at dawn on the three preceding days.

Meticulous observations are particularly important throughout the entire lunar month of *Ramaḍān*, a period of fasting and meditation, the religious observations of which affect all members of society. Although observance of *Ramaḍān* is on the decline in certain parts of the Moslem world, particularly in the towns, this month remains a month of spiritual regeneration for the entire

Community in the Maghreb. Even non-practising Moslems are obliged to practise at this time if they wish to avoid violent disapproval from their people. Everyday life is indeed totally disrupted, most daytime commercial and cultural activities ceasing and being carried on more intensely by night. There are even some activities which are carried out only during this month.

However, during holy months and religious festivals, and on Fridays—the day of communion in prayer—each portion of time which is 'densified' by particular acts (fasting or breaking of the fast, the sacrifice of the sheep, collective prayer) is a kind of landmark which breaks the undifferentiated passing of time. It fixes in the memory of the common people a very precise mental time-table which often remains the best calendar to which they can refer.

But these divisions are not the only ones which mark significant stages in the passage of life. Human time, which is a tissue of events of personal, family or community significance, comprises certain occasions which mark the succession of days. Birth, circumcision, the progression from one level of education to another in the traditional system, puberty which marks the religious coming-of-age, marriage and death are all events which are assimilated into the religious life of the entire Community. No individual can stand aloof and even if he is in rebellion against society, society pretends not to notice. Thus, the religious community solemnizes each important moment in human life; the moral outcast is formally integrated in order to preserve social cohesion.

On a higher cultural level, the man of the people derives his conceptions of absolute time from his religion. The concept of eternity, for example, which is at first sight the hardest to grasp, is linked in this religious framework with 'divine time' which has neither beginning nor end. Man himself, according to religious teaching, is eternal, since his life has been written down in the Book of Eternity, and he is imperishable. Earthly life is no more than one stage of existence. The infinite world is the world of heaven and hell. Furthermore, even in the world below, both good and bad actions are imperishable: they continue to exist in the memory of time and are written in the book of his deeds with which every man will appear before God on the Day of Retribution.

But this eternal and almost transcendent time is itself punctuated by notable events which interrupt its inapprehensible duration: the creation of the universe, the creation of man, the ages of prophecy which are the basis of universal history, the only one which has both human and divine dimensions. The end of time, which is the supreme event, the 'hour' *par excellence*, is not a stopping point but a resumption of life in other climes. The arresting images of the Koran on this subject strike the imagination of ordinary people and powerfully impress upon them notions which are genuinely metaphysical. The idea of divine transcendence and eternity is illustrated by the obliteration of everything which exists: '. . . But will abide forever the face of thy Lord, full of majesty, bounty and honour'.[51] The earth will dissolve, the stars will leave their courses and God will make new heavens and a new earth. No particle of the universe, no being, whatever his place in the hierarchy of existence, will escape this destruction.

The idea of a relative time, with differing notions of duration, may be perceived through the images used in the Koran of the day which is, in the sight of God, 'of fifty thousand years', and of the intense instant of creation. The latter is sometimes equal to the 'six days' during which God created the heavens and earth and at other times compressed into the fraction of a second between the *kāf* (k) and the *nūn* (n) of the word *Kun!* ('Fiat!') uttered by the Creator.[52] Explanatory folk legends concerning the experience of duration tell of one Tamīm al-Dārī, a contemporary of the Prophet, who is supposed to have lived two different lives: the more important for him was not his real life in society but a life which was rich, varied and of very long duration in subjective terms and which he lived in a few moments. According to the story, Tamīn al-Dārī was unable to understand how a vast number of events could occur in an instant such as that between the *kāf* and the *nūn* of the divine decree *Kun!* He was alone in a washroom making his ablutions when this doubt assailed him. He was then transported in spirit to another world, not an imaginary world but a real one, in which time was not the time of our own world. There he was metamorphosed into a woman. He married, had two children and died. His life in this other world was so rich, so intense and so long that he felt the burden of years weighing down heavily upon him. When he returned to his normal self, he asked the servant who was waiting outside the door if he had been a long time: 'No longer than usual', she replied. However, he had lived in this 'other world' for thirty eventful years. He then realized how wicked he had been to doubt and repented of the intellectual sin which he had thus committed.[53]

To sum up, we may say that the religious apperceptions of time among simple people exist on levels of knowledge which range from practical to theoretical and that the popular explanatory images are not as unsophisticated as might have been expected. Furthermore, although the intellectual ability of the men of religion who disseminate this form of culture varies considerably, one may assume that they have a certain minimum standard of knowledge below which they would be liable to the charge of ignorance. It is this daily ritual, these ceremonies which mark the successive stages in a person's life, these annual festivals and these fundamental theoretical conceptions, often supported by symbolic legends, which the man of average education shares with the illiterate and which women and children absorb within the context of family life. Thus, not even the most practical aspect of ordinary people's conceptions of time is independent of religious inspiration and values.

'PRACTICAL' TIME

The practicalities of rural life. The empirical apperceptions of time are inseparable from a knowledge of the climate and of agricultural life. They are generally enshrined in popular sayings or in symbolic legends which teach a lesson but which are never taken literally. There are, it is true, various influences at work. The populations of the Maghreb sometimes borrow from the Coptic calendar as well as from the Roman calendar, and draw on the wisdom of ancient Arabia as much as on the old Berber tradition. In addition to the religious calendar there is a solar calendar which divides the year either into months of thirty days, or into periods of cold and heat of forty days or, lastly, into climatic periods of ten days. We shall now look at this in greater detail.

The depth of winter lasts forty nights *al-layāli*,[54] divided into 'white nights', illuminated by the moon, and 'black nights' in which the moon does not appear from behind the clouds. The forty days of great heat (*as-sama'in*: hot winds) are divided into hot days and temperate days. *Nāyer* (*Yanāyer*: January), considered as a climatic period, may refer to a period of ten days or may correspond to the month of January. It is also used to denote one particular day which corresponds exactly with the Coptic New Year. For this reason it is still observed as a holiday on which children are given baskets of fruit as New Year presents.

The above examples show the wide variety of borrowings; it can also be seen that these borrowed elements, in being adapted to practical ends, are modified by a knowledge of the climate. Thus, *Nāyer* denotes the end of the ploughing season. Days when the earth is not tilled are so long that 'the lazy ox gets bored',[55] as the saying goes. *Nāyer* is a cold month but *Fabrāyer* (February), which follows it, is also unreliable. There is a complicity between the two months which is illustrated by the following folk tale. An old woman who was pleased at having got through to the end of January without loss to her modest herd exclaimed jubilantly: 'I've got to the end of you, *Nāyer*, and my calves are still there.' Thereupon *Nāyer*, angry with the old woman, asked *Shabrāyer* (a variant pronunciation of *Fabrāyer*) to lend him a day, a request which was readily granted. Since that time *Fabrāyer* has only twenty-nine days whereas *Nāyer* has thirty-one. It was during this borrowed day, which has become 31 January, that wind, hail and cold weather finished off the old woman and her calves. 'Beware of the days of the old woman' (*ayyām al-'ajūz*), runs the proverb, in other words the end of *Nāyer* is not the end of winter and you risk losing your livestock in the severe weather of February.

Fabrāyer is also a variable month: 'Sometimes it laughs, sometimes it empties its sacks of snow.'[56] For people living in the mountains, March is just as harsh a month as January. It is called *Mārs bū thlūj*, 'snowy March'. Fruit-growers fear it more than any other month, for the frequent frosts may destroy the blossoms. But it is also the ideal month for planting fruit trees and is, moreover, the last chance for doing so. 'The opportunity for planting passes in March', runs the saying, which is an expression both of practical knowledge and of popular wisdom.[57] *Yabrīr* (April) is the month during which the ears of grain are formed: 'April tells the wheat from the barley.'[58] It is also the month of the cuckoo, *ṭakūk*. It is at this time that cattle, which are believed to be irritated by the cry of this bird, run wild and may wander off: 'Don't count your calves until after the *ṭakūk* has gone by'[59] says the proverb. *Yabrīr* is a propitious month for country people, who consume large quantities of health-giving dairy products at that time, but it remains a difficult month for town dwellers who are to be pitied for the privations which they endure during spring: 'The townswoman should take care of her dried meat,' as the saying goes, 'her winter continues during spring'.[60] The spring equinox is noteworthy for the appearance of the first leaves in the fig trees: 'Day and night will be equal when the fig leaf is as long as the ear of a mouse.'[61]

Yulyūz (July) is the month for harvesting and threshing the grain. *Ghust* (August) and *Shutenbīr* (September) are generally the months of rest and of family celebrations. Marriages, circumcisions, the purchase of family trousseaux (*jihāz*), ceremonies at the tombs of saints, all take place at this time. For mountain dwellers, *Khtūber* (October) is a propitious but, at the same time, a rather sad month. It is a month for laying in stores and is therefore a time of intense activity in preparation for the long winter to come. In October the various autumn fruits and vegetables are picked and dried: figs, grapes, walnuts, almonds, jujubes, pumpkins, peppers, maize. But October is also the month in which the first cold winds bring nostalgic memories of summer: 'Tell me the almond trees are in blossom, but do not tell me it is time to shake down the walnuts', runs the saying.[62]

This division of the year into seasons and sub-seasons, in accordance with the regular changes in nature and in agricultural life, is expressed in *mawāsim* (plural of *mawsim*, time of the year, season). There is a *mawsim* or *zamān* (period, time) for ploughing, a *mawsim* for the blossom, a *mawsim* for harvesting and a *mawsim* for shaking down the olives, each of which are marks (the root verb being *wasama:* to mark or stamp) made by time and by man's labour on nature.

Both in the case of the calendars of various origins and of the seasonal rhythms of agricultural life, popular apperceptions are expressed by meaningful sayings and easily transmitted symbols. These are the basic elements of the conception of time which is enriched, but not substantially altered, by religious knowledge. Climatic and practical considerations justify any borrowing, whether Coptic, or Roman or African; and these borrowings thrive so in Maghrebian Islam that the man of religion must be as familiar with his agricultural calendar as with his lunar calendar. The reason why the various Mediterranean cultures have amalgamated in the popular apperception with Islam is that the cultural climate here is far more favourable to open-minded assimilation than to closed parochialism.

Receptivity to scientific knowledge. Weather lore based on centuries-old contact by the Maghrebian peoples with different climates ranges from ordinary observations to the conceptions and calculations of specialists. This is the field of the *anwā'* (traditional climatology) and of the *abrāj* (the phases of the moon as related to the seasons) and of all their practical applications. There is a difference in the mode of knowledge between the *muwaqit* of the towns, who is often an astronomer and a mathematician, and the layman who observes the weather direct, but the former does not reject popular wisdom, any more than the latter is closed to or estranged from the findings of *'ilm* (science).

The average *fallāḥ* (peasant), observing the weather, knows, for example, that the month of April is a time of thunderstorms and hail, and that October is the month of the first rains 'beneficial to the stockbreeder, harmful for the fruit-grower',[63] that the late fogs of spring cause rust on the corn, that if the end of winter is dry it causes epidemics among cattle, that the sirocco destroys the blossom and the growing vegetables, that the north-east wind heralds the coming of rain and that low white clouds mean snow; but in order to make his forecasts on the basis of the signs he sees in the sky, the position of the clouds the exact direction of the wind, and the various climatic zones, determined by altitude and distance from the sea, he will turn to specialists who have generally acquired their knowledge through the oral tradition.

Such experts rely more on detailed observation and their sensitivity to natural phenomena than on traditional weather lore. They are observant for the heaviness which heralds a storm, the red evening sky which predicts the end of the rains and the hush falling on nature which denotes a change in the direction of the wind. Such observations have been codified into laws or exact knowledge only from long and constantly enriched individual experience. In this field, knowledge remains empirical and practical but pays due deference to book learning. The role of popular astronomer is often filled by the *faqīh* (lawyer) of the village who is also the school-teacher, the judge, the Imam of prayer and the scribe; he does not, however, think it beneath him to appeal to the old experts for help. He is expected to provide answers to questions which he is asked concerning various practical matters. If he provides the *fallāḥs* with information on the religious calendar he is also expected to inform them concerning the solar calendar and weather conditions. Nevertheless, religion carries greater weight than empirical or astronomical knowledge and the weather forecast, even if it is announced on the radio, on television or in the newspapers, is not yet fully accepted as scientific. It is no more than the result of approximate calculations and God is the master of *ghayb*, the hidden future, which is in his power alone.

In market towns and in the old villages, *tawqīt* (from the root *waqt*), the reckoning of the movable time-table for prayer in accordance with the positions of the sun, is the province of the *faqīh*. The traditional town *muwaqit*, however, is a specialist whose role is to establish the annual table of hours of prayer; in many cases it is he who supervises the setting of the mosque clocks. In certain areas in the Maghreb, people still talk of 'Arab time', which applies to that country, and *franjia* (European) time, which is recognized as universal. In connexion with the technical means of measuring time, it is worth recalling here that the water clock, which has now disappeared, had been very widely used in the towns of the Western Moslem countries since the tenth century.

At a more rudimentary level, it may be pointed out that the times for watering crops in country areas were, until quite recently, established in accordance with the readings provided by a makeshift sun-dial, a small straight stick, one cubit in length, pushed into the earth which enabled the *fallāḥ* to tell the approximate time by the length of its shadow. Moreover, the peasants are still able to reckon the principal divisions of time during the hours of darkness by observing the stars, but need the help of guides and experts on time in order to find their direction in open country or to establish the exact time by the stars. In fact, the main repositories of these traditions of popular practical astronomy are herdsmen and those who travel the caravan routes.

Nowadays standardized calendars are published in advance, showing the phases of the moon, the variable hours of prayer and religious festivals. *Hijrīya*, Gregorian, Julian and agricultural calendars are available to the public at large. The press and radio announce the hours of worship. Traditional lore has thus become of secondary importance. Although it is still illegal to establish fast days or feast days on the basis of forward calculations, the calendar is hardly ever totally ignored. The watch and the alarm clock have become the only infallible instruments for measuring time and the peasant, instead of looking at the sky, glances at his watch or listens to his transistor radio. The weather forecasts announced by the radio are not yet followed with much interest but their value and accuracy are no longer disputed. Contrary to what one might assume, no special effort has ever been made to adapt the traditional outlook to make it receptive to scientific and universal knowledge; traditional popular culture, which has always had a practical bent, continues to be open to any useful knowledge which science has to contribute. Here again, the local heritage willingly draws on sources of universal learning.

THE SOCIO-HISTORICAL CONCEPTION OF TIME

It is particularly the unpleasant aspects of time which find an echo in popular language and literature. In most regions of the Maghreb the word *zamān* (time) suggests misfortune and pessimism. One says of a person who behaves badly that 'he is time' (i.e. 'as bad as time') or that he has 'a face like time'. The same term denotes wretchedness, and the popular expression 'time is killing me' is a reference to the hardships of life.[64]

The full significance of these expressive terms can probably only be grasped if they are seen in the context of the social and political conditions in which they seem to have arisen, for there is no doubt that these are modern, and perhaps specifically Maghrebian expressions. Be this as it may, these turns of phrase do not occur in popular pre-colonial literature nor in the classical language which is common to all Arabs. The association of time with misfortune is, however, very ancient and seems to date from the periods of decline. One flourishing genre of classical literature was that of 'complaints against time'.[65] In the Western Moslem countries, in which political misfortunes were felt more intensely from the fourteenth century onwards, all the blame for such misfortunes was, at a very early stage, attributed to time. The descendants of the emigrants from Spain, who settled in the cities of the Maghreb, have preserved an ancient Andalusian literature which refers to 'treacherous time',[66] and which expresses a painful nostalgia for the time 'of happiness and fulfilment',[67] in the lost homeland. It was, however, at the end of the nineteenth century and during the colonial twentieth century that there was an explosion of literature in the tragic vein in which time bears equal responsibility with men for the defeat and collapse of the Arab-Moslem world. A vast number of expressions voicing pessimism and resignation reflect this political situation, of which the people were painfully conscious. Hardly a single conversation, however short, does not include such sayings as: 'fickle time which leaves nothing as it was before', or 'villainous time when villains prosper', or 'time is succession, the hours are fickle and the wheel of history turns' or, lastly, 'the days have become for us like misfortune'.[68]

The language of the poets of this peasant world is more violent and more direct. It glorifies past times of victorious Islam in which the 'idolater' and the 'Roman' (*rūmī*) were overcome by 'the men of God'. This time was itself 'a lordly time, because it bred lords'; whereas 'our time is vile because it breeds villains'.[69] History, according to such peasant literature, has known only one golden age, that when the Companions of the Prophet conquered the world, and that age is gone for ever, for the men who constructed it were a superior breed: 'A race of ivory and not of flesh, a race of eagles' says a poet contemporary with 'Abdelkader.[70]

However, one must not despair. Time is fickle by nature and will turn against the present conquerors and the saviour will come. He is not far away. He will appear before the end of the fourteenth century of the Hegira (*qarn arbataash*) and will be the 'Master of the Hour', *mawla assāa.* Thus, resignation in the face of defeat is, as it were, counterbalanced by the evocation of past glories and by the expected downfall of the enemy which was already being confidently predicted at the end of the nineteenth century.

Certain expressions, however, reflect an attitude of resignation towards the decline, in so far as time is regarded as an almost sovereign power which deals out to each nation its fate as the ages go by. 'Our *dawla* is past' means 'we have had our share', our 'turn', our 'government' have passed. The chivalrous spirit of the Bedouin affirms that one must play the game whether it be won or lost and that everyone has 'his hour' or 'his age'. Indeed, as the poets say, 'the hour of the Roman has come' following 'the hour of the Arab'.

Proverbs and poetry are thus an inexhaustible source of popular wisdom which transcends suffering. 'The days of the wicked world are to be forgotten', runs the saying,[71] and, in order not to know despair, one must learn to expect nothing. The experience of time here reaches the depths of pessimism, for time hounds us mercilessly and the 'few moments of happiness' which it allows us to experience are ephemeral. Indeed, the whole of life is reduced to 'a few hours'.[72] But an analysis of this subjective duration in popular literature makes it clear that such pessimism with regard to time had its origin in political events which weighed heavily on the Maghrebian consciousness during the colonial period. This literature perhaps takes us rather far away from the practical awareness of time, but it has the advantage of opening windows on to an area of human reality which, far better than mere empirical behaviour, reflects popular apperceptions which are intensely experienced and loaded with a wealth of meaning.

NOTES

1. This is a specifically Arabic term which, unlike *zamān*, is not part of the common Semitic lexicon.
2. A *ḥadīth* is a saying attributed to Muḥammad. The entire body of *ḥadīth(s)* is the '*Sunna* (tradition) of the Prophet'.
3. cf. W. Montgomery Watt, '*Dahr*', *Encyclopedia of Islam*, 2nd ed.
4. cf. L. Massignon, *Essai sur les Origines du Lexique Technique de la Mystique Musulmane*, 3rd ed., p. 66–7, Paris, Vrin, 1968.
5. cf. M. Gaudefroy-Demonbynes and R. Blachère, *Grammaire de l'Arabe Classique*, 3rd ed., p. 36, Paris, Maisonneuve, 1952.
6. In his *Āthār*, quoted by Willy Hartner, '*Zamān*', *Encyclopedia of Islam*, 1st ed.
7. L. Massignon, 'Le Temps dans la Pensée Islamique', *Eranos Jahrbuch, 1951*, Vol. XX, p. 142, Zurich, Rhein Verlag, 1952.
8. J. Chelhold, *Les Structures du Sacré chez les Arabes*, p. 238, Paris, Maisonneuve et Larose, 1964.
9. The division of the day into twenty-four hours seems to be due to Greek influences.
10. On the importance of the moon in the pre-Islamic world and in the life of Moslem communities (whether educated or otherwise), see Maxime Rodinson, 'La Lune chez les Arabes et dans l'Islam', in the collection: *La Lune, Mythes et Rites*, p. 153–215, Paris, Éditions du Seuil, 1962.
11. The exact date of this 'emigration' (*hijra* or hegira) is disputed. It is generally situated on the eighth day of *Rabī'* I, the third lunar month of the same year (20 September 622). *Hijra*, as is often said, should be understood as implying 'emigrating' far from all infidelity.
12. A very Semitic notion of the value of direct testimony.
13. The '*umra* (including visits to the holy places of Mecca) may be performed separately and is allowed on a private basis at any time of the year, whereas the *ḥajj* (which takes place outside the walls of Mecca and includes a pause on the hill of '*Arafāt* and the sacrifice of animals), an act of community worship obligatory 'at least once in a lifetime', barring some major obstacle, and one of the 'pillars of Islam', has a rigorously established date.
14. This is the '*Īd al-aḍḥā*, 'the sacrificial festival', which is solemnly celebrated on the same day throughout the entire 'Islamic world', which forms a single community with the pilgrims of Mecca.
15. Massignon, op. cit.
16. ibid., p. 141.
17. A reference to the account given in the Koran 7: 172.
18. Jurjānī, *Ta'rīfāt*, p. 111, Leipzig, Flügel, 1845.
19. *Dīwān d'al-Ḥallāj*, Arabic edition with French translation by L. Massignon, in: *Journal Asiatique*, January-March 1931, p. 29.
20. Ḥallāj, quoted by L. Massignon, *La Passion d'al-Ḥallāj*, p. 557, Paris, Geuthner, 1922.

21. Hujwīrī, *Kashf al-mahjūb* (Persian text of the eleventh century). cf. English translation by R. A. Nicholson in 'E. J. W. Gibb Memorial Series', p. 367, Leyden and London, 1911.
22. ibid., p. 368.
23. Whereas Iraq, an Arab country, has a slight Shiite majority, and the Moslems of Lebanon, for example, include Sunnites, Imamite Shiites, and sects deriving from Ismailism. (In Pakistan, however, there is a preponderance of Sunnites.)
24. *Najāt*, 2nd ed., p. 118, Cairo, 1357/1938. The two chapters on time and space (p. 115–24) repay close analysis, as do the corresponding texts of the *Shifā'*.
25. *Al-Risāla fī l-ḥudūd* (Treatise on Definitions), in *Tis' rasā'il*, p. 92, Cairo edition, 1326/1908. French translation by A. M. Goichon, *Introduction à Avicenne*, p. 135, Paris, Desclée de Brouwer, 1933.
26. *Kitāb al-mashā'ir* (*Livres des Pénétrations Métaphysiques*). Arabic edition (with Persian text), p. 65–212 and French translation by Henry Corbin, p. 210–11, Teheran and Paris, Bibliothèque Iranienne, 1964.
27. ibid., p. 64–210 (translation p. 209).
28. See the analysis of the thesis of 'Alā' al-Dawla Semnānī and Sa'īd Qummī made by H. Corbin in *En Islam Iranien*, I, 'Le shī'isme duodécimain', p. 176–83, Paris, Gallimard, 1971. (The Ismaili Qummī was to add the 'very subtle time' of the 'superior spiritual beings', p. 180–1.)
29. cf. Plato's definition, 'time, image of eternity'.
30. See below, note 47.
31. cf. Muḥammad Iqbāl, *Paymā-i-Mashriq* (Message de l'Orient), translated from the Persian by E. Meyerovitch and M. Achena, respectively, p. 138, 92, 77, Paris, Les Belles Lettres, 1956.
32. ibid., p. 179.
33. *Djāvīd-Nāma, Le Livre de l'Éternité*, translated from the Persian into French by E. Meyerovitch and M. Mokri, p. 33 and 150, Paris, Albin Michel, 1962 (Unesco).
34. *Payām-i-Mashriq*, trans. cit. note 31.
35. However, each prophet, as a prophet, is always highly personalized. (cf. Louis Gardet, *Les Grands Problèmes de la Théologie Musulmane: Dieu et la Destinée de l'Homme*, p. 150–1, Paris, Vrin, 1967.)
36. Henry Corbin, *Trilogie Ismaélienne*, on *Ta' wīlāt* [La Roseraie du Mystère] by Maḥmūd Shabestarī, p. 83, Tehran and Paris, Bibliothèque Iranienne, 1961.
37. ——. Persian edition and commentary on the *Kitāb jāmi' al-ḥikmatayn* (*La jonction des deux Sagesses*) by Nāṣir-e Khusraw, 'Étude Préliminaire', p. 5, Tehran and Paris, Bibliothèque Iranienne, 1953.
38. According to the Ismaili tradition of the 'Reform of Alamūt' when in the year 669/1164, was proclaimed the 'Resurrection of Resurrections'. (cf. Corbin, ibid., p. 4–36.)
39. Massignon, op. cit., p. 143.
40. ibid.
41. Apart from the Ismaili gnoses, according to which a blissful cycle of 'unveiling' preceded- (and will follow) the dark historical cycle of the present 'eclipse'.
42. 'The oriental historian', writes Henry Corbin, 'sees himself as a chronicler whose task is faithfully to record and collate the "chains" of authorities (*isnād*).' *En Islam Iranien*, I, p. 183, note 148.
43. Born in Tunis of an Arab family in 732/1332; died in Cairo in 808/1406.
44. *Muqaddima* (*Prolegomena*), p. 26, Cairo edition, n.d. (Trans. Slane, Vol. I, p. 71); the most recent translations of the *Muqaddima* are, in English, that of F. Rosenthal, New York, 1958, and in French, that of V. Monteil, Paris, 1970.
45. ibid., p. 2 (trans. I, 4).
46. ibid., p. 24 (trans. I, 67). Although the diagnoses a cultural decline in Andalusia and in the Maghreb, Ibn Khaldūn suggests a possible resurgence on the one hand in the Eastern Arab countries and on the other hand, on the north coast of the Mediterranean 'in the land of the Franks' (dawn of the Renaissance . . .), p. 337 (trans., Vol. III, p. 128–9).

47. *The Reconstruction of Religious Thought in Islam*, new edition, p. 141, Lahore, Ashraf Press, 1960.
48. 'Its cyclical character is that of a three-dimensional universe: it is spiroidal', Muḥammad Ṭalbī, 'Ibn Khaldūn et le Sens de l'Histoire', *Studia Islamica*, XXVI, Paris, 1967, p. 138.
49. A Koranic expression. See page 198, Waqt, above, for the references and eschatological significance of these verses.
50. Among the many books and articles concerning Ibn Khaldūn we shall cite the following which provide illustrations of what we have said: Muḥsīn Mahdī, *Ibn Khaldūn's Philosophy of History*, London, Allen & Unwin, 1957; and the remarkable study by Muḥammad Ṭalbī which has already been mentioned (*Studia Islamica*, XXVI, p. 73-148. See note 48). Also worth mentioning is *La Pensée Réaliste d'Ibn Khaldūn*, Paris, Presses Universitaires de France, 1967, by N. Nassār; this contains a pertinent analysis which seems to us, however, to be somewhat biased towards Hegelian dialectic; and, lastly, the excellent study by Muhammad 'Azīz Laḥbabī, *Ibn Khaldūn*, Paris, Seghers, 1968.
51. Koran 55:27.
52. بين الكاف والنون يكون ما يكون, 'bayn al-kāf wa l-*nūn* yakūn mā yak*ūn*' as the saying goes. (As such sayings are almost always in verse or in rhymed prose, we have underlined the rhyme.)
53. A legend which is current (with variations as to the name of the hero and the experiences he goes through) in several areas of western Algeria.
54. The Arabic words of these sayings and proverbs are those of the language most commonly spoken in the countryside. The transcription, while not entirely 'phonetic', is intended to give an approximate idea of the usual pronunciation.
55. نهارات الناير يقلق فيهم الثور الحاير, 'nāhārāt annā*yer*—yeqleq fīhum althawr alḥā*yer*'.
56. شبراير مرة يضحك مرة يرمى الثلج بالغراير, 'shabrā*yer* marra yaḍḥak marra yarmī athalj belgharā*yer*'.
57. فاتك الغرس فى مارس, 'fātek algher*s* fī mar*s*'.
58. يبرير فراز القمح من الشعير, 'yebr*īr* ferrāz alqamh men ashsha '*īr*'.
59. ما تحسب عجولك حتى يفوت الطكوك, 'mātehsseb 'ajūlek hattā yefūt aṭṭakūk'.
60. قد : للحضرية تستحفظ بخليعها شتاء فى ربيعها, 'qul: lalḥaḍriyya testaḥfeẓ bekhlī' *ihā*—shetā' fī rabī' *iha*'.
61. حين تكون ورقة الكرمة قدر أذن الفار يستوى الليل مع النهار, 'ḥīn tekūn warqat alkarma qadr udhun alf*ār*—yestawī allayil ma 'annah*ār*'.
62. بشرنى بأنوار اللوز لا تخبرنى بنفض الجوز, 'bashernī bianwār al*lūz*—lā takhbernī binafd al*jūz*'.
63. أمطار اول الخريف تفرح صاحب العتروس (التيس) وتنكد صاحب الكرموس (التين) 'amtar awal alkharīf teferreḥ ṣāḥeb al'atr*us* (var. attīs)—we tenekked ṣāḥeb alkarm*ūs* (var. attīn)'.
64. فلان زمان – وجه الزمان – قتلنى الزمان, 'fulān zamān—wejh ezzamān—qutalnī ezzamān'.
65. شكوى الزمان والحال, 'shakwā ezzamān wa-lhāl'.
66. الزمان الغدار – الزمان الخوان, 'ezzamān alghaddār—ezzamān alkhawwān'.
67. زمان السعود والانشراح, 'zamān assu 'ūd wa-linshirāh'.

68\. (a) الزمان البدال ما يخلي حال على حال, ‘ezzamān albadd*āl* mā yekhellī ḥāl ‘alā ḥ*āl*’.

(b) زمان الشمايت للشمايت, ‘zamān ashsha*māyet* lishsha*māyet*’.

(c) الحالة دالة و السوايع بدالة والفلك يدور, ‘alḥāla dāla wa-ssawāye‘ baddāla wa-lfalk yedūr’.

69\. The traditional expressions, particularly in Algeria are: الزمان الحر (noble time), ‘ezzamān alḥurr’ and الزمان البرهوش (mongrel time), ‘ezzamān albarhūsh’.

70\. This is a reference to Ben Raho, a popular west Algerian poet whose epics are panegyrics in honour of the Companions of the Prophet and, more particularly, of ‘Alī, here transformed into a super-human hero. His attacks on ‘the Romans’ (*rūmī*) are set in about 1850 and therefore post-date the victory of the colonial armies which were referred to as ‘Roman’ by the people. ‘Race of ivory’, عظام الفيل, ‘*iẓām al-fīl* (literally: ‘elephant bones’); ‘eagles, offspring of eagles’, العقبان و لادة | العقبان, ‘*al-‘uqbān wilādat al-‘uqbān*, literally: ‘falcons children of falcons’.

71\. انس الزمان ينساك, ‘ansa ezzamān yensāk’—‘forget time and it will forget you’.

72\. الدنيا ساعات, ‘addunyā sā‘āt’.

TIME AS A PROBLEM OF CULTURAL HISTORY

A. J. Gurevich

Representations of time are essential components of social consciousness, whose structure reflects the rhythms and cadences which mark the evolution of society and culture. The mode of perception and apperception of time reveals many fundamental trends of society and of the classes, groups and individuals composing it. Time occupies a prominent place in the 'model of the world' characterizing a given culture, along with other components of this model, such as space, cause, change, number, the relation between the sensible and the suprasensible world, the relation of the general to the particular and of the part to the whole, fate, liberty, etc.

Every civilization perceives the world through language and other semiotic systems peculiar to itself (the 'languages' of art, religion, science, etc.), systems which are formed in the course of men's practical activity, on the basis of their own experience and of the tradition inherited from preceding generations.

Every stage in the development of production, in the evolution of social relations and in the progress of man's autonomy in relation to his natural environment is matched by special ways of experiencing the world. In this sense, all the categories enumerated above, including 'time', reflect social practice. But they also contribute, at the same time, to moulding practice in forms fixed by the existing 'model of the world'. If it is true that culture is 'second nature' to man, it would appear to be equally true that it is impossible to understand a particular historical type of structure of the human personality without having studied the modes of perception and apperception of time pertaining to the corresponding culture. The sense of time is one of the essential 'parameters' of personality.

Since the attitude to time and the way in which it is apprehended and experienced vary according to epochs and civilizations, the problem posed by time in relation to cultural history differs from those which it poses in philosophy, modern physics, psychology and literature.

Contemporary man lives *sub specie temporis*. He handles the 'time' category with ease, and has little difficulty in taking stock of the most remote past. He claims to foresee the future, to plan his activities and to determine far in advance the development of science, technology, production and society. That he possesses this faculty is due to the very elaborate stage reached by the time systems we use. Time and space are seen as abstractions which alone make it possible to form the image of a unified cosmos, to conceive the idea of a single, coherent universe. In the modern age, these categories have acquired an autonomous character, and they can be used as instruments without reference to specific events of which they are absolutely independent. Time, in our minds, is linked not so much to the phenomena which occur in time as to the instruments by which the passage of time is measured. Having mastered time, having, that is to say, learned to measure time and divide it up with great precision, to save it and to spend it, man finds himself, at the same time, a slave to it. And indeed, the idea of time, with its passing and its irreversibility, is continually present in the mind of modern man 'in a hurry'.[1] Contemporary civilization has witnessed an immeasurable increase in the value and importance of speed, and a radical transformation of the very pace of life, a pace which is now regarded by the inhabitants of the industrialized countries as normal and inevitable. Time which is irreversible, vectorial and divisible into segments of equal size and equivalent value, the time of our chronometers, watches and calendars, time conceived as a form of existence of matter, as 'pure duration', forms an integral part of the scientific image of the world which has developed in the course of the last centuries and is at present in the process of being modified (but within the framework of this same scientific thought).

Never before in the whole of its history has mankind had a feeling of time such as now prevails in the developed countries.

The present perception of time bears very little resemblance to that of other epochs. In the so-called primitive or mythological consciousness, the time category does not exist in the form of an abstraction, in so far as thought itself, at the archaic stages of development, is mainly concrete, object-related and sensible.[2] Consciousness perceives the world simultaneously in its synchronic and diachronic totality, and is thus 'in temporal'. An event which took place before and one taking place now can, in certain circumstances, be perceived by the archaic consciousness as phenomena situated on the same plane, occurring in the same temporal duration. It is for this reason that the perception of time by primitive man appears to the modern mind as unorganized. The fact is that time, in the archaic consciousness, has a completely different structure, corresponding to the fundamental concepts and needs of primitive society. For all intents and purposes, the sentiment of time, in this society, extends only to the immediate future, the recent past and present activity, to phenomena occurring in man's immediate environment; beyond these limits, events are perceived more vaguely, are little co-ordinated in time, and belong already to the realm of legend and myth.

In the consciousness of the men of primitive societies, time appears not in the form of neutral co-ordinates but as a powerful, mysterious force governing everything, the life of man and the existence of the gods alike. This explains why time is impregnated with affective associations: it can be good or bad, favourable to certain forms of activity and fatal to others; there exists sacred time, the time of festivals, of sacrifice and of re-enactment of the myth relating to the return of the 'original' time, which has the effect of 'switching off' profane time.[3] In this society, time does not proceed in linear fashion from the past to the future; it is either immobile or cyclical. That which has already been returns at fixed intervals. This cyclical conception of the apperception of time, which is also found much later, in a new form, and in far more evolved social systems, is linked in large measure to the fact that man has not freed himself from nature and his consciousness is subordinated to the periodical changes of the seasons. The rhythm of social life is governed by the alternation of the seasons and of the corresponding production cycles. As a result, the interpretation of both the natural and also the social world in accordance with mythical categories leads to the belief in 'eternal recurrence'.[4] Human acts are a repetition of acts committed previously by the divinity or the 'cultural hero', ancestors are born again in their descendants. The consciousness of primitive man is not directed towards the perception of changes, but inclines to find the old in the new. This explains why the future, for him, is not differentiated from what has already been.

It is clear that this kind of perception of time reflects a specific appraisal of the human being, attaching no value to independence and originality. The rule in primitive societies is to conform strictly to traditional models; all innovation is anathema, precise observance of the rites of existence compulsory. The very nature of this society makes its capacity for change extremely limited, and its stability can only be guaranteed by a rigid and total control mechanism. The idea of the eternal recurrence of time forms part of this mechanism. The individual, like time, is not unique of his kind. G. J. Whitrow rightly draws attention to archaic man's aspiration to overcome time or set it aside.[5] The attempt to abolish passing time by a return to a mythical prototype, to an original *illud tempus*, was perhaps nothing but an attempt to overcome the isolation and solitude of individual existence. With the myth of the renewal of time, archaic culture gave man the possibility of transcending the briefness and oneness of his life. By identifying himself both in his thoughts and in his behaviour with the society of the clan, man cheated death . . .

Linked also with the mythological concept of time is the idea that all modes of time, past, present and future, are so to speak situated on the same plane, in a sense 'simultaneous'. This brings us up against the phenomenon of 'spatialization': time is perceived in the same way as space, and the present is not separated off from the temporal unity of past and future.[6] Archaic man sees the past and the present extending around him, intermingling and mutually explanatory.[7] The past never ceases to exist, which is why it is no less real than the present. It is this representation of time that underlies ancestor worship and all the archetypes which constantly gain a fresh lease of life through the celebration of myths and rites at festival times. Traditions piously observed are the materialization and perpetuation of the past, dominating the present. But the future also participates in the present: man can look into it and exercise a magic influence on it; and from this stem fortune-telling, soothsaying, prophetic dreams and also the belief in fate. Fate is irrevocable since, in a certain sense, what is to come to pass is already a fact. At all events the future, perceived as fate, can be felt in the present: thus a man doomed to die is marked in advance by its imprint; death casts its shadow on him; the wounds he is about to receive in the coming battle can be felt on his body; he 'smells' of death. With this attitude towards time, there is no clear dividing line between the past, the present and the future.

Time, in this conception, is not an 'empty' abstract duration. It is the very life of man, and changes its quality as life goes on. Time is the link between human generations, succeeding one another and returning, recurring like the seasons. Time is as real and tangible as the rest of the world. This conception of time reflects the feeling of the fullness of being which is characteristic of archaic man. Being is not divided up by the spirit of analysis into separate categories, devoid of objective content. Time and space are considered not as being outside experience or prior to experience, but as existing solely within actual experience itself, forming the elements which constitute it and which are inseparable from the tissue of life. This explains why time is not so much apprehended by consciousness as directly experienced.

It is not possible to draw a clear distinction between past, present and future until the linear perception of time, linked to the idea of its irreversibility, comes to predominate in the social consciousness. This is not to say that this kind of distinction is entirely lacking in archaic societies: the experience of life provides man with the elements from which to elucidate the sequence of his actions and of natural phenomena.

The chronological series formed by the events of men's everyday life are separated, in their minds, from mythical time; ancestors and their living descendants exist in two different systems of time. Rites and festivals, however, form the link which connects these two different perceptions of time, these two different levels of apprehension of reality. Thus linear time does not predominate in the human consciousness; it is subordinated to a cyclical perception of the phenomena of life, to a mythical image of the world.

The union of the linear perception of time with a cyclical, mystical and poetical conception, a 'condensation of time through dreams' (Thomas Mann), occurs all through history; the problem is how to link up these various forms of experience with the apperception of the passage of time. In varying degrees, many of the peoples who created the great civilizations of antiquity had a cyclical consciousness of time. The systems of values underlying various ancient oriental cultures are based on the idea of immobility, of an eternal present indissolubly linked to the past. The cyclical succession of eras, dynasties and reigns, which obey a liturgical order and are subject to a rigid rhythm,[8] the wheel of the cosmic order revolving through all eternity, the perpetually recurring cycle of birth and death[9]—all these bear witness to the absence of any absolute difference between the past, the present and the future. Changes affect the surface of life rather than its essence. In everyday life, time passes, but this time is only a semblance of the world; real time is the eternity of a higher reality not subject to change. The world, in the representation of the ancients, emerged complete from the hands of the creator, the past and the future existing in the present.

Antiquity is rightly regarded as the cradle of European civilization. Yet nothing, it would appear, indicates more clearly the profound difference between ancient culture and the modern than their interpretation of time: whereas contemporary society is wholly dominated by vectorial time, time in Hellenic consciousness played only a minor part. The Greek perception of time was still strongly influenced by a mythical interpretation of reality.[10] The Greeks perceived and experienced the world not in terms of change and evolution, but as being at rest, or effecting a revolution in the 'great circle'. The events occurring in the world are not unique: the successive epochs recurred and the men and events of former times will arise again at the expiration of the 'Great Year'—the era of Pythagoras.[11] Man contemplates a harmonious, perfect cosmos, 'material, sensible and living', 'appearing like an eternal cyclical rotation of matter, now emerging out of formless chaos, striking in its harmony, its symmetry, its rhythmic disposition, its sublime and peaceable grandeur, now rushing to its destruction, wrecking its equilibrium and transforming itself into chaos once again.[12] The plastic arts of antiquity are impregnated with this attitude to time: the interpretation of the body in ancient art shows that men saw in the present moment the fullness of being complete in itself and not subject to evolution. The same is true of philosophy: the dialectic transitions from one state to another do not interrupt the rotation of the world and of matter. 'Was', 'is' and 'will be' are forms of the time which imitates eternity and progresses in circles according to the laws of number (Plato).[13] The Hellenic consciousness is turned towards the past; the world is governed by fate, to which the gods too are subordinated, and consequently there is no room left for historical evolution. Antiquity is static, 'astronomical' (A. F. Losev). According to the representations of the ancient world, the 'golden age' lies behind, in the mythical past.[14] The men of antiquity seem to 'advance towards the future backwards, with their faces turned away from it.[15]

This mytho-poetical, static and cyclical conception of the world, so characteristic of the Hellenes, was to be transformed in Rome. The Roman historians are far more alive to the linear passage of time, and they interpret history no longer through the categories of myth, but on the basis of specific historical events (foundation of Rome, and so on). However, despite the progress of philosophical thought, the ancient world produced no philosophy of history beyond a general historical pessimism: the men of antiquity, in their contemplation of the world, did not perceive history as a drama, a field of action for the exercise of man's free will.[16]

In antiquity, man was not yet in a position to detach himself from his natural existence and stand resolutely over against his environment. His dependence on nature and his inability to perceive it as an object on which he acts from without find concrete expression in the idea of the analogy between man as 'microcosm' and the world as 'macrocosm', each with a peculiar structure and composed of the same elements;[17] also in Rabelais' image of the 'grotesque body', inchoate, not wholly separated from the surrounding world, but engulfed in and pervaded by it. As shown by M. M. Bakhtin, this image played a primordial role in ancient and mediaeval culture, remaining unchanged in the popular consciousness for several epochs, until the Renaissance, which marks the transition to a new conception of the world and a new apperception of man by himself (individualism and a body 'withdrawn', 'isolated' from the world).[18] It is probable that this specific perception of reality corresponded to a particular attitude towards time.

N. I. Konrad has shown that Polybius and Ssu-ma Ch'ien, who lived in totally different socio-cultural regions, were astonishingly alike in their interpretation of history as a circular process; though it is true that these two great historians of antiquity both held that the circle does not signify more repetition, and that it encloses a new content.[19] But for all this, neither of them was able to escape from the conception of the world and the perception of time characteristic of his own epoch and culture: history for them and their compatriots was nothing more than an eternal recurrence of the same political forms in a specific order.

Linear time is one of the possible forms of social time which has prevailed, as the sole system of calculation, in the European cultural region only. But this happened only after a very lengthy and complex process of evolution. Christianity, breaking with the pagans' cyclical vision of the world,[20] took from the Old Testament the notion of time experienced as an eschatological process, a fervent waiting for the great event in which history is fulfilled—the coming of the Messiah. While sharing the eschatological approach of the Old Testament, the teaching of the New Testament transformed this conception and entirely renewed the concept of time.

In the first place, in the Christian vision of the world, the concept of time is distinct from the concept of eternity which, in other ancient systems of thought, comprehended and subsumed terrestrial time. Eternity cannot be measured in segments of time, it is an attribute of God who 'was not, will not be, but always is'. Terrestrial time is described as the 'shadow of eternity', the 'succession of things' (Honorius Augustodunensis).[21] It was created, and it has a beginning and an end which set bounds to the duration of human history. Terrestrial time is in correlation with eternity and, at certain decisive moments, human history, as it were, 'irrupts' into eternity. The Christian aspires to pass from time on earth to eternity, the realm of eternal beatitude.

Then secondly, historical time acquires a definite structure, being clearly subdivided both quantitatively and above all qualitatively, into two main epochs, before and after Christ. History is in movement, from the act of divine creation to the last judgement. In the centre of history is a decisive sacramental event which determines its course and gives a new and predetermining sense to the whole of its subsequent evolution: the coming and the death of Christ. The history of the Old Testament is that of an epoch preparing for the birth of Christ, and subsequent history is the result of his incarnation and his sacrifice. This is an event of exceptional and unique significance.[22] Thus the new apperception of time is based on three decisive moments: the beginning, the apogee and the end of the human race. Time becomes definitively vectorial, linear and irreversible. The Christian vision of time differs both from the archaic vision, centred wholly on the past, and from the messianic, prophetic vision, looking to the future, characteristic of the Judaic conception of time as expressed in the Old Testament. The Christian conception of time attaches importance both to the past, in that the tragedy of the New Testament is already enacted, and to the future, which brings reward or punishment. It is precisely the existence of these points of reference in time which, with extraordinary force, 'straightens it out', 'draws it into line', at the same time forging close links between different times and inscribing the course of history in an immanent, restricted plane, which is the only possible one (in the context of this conception of the world). It will be noted however that time, in Christianity, though vectorial, is nevertheless not freed from the cyclical conception. It is only the interpretation of this conception which has radically changed. The point is that, since time has been separated from eternity, man examining the segments of the earth's history sees it in the form of a linear succession; but the history of the earth itself, considered as a whole, in the context of the creation and the end of the world, constitutes a complete cycle: man and the world return to the Creator, time to eternity.[23]

The historical time of Christianity is dramatic. The drama begins with the first free act of man: the fall of Adam. This is closely linked to the coming of Christ, sent by God to save mankind. Reward and punishment await man at the end of his earthly existence. The interpretation of the history of the earth as the history of the salvation of mankind has given it a new dimension. Human life takes place simultaneously on two temporal planes: that of the empirical, passing events of earthly existence, and that of the fulfilment of the divine command. As a result, man takes part in the drama of the history of the universe, in the course of which the fate of the world and that of his soul is decided. This consciousness of playing a direct part in history coloured mediaeval man's attitude to the world. The dramatic character of the Christian apperception of time is based on a dualist vision of the world and its history: life on earth and the whole of history are an arena where good and evil meet in conflict.

But good and evil are not impersonal, cosmic forces; they are rooted in man himself, and to ensure the triumph of good in his soul and in history, man's free will is necessary. It is the recognition of the freedom of human choice that makes the Christian perception of time and history so irrevocably dramatic. Life on earth, with its passing joys and sorrows, is not an end in itself; it has meaning only in the context of the sacramental history of the salvation of mankind.[24] This explains why the past and the future have a value greater than the present, which is fleeting. This attitude towards the passing events of the present is characteristic of the mythological mentality, which regards them merely as the reflection of original models, a replica of the divine archetype. But the Christian conception of the world is also a mythological one, though the Christian myth differs basically from the 'natural' pagan mythologies in that it is a historical myth which does not dissolve earthly history in the interplay of suprasensible essences, but constructs, from the sacred and the terrestrial, a specifically dualist image of historical evolution. That is why it is possible, in the context of the Christian conception of the world, to create a philosophy of history and to perceive time as an irreversible historical continuum.

Christian historicism is specific. It admits of evolution, change; but this evolution is not unlimited, it does not contain possibilities freely realizable, and it cannot lead to unexpected results not foreseen beforehand. Christian history is directed towards a limit established in advance. The symbolic 'symmetry' of the events and personages of the Old and the New Testament (since the first is the prefiguration of the second, the two series are in perfect harmony), the Augustinian doctrine of the six 'ages' of mankind, Saint Jerome's theory of the four monarchies, precluding the advent of a fifth—all these bear witness to the divine purpose of history, whose rhythm, content and outcome are inevitable and predetermined by a rational God. In this system of thought, it was perfectly logical for the chronicler, after bringing his historical account up to the events of his own time, to add, as did for instance Otto von Freising, a picture of the end of the world; only thus was history regarded as being completed, and its meaning revealed.[25]

But this religious historicism went hand in hand with a certain 'antihistoricism'. The mediaeval chroniclers, while recounting the facts of political and religious history and the cosmic phenomena which, they believed, played a mysterious part in human affairs, ignored all the other aspects of social relations and usually failed to note changes occurring in either the material or the spiritual domain. This feature of mediaeval historiography is due not only to the historians' preference for royal personages and the events concerning them: the men of this time took the view that the whole texture of real life remained outside history, immobile, untouched by time. Time passes, they thought, but not in all spheres of existence. It is but an external variation on the basis of the immobile world. 'Times change, words also change, but not faith', since 'a proposition once true will remain for ever true'. That is why, it was believed, 'Christ will come, is coming and has come' (Peter Lombardus).[26] Truth is not linked to time, and does not change with it.

The Christian conception of time, which dates from Saint Augustine, is characterized by its psychologism. Time is perceived not so much as a pure notion, an abstract measurement (Saint Augustine contested Aristotle's statement that time is a measure of movement and is itself measured by the movement of the heavenly bodies), but rather as a psychological fact, an inner experience of the soul.[27] Man must be prepared at any moment to die and appear before the Creator; his attitude to time and eternity was thus specific, immediate and personal. Time became an essential aspect of his spiritual life, an integral part of consciousness. Is not this psychologization of time linked to the general 'dematerialization' of the world by Christianity, and is it not a reaction against the ancient pagan corporeal and physical perception of the world?

Although the sentiment of time was thus substantially transformed under the influence of Christianity, the perception of time as a cyclical phenomenon, an eternal recurrence of the seasons and a repetition of the same human individualities from generation to generation, was inherent among the European peoples. Time was thought of in terms of time in man's life, having no existence outside; the mind of the peasant was incapable of seeing beyond the implacable rhythms of nature. Throughout the whole of the Middle Ages, people believed indefectibly in fate, and in the ability of certain persons to foresee the future, prophesy and influence the course of time by magic means. The ancient concepts —the cyclical recurrence of time, the 'wheel of fate' and the domination of 'dame fortune'—were preserved and revived.[28] Time, instead of being the neutral span of the real processes of life, formed an integral part of life, possessing objective materiality and reality in the medieval conception of 'realism' and having the characteristics of all 'transitory things'. Thus Christianity did not succeed in overcoming antiquity's characteristic attachment to the mythical archetype, or changing its ritual, magic attitude towards reality and in particular towards the passage of time.

Mediaeval man's inability to see the world and society as evolving entities was the corollary of his attitude towards himself and to his own inner world. As a member of the group and an embodiment of the function he performed or the position he occupied, the individual aspired above all to conform as closely as possible to an established type and to do his duty before God. His road through life was plotted in advance, 'programmed', so to speak, by his earthly vocation. There could therefore be no question of the interior development of the individual. The lives of the saints, which are the form of biography most typical of the Middle Ages, usually say nothing about man's progress towards saintliness: either the hero is converted suddenly, passing immediately and without preparation from a state of sin to saintliness; or else saintliness is given in advance, and is only revealed gradually. Since man did not perceive his own essence in terms of the categories of development, he could clearly not regard the world as a process. In this system of thought, neither the individual on the psychological plane, nor society or the universe on the historical plane presents any problem.

It is no less significant that the portrait was long neglected in mediaeval painting. Painters observed the individual features of human faces and were capable of reproducing them,[29] so that the absence of portraits was due neither to inability nor to lack of observation; they failed to produce a likeness because they were concerned to depict the general rather than the particular, the suprasensible rather than the actual features of the individual. But the absence of portraits in the Middle Ages was due also to the taste of the epoch for the incarnation of eternal truths and values, and it throws further light on the mediaeval perception of time. De-concretization is the reverse of a-temporality. Man did not see himself as existing in time; existence for him meant being and not a process of becoming. But a portrait depicts one of the numerous states of man in concrete space and time. Moreover, mankind does not live in one time only: besides natural being there is the supernatural, and the function of art was to reflect both life on earth and the reality of a higher plane, the former being regarded as deriving from the latter.

A clearer idea of mediaeval man's view of the passage of life and history could be obtained by analysing the interpretation of time in the literary works of this period. However, this is a problem which would warrant a study on its own.[30] We shall confine ourselves here to mentioning Dante, who, perhaps, most forcefully expressed the mediaeval conception of time: the contrast between the time of ephemeral life on earth and eternity, and the ascension from the first to the second, determine the 'space-time continuum' of the *Divine Comedy*, where the whole history of mankind appears synchronically. Time is immobile, and exists wholly—present, past and future—in the present. By filling the Inferno with his contemporaries and his compatriots, Dante drew the different strata of time as close as possible not only to one another but also to eternity. The system of thought of the *Divine Comedy* is based on the contrast between 'eternity' and 'earthly time'.[31] The time of human existence is contrasted with divine eternity: 'A thousand years . . . is shorter space to eternity than the twinkling of an eye to the circle which slowest is turned in heaven'.[32] Beatitude can only be attained in Paradise, 'where every *where* and every *when* is focussed', where reign 'beginning and continuity and end', and 'nor before nor after', where 'a single moment maketh a deeper lethargy for me than twenty and five centuries . . .'.[33]

Social time differs not only as between different cultures and societies, but also within each socio-cultural system as a function of its internal structure. It does not pass uniformly in the consciousness of the various classes and groups, which all perceive and experience it in their own way, functioning as they do at a different rhythm. In other words, in every society there exists not one single 'monolithic' time, but a whole series of social rhythms governed by the laws of the different processes and by the nature of the various human groups.[34]

In the Middle Ages, there were differing attitudes to time, depending on whether the reference was to agrarian time, genealogical time, biblical (or liturgical) time, cyclical time or, lastly, historical time. But, even as the different social phenomena and the institutions and mechanisms operating in society are interlinked and form a global system in which a certain type of determinism predominates, so the rhythms at which these mechanisms operate and these social forms function constitute the hierarchy of the social time of a given system. Society is unable to exist unless the multiple social rhythms have attained a certain degree of co-ordination. It is for this reason that we can speak of the social time predominating in a society. In an antagonistic social system, the social time of the dominant class will naturally be determinant so long as this class has not lost real control of social life, and remains an influential ideological force. Social time is an important element of the mechanism of social control, which is wielded by the ruling class. Conversely, a change in the time structure prevailing in a society is one of the signs indicating that the ruling class is losing control over social life.

In the Middle Ages, the Church was mistress of social time. It was the clergy who fixed the entire system applied to the calculation of time. The chronology of historical time was counted from the creation of the world and the birth of Christ. The astronomical year was also the liturgical year, punctuated by religious festivals; and even the day was regulated by the Church, with its offices and prayers. The population was informed of the passage of time by the church bells summoning them to matins, mass, vespers and so on. Thus it was that the clergy established and oriented the whole course of time in feudal society, and regulated its rhythm. All attempts to remove time from their control were vigorously repulsed: the Church forbade work on feast days (the observance of religious interdictions was considered more important than the supplementary output that might have been achieved by working on holidays, which represented more than a third of the year); decided what foods were authorized during the various periods (fast days); and interfered in sexual life, indicating when sexual relations were permitted and when they were a sin. The total control exercised over social time led to the subjugation of man to the ruling social and ideological system. Time for the individual was not his own individual time, it belonged not to him, but to a higher, dominating force.

This explains why the opposition to the ruling class, in the Middle Ages, assumed the form of a protest against the Church's control over time: the eschatological sects, by prophesying the forthcoming end of the world and calling on people to repent and reject earthly treasures, were casting doubt on the validity of ecclesiastical time. The millenarian's interpretation of history was contrary to the official doctrine of the Church; they asserted that the Last Judgement would be preceded by the thousand years of Christ's reign on earth, and rejected all feudal and ecclesiastical institutions, property and the social order. The apocalyptic expectation of the imminent 'end of all time' symbolized the sectarians' hostility to the orthodox conception of time. The eschatological sects represented a danger to the dominant Church because, by prophesying and 'hastening' the end of the world, regarded as imminent, they removed all internal justification for the terrestrial order, which the Church declared to be divinely instituted.[35] The members of these sects did not precisely accelerate the passing of time, but denied time, by prophesying its imminent end. The mystics even affirmed that it was possible to overcome the irreversibility of time and revert to the original status of communion with the Holy Trinity: at this instant, according to the words of Meister Eckhart, all 'lost time' can be recovered.[36]

Ecclesiastical time could remain preponderant so long as it corresponded to the slow, measured rhythm of the life of feudal society. The measuring of time by generations, reigns and pontificates had more meaning for the men of this epoch than the precise calculation of short periods of time unconnected with religious or political events. In the Middle Ages, there was no need to make the most of time and save it, to measure it exactly and know its minutest intervals. This majestic pace of mediaeval life was governed by the essentially agrarian character of feudal society. But there arose and developed within it another focus of social life, characterized by a particular rhythm and necessitating more precision in the measurement of time and more care in the spending of it: the town.

The production cycles of the craftsman were not determined by the alternation of the seasons. Whereas the farmer was directly dependent on the cycle of nature, from which he could never completely escape, the town-dwelling craftsman had more complex and contradictory relations with nature, from which he had sundered himself by creating an artificial milieu constituted by the various tools of his trade and by a variety of devices and mechanisms, interposed between him and the natural environment. In the emerging urban civilization, man was already governed more by the system which he himself had established than by the rhythms of nature. He detached himself increasingly from nature, which he treated as an external object. The development of the urban population, with its new, more rationalist style of thought, began to modify the traditional perception of nature. The growing complexity of man's practical activity, together with his more active and more deliberate influence on nature, posed him fresh problems. Nature was losing the character of something holy. Certain theologians, reflecting man's new situation in the world, began to ask themselves whether the works of man were divine creations.[37] Man saw himself as the independent creator of his own artificial world, distinct from the world of nature.

In these conditions, the need for making more precise and standardized measurements of bodies and surfaces, space and time, also began to be felt. Merchants, in carrying out their work, needed to be able to cover the distance between trading centres more quickly. Entrepreneurs were anxious to produce as much as possible within a given time and to increase the length of working hours; small craftsmen and workmen were interested in seeing that the hours of work were precisely measured. Work came to be measured by time (or more precisely the clock), which acquired great importance, becoming an essential factor of production. The appearance of the mechanical clock was the perfectly logical outcome of the new feeling of time, which it also served to strengthen. Invented at the end of the thirteenth century, clocks were, in the words of Spengler, a 'terrifying symbol of passing time . . . the *nec plus ultra* expression of a historical sentiment of the universe'.[38] In the fourteenth and fifteenth centuries, clocks adorned the towers of the town halls of numerous European cities. Inaccurate though they were, and lacking a minute-hand, they nevertheless marked a veritable revolution in the perception of social time. The striking of the town clock symbolized 'secular' time, as opposed to the bells of the churches and monasteries which measured the time of the religious offices. The urban community became master of its own time with its own particular rhythm. It was then, to use the words of Jacques Le Goff, that the transition from 'biblical time' to 'the time of the merchants' began.[39]

If we consider these events in a wider historical and cultural context, however, the emancipation of urban time from the authority of the Church will possibly no longer seem the main consequence of the invention of mechanical clocks.[40] That it was not felt necessary, for a great part of history, to measure time constantly and exactly and divide it up into equal parts was not solely due to the lack of adequate devices for making such measurements. Where a social need exists, there are generally means of satisfying it. Mechanical clocks were installed in the towns of Europe at a moment when the influential social groups had become aware of the need to know the exact time. These groups broke away (this did not happen all at once of course, but there was a move in this direction) not only from 'biblical' time but from the entire way of perceiving the world which characterized the traditional agrarian society. In this ancient perception of the world, it should be stressed once again, time was not an autonomous category, experienced independently of its real object-related content, it was not a 'form' of the existence of the world: inseparable from existence itself, it was apprehended through natural, anthropomorphic concepts. Hence its qualitative determination: it could be either 'good' or 'bad', sacred or profane. The notion of a time of unspecified quality, neutral as to content and unconnected with those who experience it and lend it emotional tone, was, in general, alien to the consciousness of the men of antiquity and the Middle Ages. This explains why the division of time into commensurable, interchangeable segments was impossible.

Lastly, the invention of an instrument for measuring time created the conditions necessary for evolving a new attitude towards time, regarded as something flowing at a uniform, regular pace, divisible into equal, non-qualitative units. It was in the European city that time began, for the first time in history, to be 'isolated' as a pure form, exterior to life. The mechanical clocks used by nobility, sovereigns and great city families as symbols of social prestige always served a practical purpose. Europeans gradually ceased to contemplate the world *sub specie aeternitatis* and began to take an active view of it *sub specie temporis*.

Possessing the means of measuring time precisely, and so of dividing it up into equal periods, men were bound, sooner or later, to become aware of the radical transformations the concept of time had undergone as a result of the evolution of society as a whole, and of the town in particular. Time for the first time, and for good, 'extended' in a straight line, from the past to the future, passing through a point called the present. In earlier ages, the differences between past, present and future had been relative, and the dividing line between them had been movable (in religious and magic ritual, at the moment of the fulfilment of the myth, the past and the future dissolved in the present, in an eternal moment suffused with supreme significance); but with the triumph of linear time these differences became very precise, and present time was 'compressed' until it was merely a point sliding continously along the line which runs from past to future, transforming the future into the past. Present time became fleeting, irreversible and elusive. Man for the first time discovered that time, whose passing he had noted only in relation to events, did not cease even in the absence of events. As a result, an effort had to be made to save time, to use it rationally and to fill it with actions useful for man. The bells from the belfry, ringing out at regular intervals, were a constant reminder of the brevity of life, and a call to great actions which could give time a positive content.

The transition to the mechanical measurement of time helped to reveal those qualities of time which were calculated especially to attract the attention of the agents of the new mode of production: entrepreneurs, manufacturers, merchants. Time was seen as a thing of great value and a source of material values. Manifestly, the significance of time was increasingly realized as the individual became aware of himself, and began to see himself not as a generic being but a unique individuality, a person situated in a specific temporal context and exercising his capacities in the limited span of life allotted to him. The mechanical counting of time does not involve any direct action by man, who is obliged to recognize that time is independent of him. We said above that the town had become master of its own time, which is true in the sense that time had been wrested from the control of the Church. But it is true also that it was precisely in the town that man ceased to be master of time, for time, being now free to pass by independently of man and events, established its tyranny, to which men are constrained to submit. Time imposes its rhythm on them, forcing them to act more quickly, to hurry, not to allow the moment to escape. In former days, time was regarded as the property of God (this was one of the main bases for the criticisms directed against usury, regarded as misuse of the property of God—that is to say, of time);[41] time henceforward is regarded as the undeniable and inestimable property of man, in the same way as his body and soul (L. B. Alberti).[42]

The 'alienation' of time from its concrete content made it possible to see it as a pure categorial form, duration, not 'burdened' by matter. During the pre-capitalist era, time was always local. There was not a single scale of time for wide expanses of territory, not to say States or whole regions. The particularism of social life was also manifest in the systems for computing time. And this lingered on after the transition to the mechanical measurement of time; each town had 'its own' time. But inherent in this new way of determining time was the possibility of unifying it, and with the responsibility for measuring time passing to the State, the State began to proclaim its time as the only true time and impose it on all its subjects. Local time was split up, while nation-wide—and subsequently zonal—time became a means of intensifying relations. There arises a uniform conception of time. In this way, the importance attached to time in cities is sharply increased. However, the view expressed by more than one historian that the preceding phase of history was characterized by 'indifference to time'[43] can be accepted only with a reservation: people of the Middle Ages were indifferent to time as we now understand it, but they had their own specific ways of experiencing and reflecting on it. They were not so much indifferent to time, as imperceptive to its change and development. Stability, tradition, repetitiveness, these were the categories in which their consciousness moved, and in terms of which they interpreted the actual historical development which for so long they could not apprehend.

The perception and apperception of time relate to the very essence of cultural life. This concept is closely linked to the idea of evolution. It is possible, however, that we sometimes lose sight of the fact that in history, side by side with evolution, the static element has played an important part. The three great epochs of history are characterized by extremely slow changes, the stagnation of production and social life and, accordingly, the tendency to perceive the world not in the process of becoming, but in a state of repose, or of 'eternal recurrence'. It is possible that certain contemporary scholars may underestimate this factor, because they belong to a civilization developing at tumultuous speed, forcing them to view the past itself through the prism of change.

We have seen that, in primitive societies and the civilizations of antiquity, as also among certain non-European peoples, the predominant concept of time was not vectorial but cyclical, engendered by another style of life, by a particular view of the world and a certain type of personality preponderant in society. Conceptions of time in any society or cultural region reflect the pace of social evolution. Whether cyclical time predominates over linear time in the social consciousness depends on the specific relation between the dynamic and the static elements in the historical process.

NOTES

1. H. H. Parkhurst, *The Cult of Chronology, Essays in Honor of John Dewey*, p. 294, New York, 1929; R. Alexander, *Space, Time and Deity*, Vol. I, p. 36, London, 1947; W. Lewis, *Time and Western Man*, p. x et seq., 211 et seq., Boston, 1957; W. Weischedel, 'Das heutige Denken zwischen Raum und Zeit', *Universitas*, 22. Jg., H. 12, 1967, p. 1234 et seq.; R. Melka, 'Punctuality. An Inquiry into the Psychology of Modern Man', *Diogenes*, Vol. 65, 1969.
2. H. Werner, 'Raum und Zeit in den Urformen der Künste', *Vierter Kongress für Ästhetik und Allgemeine Kunstwissenschaft, Berichte*, p. 69 et seq., Stuttgart, 1931.
3. E. Cassirer, *Philosophie der Symbolischen Formen*, Vol. II, p. 103 et seq., Berlin, 1925; A. Hallowell, *Culture and Experience*, Philadelphia, 1955; B. L. Whorf, *Language, Thought and Reality*, New York, 1956.
4. M. Eliade, *Le Mythe de l'Éternel Retour, Archétypes et Répétition*, Paris, 1949; cf. P. Vidal-Naquet, 'Temps des Dieux et Temps des Hommes', *Revue de l'Histoire des Religions*, Vol. 157, 1960.
5. G. J. Whitrow, *The Natural Philosophy of Time*, London, 1961.
6. M. I. Steblin-Kameskij, *Mir Sagi* [The World of Saga], p. 110 et seq., Leningrad, 1971; by the same author, 'Tidsforestillingene i Islendingesagaene', *Edda*, Vol. LXVII, No. 6, 1968, p. 351 et seq.; E. Leisi, 'Die Darstellung der Zeit in der Sprache', in : R. W. Meyer (ed.), *Das Zeitproblem im 20. Jahrhundert*, p. 17 et seq., Bern and Munich, 1964.
7. W. Grönbech, *Kultur und Religion der Germanen*, Vol. I, p. 150–1, Darmstadt, 1961.
8. M. Granet, *La Pensée Chinoise*, p. 86, 90, 97, 103, Paris, 1934.
9. S. G. F. Brandon, *History, Time and Deity*, Manchester, 1965; 'The Deification of Time', in *Studium Generale*, Vol. 23, fasc. 6, 1970, p. 493 et seq.
10. J. P. Vernant, *Mythe et Pensée chez les Grecs, Études de Psychologie Historique*, p. 22 et seq., 57, 71 et seq., 99 et seq., Paris, 1965.
11. Ch. Mugler, *Deux Thèmes de la Cosmologie Grecque; Devenir Cyclique et Pluralité des Mondes*, p. 148 et seq., Paris, 1953.
12. A. F. Losev, *Istorija antičnoj ěstetiki, Sofisty, Sokrat, Platon* [History of Classical Aesthetics. The Sophists, Socrates, Plato], p. 598–600, 612–13. Moscow, 1969; cf. S. S. Averincev, 'Grečeskaja' 'Literatura' 'i Bližnevostočnaja' 'Slovesnost' (Protivostojanie i Vstreča dvuh Tvorčeskih Principov)', *Tipologija i Vsaimosvjazi Literatur Drevnego Mira*, [Greek and Near Eastern Literature (The Contrast and Convergence of two Artistic Principles), Different Types of Ancient Literature and the Interaction between Them], p. 229–31, Moscow, 1971.
13. Plato, *Timaeus*, 38a.
14. B. A. Van Groningen, *In the Grip of the Past, Essay on an Aspect of Greek Thought*, Leyden, 1953.
15. P.-M. Schuhl *et al.*, 'Espace et Temps dans la Cité, la Littérature et les Mythes Grecs', *Revue de Synthèse*, No. 57–8, 1970, p. 96.
16. W. den Boer, 'Graeco-Roman Historiography in its Relation to Biblical and Modern Thinking', *History and Theory*, Vol. VII, No. 1, 1968, p. 72; cf. E. C. Welskopf, 'Gedanken über den Gesellschaftlichen Fortschritt im Altertum', *XIII. Internationaler Kongress der Historischen Wissenschaften*, Moscow, 1970.
17. A. Meyer, *Wesen und Geschichte der Theorie vom Mikro-und Makrokosmos*, Bern, 1900; G. P. Conger, *Theories of Macrocosms and Microcosms in the History of Philosophy*, New York, 1922; R. Allers, 'Microcosmus', *Traditio*, 2, 1944.
18. M. M. Bakhtin, *Tvorcestvo Fransua Rable i Narodnaja Kultura Srednevekov'ja i Renessansa* [The work of François Rabelais and Popular Culture during the Middle Ages and the Renaissance], Moscow, 1965. (French trans.: *L'Œuvre de François Rabelais et la Culture Populaire au Moyen Age et sous la Renaissance*, Paris, 1970).
19. N. I. Konrad, *Zapad i Vostok* (West and East), p. 79, Moscow, 1966.

20. St Augustine, *De Civ. Dei*, XII, 13, 17.
21. Honorius Augustodunensis, *De Imagine Mundi*, II, I–3.
22. O. Cullmann, *Christ et le Temps*, Neuchâtel and Paris, 1947.
23. Duns Scotus, *De Divisione Naturae*, I, 1.
24. H.-I. Marrou, *L'Ambivalence du Temps de l'Histoire chez Saint Augustin*, p. 22, Montreal and Paris, 1950.
25. A. Dempf, *Sacrum Imperium, Geschichts- und Staatsphilosophie des Mittelalters und der politischen Renaissance*, p. 251, Munich and Berlin, 1929; P. Roussel, 'La Conception de l'Histoire à l'Époque Féodale', *Mélanges d'Histoire du Moyen Age Dédiés à la Mémoire de Louis Halphen*, p. 630–3, Paris, 1951; A.-D. v. den Brincken, *Studien zur Lateinischen Weltchronistik bis in das Zeitalter Ottos von Freising*, p. 38, Düsseldorf, 1957.
26. M.-D. Chenu, *La Théologie au XII*e *Siècle*, p. 93, Paris, 1957.
27. St Augustine, *Confessions*, XI, 27.
28. A. Doren, *Fortuna im Mittelalter und in der Renaissance*, Leipzig, 1924; K. Hampe, 'Zur Auffassung der Fortuna im Mittelalter', *Archiv für Kulturgeschichte*, 17, 1927; D. M. Robinson, 'The Wheel of Fortune', *Classical Philology*, Vol. XLI, No. 4, 1946; H. R. Patch, *The Goddess Fortuna in Mediaeval Literature*, 2nd ed., New York, 1967.
29. M. Kemmerich, *Die Frühmittelalterliche Porträtmalerei in Deutschland bis zur Mitte des XIII. Jahrhunderts*, Munich, 1907.
30. L. S. Lihacev, *Poétika Drevnerusskoj Literatury* [Theory of Poetry in Early Russian Literature], Leningrad, 1967; E. Kobel, *Untersuchungen zum Gelebten Raum in der Mittelhochdeutschen Dichtung*, Zurich, 1950; U. Ruberg, 'Raum und Zeit im Prosa-Lancelot', *Medium Aevum, Philologische Studien*, Vol. 9, Munich, 1965; P. Ménard, 'Le Temps et la Durée dans les Romans de Chrétien de Troyes', *Le Moyen Age*, Vol. 73, Nos. 3–4, 1967; S. Hinterkausen, *Die Auffassung von Zeit und Geschichte in Konrads Rolandslied*, inaugural address, Bonn, 1967.
31. Inferno, XV, 85–7.
32. Purgatorio, XI, 106–8.
33. Paradiso, XXIX, 12–32; XXXIII, 94–5.
34. G. Gurvitch, *La Multiplicité des Temps Sociaux*, Paris, 1962.
35. N. Cohn, *The Pursuit of the Millennium*, London, 1970.
36. M. de Gandillac, *Valeur du Temps dans la Pédagogie Spirituelle de Jean Tauler*, p. 42, Montreal and Paris, 1956.
37. M.-D. Chenu, L'homme et la Nature, Perspectives sur la Renaissance du XXIe Siècle; *Archives d'Histoire Doctrinale et Littéraire au Moyen Age*, 27, 1953, p. 62.
38. O. Spengler, *The Decline of the West*, English trans., Vol. I, London, 1926.
39. J. Le Goff, 'Le Temps du Travail dans la "Crise" du XIVe siècle: du Temps Médiéval au Temps Moderne', *Le Moyen Age*, Vol. 69, 1963.
40. P. Wolff, 'Le Temps et sa Mesure au Moyen Age', *Annales E.S.C.*, 17th year, No. 6, 1962, p. 1143 et seq.
41. J. Le Goff, 'Temps de l'Église et Temps du Marchand', *Annales E.S.C.*, 15th year, No. 3, 1960.
42. L. B. Alberti, *Della Famiglia*, p. 183 et seq., Milan, n.d.
43. G. Paris, *La Littérature Française au Moyen Age*, 2nd ed., p. 30, Paris, 1890; L. Febvre, *Le Problème de l'Incroyance au XVI*e *Siècle. La Religion de Rabelais*, p. 426–34, Paris, 1942; M. Bloch, *La Société Féodale*, p. 118, Paris, 1968.

[A·45] SHC·74/XXII·1/A